CROMFORD
REVISITED

Doreen Buxton and Christopher Charlton

Published by The Derwent Valley Mills World Heritage Site Educational Trust
Registered charity number 1099279

ISBN 978-0-9541940-6-2

Designed by Ian Lane, Mill Design and Advertising, Duffield DE56 4FY

Printed by Pyramid Press, Quorn Road, Nottingham, NG5 1DT

Published by The Derwent Valley Mills World Heritage Site Educational Trust, a registered charity funded initially by the Derbyshire Building Society and the University of Derby, publishing material relating to the history of Derbyshire's Derwent Valley.
Registered Charity number 1099279
Address for Correspondence. c/o Cultural and Community Services, County Hall, Matlock, Derbyshire DE4 3AG or e-mail: info@derwentvalleymills.org

Contents

Acknowledgements

Many people have contributed to this book. Thanks are due for the generosity and patience of Ken Askew, Tony Holmes, Ken Smith and Glynn Waite who have allowed their collections of photographs to be used for reference and for reproduction; to the late Frank Clay, to Ron Duggins, Mrs Garth, Mr and Mrs Gerish, Betty Gregory, Trevor Griffin, Frank Hawley, the Mee family, John Millward, Ron Wood, Scarthin Books and John Smedley Ltd for lending images and to Trevor Steed who helped to reproduce many of them. Photohistorian, Dr John Bradley kindly contributed the earliest photographic images from his collection of stereoscopic photographs. Thanks also to the people who have shared their memories of the twentieth century especially Martin Bibby for his description of the Troy Laundry and Ron Wood for summarising the work of the Cromford Colour Company, to Roger Flindall for reference to his painstaking newspaper and mining record indices, to Sue Graham for access to her Wheatcroft family history, to David Hool for the many valuable contributions from his extensive research material and for his interest and advice, to Barry Joyce for sharing his surveys of significant houses in the village and to Dr Patrick Strange for details of his archaeological exploration of the Arkwright Mills' site. Darrell Clark, Sally Hargreaves, Frank Hawley, John Hirst, Judy Jones, Terry Moore, Sue Moseley, Hugh Potter, Dr Jim Rieuwerts, John Robey, Tim Rogers, Glynn Waite, Angus Watson and Lynn Willies have added valuable information and advice. The contribution of images from Derby Museum and Art Galleries and Derbyshire County Council Buxton Museum and Art Gallery, the Derbyshire Archaeological Society, the Royal Commission on the Historic Monuments of England, the National Gallery of Scotland, the National Portrait Gallery, London and the Harris Museum and Art Gallery, Preston, Tate Images, the Waterways Archive, Gloucester and Brunel University: Clinker Collection is gratefully acknowledged. Derby Local Studies Library, the Derbyshire Records Office and the Arkwright Society have supplied pictures and information as has the Derbyshire County Council Local Studies Library, Matlock along with a bonus of steady encouragement. Members of the Derwent Valley Mills World Heritage Site Research and Publications Panel made valuable comments on the draft script and Ian Lane patiently dealt with the layout. We must also thank the Trustees of the Derwent Valley Mills World Heritage Site Educational Trust for undertaking the publication of our work.

The authors are grateful to all.

Preface

This book is not a history of Cromford; that has yet to be written. But we would like to think that whoever attempts that task will find the themes and episodes we explore here to be of some value. This book started life as a picture book or an annotated gazetteer with the narrative tightly focused on the content of the illustrations; but as our research achieved a greater understanding of the issues we recognised the limitations of these formats. So you will find that there are two strands; it is both a picture book and a narrative account of some aspects of the development of Cromford as an industrial village.

Our first tentative steps in collecting visual representations of Cromford and its surroundings did not prepare us for the scale and quality of this archive and it is with great pleasure we share with you some of the discoveries, many of which have not been reproduced in modern times. Cromford's popularity among amateur and professional artists owes much to its proximity to Matlock Bath whose visitors strayed from the Matlock Dale to explore the Via Gellia, the villages of Bonsall and Cromford and Sir Richard Arkwright's Mills recording what they found. There also developed a market amongst the visitors for engravings of local views and for illustrated guide books. As a result for those prepared to search the United Kingdom's galleries, libraries and private collections there are rich rewards which would not normally be available for such a small village.

We began our investigation with some scepticism as to the accuracy and historical value of the visual material we found. The level of confidence we have come to place on these drawings, sketches, watercolours and engravings will be evident in the captions. In almost every case these pictures convey an essentially truthful representation of what is in view and this extends even to those which contain a fantasy element such as the giant goats which appear to adorn Scarthin Rock in the earliest known depiction of the village. The concern for accuracy is, we believe, a reflection of the high social value polite society placed on sketching and artistic skills; nor should it be forgotten that military training included topographical drawing. And in a pre-photographic age, the engravings which were in effect the postcards of the day and which were purchased as a memento of a visit only served that purpose if they reflected what the visitor had seen.

We have rigorously interpreted the pictures we have selected by comparing one view with another and by evaluating them against a range of documentary sources. These include local newspapers, contemporary accounts, legal records, maps, plans and archaeological evidence. In the narrative sections which are not underpinned by pictorial material we have attempted to focus on issues which others have raised but which have not necessarily been answered. So, for example, we ask how far was Cromford in its early growth an Arkwright creation? Our aim is to cast new light on these questions or at least to add information to the debate.

The industrial theme to which we devote many of the pages which follow is centred almost entirely on the water power provided by the Bonsall Brook and the Cromford Sough. This limitation is deliberate; we did not feel this was the place to rehearse Sir Richard's life story or assess the value of his contribution to factory production, a path which others have followed with greater competence than we could muster but rather to concentrate on his and his descendants' effect on Cromford. The Arkwright family's imprint on Cromford is indelible. The resident squires Sir Richard (1732-1792), Richard (1755-1843), Peter (1784-1866), Frederic (1806-1874), and Frederic Charles (1853-1923) all left their mark. But Cromford was not exclusively an Arkwright family creation and there were others, outside the family, who also influenced the development of the village. We draw attention in particular to George Evans of Bonsall and Cromford, (1726-1808); Philip Gell, (1723-1795) and Philip Gell, (1775-1842) both of Hopton; Peter Nightingale of Lea (1736-1803) and German Wheatcroft (1773-1841) and his brother, Nathaniel (1777-1862).

There is one topic of the utmost significance to the history of Cromford which we have deliberately avoided. A great part of the area's history, both in importance and duration, is to do with lead mining. Much has been written about the subject by experts in the field; this account does not trespass on their ground. Their researches are ongoing and publications from the Peak District Mines Historical Society Ltd and the Peak District National Park Authority are reliable sources of information and reference. The third and fourth volumes of Dr Jim Rieuwerts series Lead Mining in Derbyshire published in 2010 and 2012 provide the most recent detailed and comprehensive account of the Cromford area orefield to date.

Finally we must explain why we have not always recorded our sources of information, a practice which we know will frustrate some of our readers. We thought hard about this but so much of our research has been conducted with privately owned picture and archive material which is currently unavailable to the public, we felt we must preserve the owner's privacy despite the scholarly conventions of which we are well aware.

Doreen Buxton
Christopher Charlton
16 March 2013

Introduction

This account begins about 1750 when Cromford was a rural hamlet or township in the ancient parish of Wirksworth. It lay scattered about the major route through the community, the road down the steep hill from Wirksworth to the crossing point over the River Derwent at Cromford bridge. Scarthin which was in Matlock parish lay alongside the road from Cromford to Bonsall. The Bonsall Brook ran into the village from the west and followed its natural course to join the river a short distance above the Cromford bridge; Cromford Sough flowed across what is now the Market Place to join the brook. The population at this time was almost entirely limited to the workers in the lead mines.

The local corn mill, which is recorded in 1276 as 'molendino de Cromford' was powered by the brook. It stood below and not far from the bridge which is now enclosed in the Arkwright's Cromford Mills' yard. Between the corn mill and the river were lead smelting mills also using the brook for power. The smelting mills had been built in 1575 by Henry Cavendish, Bess of Hardwick's son by her second husband, Sir William Cavendish. Together with the manors of Willersley and Cromford the mills became the property of the Pierrepoint family of Nottingham. In 1716 William Soresby of Chesterfield bought the manor of Cromford for £2,200 from the head of the family, the Duke of Kingston. It was Soresby's grandson, also William, who, in his will of 1758, bequeathed the estate to his sisters, Helen Monroe and Mary Milnes. He died in France in 1760. By 1771 when Richard Arkwright and his partners negotiated the lease of land on which to build a cotton-spinning mill, Mary Milnes and her husband William owned Cromford manor. Helen Monroe had died and William Milnes had bought her half share of the manor from her husband in 1765. Meanwhile, in 1746, several generations after the Pierrepoints had inherited the Willersley estate and the smelting mills, this property passed to Edwin Lascelles, (later the Earl of Harewood), when he married Elizabeth Dawes, a relative of the Pierrepoints. The map of the property which was drawn for Lascelles in 1759 is reproduced at Figure 48.

In the second half of the eighteenth century lead mining was still the predominant industry in the area and the men who would be Arkwright's neighbours, Evans, Nightingale, the Hurts and Gells all had wealth from their interests in mining, smelting and trading lead. Cromford had been at the forefront of major engineering developments in the seventeenth century when soughs, (underground tunnels), were being driven to drain water from lead mines. In 1631 Cornelius Vermuyden, the Dutch engineer, began a sough to drain mines between Cromford and Wirksworth which was long thought to be the first sough driven in Derbyshire but now has been shown to be pre-dated by three or four others, one of which, Bartholomew's Level, was also associated with Cromford mines. Of particular importance to this account and for the future development of Cromford, is the Cromford or Longe Sough, which was begun in 1657 or 1658. Dr Jim Rieuwerts' research in the Duchy of Lancaster records finds it described as 'from or neare a place called Huntley Green in Crumford ... being a worke of extraordinary difficulty and vaste Chardge to perfect'. He states the case for evidence in the sough of some of the earliest known use of gunpowder blasting in a British mine. It was nearly four miles long and still incomplete when in the early eighteenth century William Woolley, writing about 'Crumford moor' in his *History of Derbyshire*, noted the 'very rich lead mines which have for some time been drowned out, but a great sough is now carrying up to unwater them at a great expense'. In the eighteenth century, lead smelting technology advanced with the introduction of reverberatory furnaces, known as cupolas. The mills owned by Lascelles were not superseded by a cupola but after 1761 they were used to process calamine, another mineral which was found locally and which was exported for use in the production of brass.

By 1771 there had been significant improvements to the road system around the village. About 1730 the track, which ran alongside the river from Cromford bridge to Matlock Bath, had been made passable for coaches and some time before 1736 the Turners, who owned coal mines in Swanwick, had considered it worth their while to build a road from Swanwick to a depot in Cromford from which they could market their coal. The link from Cromford to Bonsall was improved in 1736 giving easier access to the village and thence to the north. Turnpike Acts of 1759 and 1766 improved the road connections from Cromford to the north along the line of the present A6 through and over Scarthin Rock to Matlock Bath (see Figure 90) and on the east side of the Derwent from Cromford bridge to Langley Mill via Crich and Ripley.

So although the structure and appearance of Cromford today is largely a legacy of the Arkwright family it is clear that there was already an established largely industrial community when Richard Arkwright arrived in 1771. The activities of the investors in the local mines and soughs had created a settlement in which the use of water power to turn the corn mill grind stones and to power the smelting mill bellows was long established, also, as a visitor noted in 1755, Cromford was home to 'an ingenious Blacksmith who had contrived a Water-wheel on one of these Streams to turn his Grindstone'.

Richard Arkwright's contribution was to introduce a new scale to the use of the same power to drive a battery of machines in a factory and to implement and support the system of employment which would successfully sustain it. In doing so he changed the industrial scene not only locally but nationally and internationally. He also built the framework of today's Cromford village which has survived almost intact.

CHAPTER ONE

The Bonsall Brook

The Bonsall Brook, the stream which flows through Cromford, rises just over four miles away to the north-west at Ivonbrook Grange and runs down the valley between Griffe Grange and Ible into the Via Gellia at Rider (sometimes Ryder) Point. Along this course and as it flows on to its junction with the brook from Bonsall at the bottom of Clatterway, it is sometimes referred to as the Ivon (Iven) Brook or the Via Gellia Brook. It is the tributary which runs down Bonsall Dale and alongside Clatterway which has given the brook its commonly used name. From under Via Gellia Mill the enlarged stream runs along Bonsall Hollow into Cromford village. Here now below the Greyhound pond most of its course is hidden from view, confined underground in culverts except for a brief appearance, glimpsed through the railings, well below pavement level, at the corner where the Cromford War Memorial Gardens meet the Lime Yard near the A6. Along the brook's course springs, including Dunsley Spring which empties into it below Tufa Cottage in the Via Gellia (see Figure 17), and lead mine drainage soughs contribute to the water it discharges into the River Derwent.

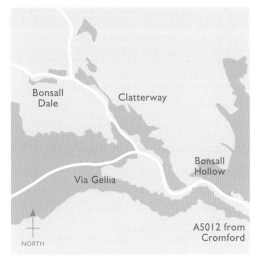

Map showing the relationship of Via Gellia, Bonsall Hollow, Clatterway and Bonsall Dale

The stream powered four mediaeval corn mills. The highest on the brook course, was at Ivonbrook Grange where, by the thirteenth century at the latest, 'the mill of the monks of Ivenbrook' was situated. These were the monks from Buildwas Abbey, a Cistercian monastery in Shropshire, who in the twelfth century had been granted rights by the de Ferrers family who held the lordships of many Derbyshire manors at that time. A corn mill remained in use at Ivonbrook Grange, perhaps on the same site as the monks' mill until some time in the last twenty years of the nineteenth century. Today the site is marked by the eighteenth century mill building which stands beside the B5056 road to Bakewell, two hundred yards from the crossroads at Grange Mill; its former mill ponds are used as fishing ponds.

FIGURE 1. **Ivonbrook Grange Mill, pencil sketch, 1974.**

Arkwright Society collection

A second corn mill was situated a little less than a half mile down the A5012 below Grange Mill crossroads. This was the Valley or Lilies mill which served the village of Ible set high on the plateau above it. Today, 2013, the mill site is marked by a small overgrown ruin standing about two hundred yards downstream from The Lilies, the house which was formerly the Flower of Lillies Inn, see advertisement overleaf. Ible's mill was served by a long goit from a pond well above the house. The mill is shown as disused on the *Ordnance Survey Map* published in 1880 but its machinery survived largely intact into the 1980s. A third mill, Bonsall's manorial corn mill stood at the foot of Clatterway on the site now occupied by Via Gellia Mill and the fourth, Cromford's manorial corn mill, was on land which is now enclosed in Arkwright's Cromford Mills' yard. These last two sites will be considered again later.

The eighteenth and early nineteenth centuries were to witness a dramatic exploitation of the power of the stream closer to Cromford and in Bonsall. The essence of the change is summed up by two contemporary descriptions. The first, from a traveller in 1755 who had come down through Bonsall, and described Clatterway and the brook as 'a steep rugged hill on the left-

FIGURE 2. **The ruins of Ible Mill, photographs, 1969 and 2011.**

The photograph (left page), taken in 1969, shows the pitwheel and main upright shaft of Ible corn mill. Note the replacement cast iron gearing attached to the inner rim of the wooden pit wheel. The photograph (above) shows Ible Mill, as seen from the A5012 in 2011.

Arkwright Society collection

hand of which runs a clear rivulet which as it descended with great impetuosity form'd the most delightful natural cascade I ever saw.' Almost 80 years later in *The Matlock Companion*, 1832, Arthur Jewitt, travelling up from Cromford commented on Clatterway 'the old Manchester road branches off to the right, in its direction to Bonsall; here then, is one of the most interesting successions of mills and wheels, and dams, for various purposes, formed by a mountain rill, that can any where be met with;'. In 1848 this 'succession' was amongst the thirteen mill sites which stood beside the brook within a distance of less than two miles from the top of Bonsall Dale to the edge of Cromford village. And there were three further mills on the brook within Cromford at this date; a colour mill on the site now occupied by Home Products and the two Arkwright cotton mills.

The brook was also a boundary feature, most significantly for this account, marking the boundary between Bonsall parish and the township of Cromford (in Wirksworth parish) from a little way above Via Gellia Mill down to the edge of Cromford village near the foot of Chapel Hill. Higher up the valley it separated Bonsall parish from Middleton township and on its course through Cromford village to the river, the brook divided Cromford township from Matlock parish. The part of Matlock parish which is relevant and important in this account is Scarthin.

The series of mills along the brook course as they were described by the Bonsall Tithe Commissioners in the Tithe Schedule of 1846 and map of 1848 is reproduced overleaf. Some of the mill sites straddled the brook so they appear not only in Bonsall's records but also in those for Cromford the Tithe Schedule and Map for which are dated 1840 and 1841 respectively; or in the Middleton Tithe Schedule and Map, dated 1841 and 1843. Considered together, the Schedules illustrate the diversity of industrial uses established on this small stream utilising the modest power supply it provided.

For ease of reference four ponds shown on the map have been given modern labels W, X, Y and Z. In the earlier Cromford Tithe Schedule, the ponds lying between X and Y are given names, New Dam and Bank next Turnpike Willows, Upper Little New Dam and Nether Little New Dam which suggest that they were constructed later than W, X, Y and Z. All the ponds are described as fish ponds in the Bonsall Tithe Schedule of 1846. The 'new' ponds may have been added for that intended use.

[556] Paint mill, yard, outbuildings, mill dam

Thought to have been a calamine grinding mill, owned by the Cheadle Calamine Company, but by 1848 when this survey was made it was described as a paint mill owned by Grace Rains and unoccupied.

Clear evidence remains of the pond, now built upon, and the dam which served this site.

[100] Corn mill, yard, gardens, outbuildings
[102] Goit, dam etc

The water corn mill was owned and occupied by Robert Clay in 1848. The mill and Nether Green House had been built by his father Francis Clay some time between 1793 and 1799. Much of the watercourse archaeology can still be traced. In March 1875 the milling equipment including a 27 foot wheel was for sale under the terms of Robert's will. A dwelling house, "Cascades", had been built by August 1877 when it was advertised to let by John Broxup Coates, of the Manor House, Bonsall. His wife was Robert Clay's niece, Mary Ann Coates.

[532] Calamine works

This mill, described as a calamine works, is shown in the possession of the Cheadle Calamine Company but unoccupied. Working calamine would usually imply the presence of powered grinding machinery and ovens but the evidence of adequate water power on this site is lacking. Unless the rivulet which runs past the building was once very much larger it is unlikely that it could have driven a wheel and grinding stones. Perhaps the site was used for washing ore and was worked in conjunction with the powered site below which may have changed hands when the company's property in Bonsall was put up for auction in 1831 while this site did not find a buyer.

[634] Part of smelting mills

In 1848 the lead smelting works was owned by the trustees of Philip Gell of Hopton who had died in 1842 and was occupied by Alfred Alsop. This water powered site on the Via Gellia brook is depicted (see Figures 14 & 15).

The site remains in a commercial use within its historic perimeter. It lies across the Middleton-Bonsall boundary so it also appears on the Middleton Tithe Map and Schedule, dated 1841 and 1843 respectively where it is recorded as Dunsley Paper Mill owned by the trustees of Philip Gell of Hopton and occupied by George Simons.

[52] Paint mill, yards etc

The paint mill was owned and occupied by William Thomisson in 1848. The mill is depicted in the watercolour (see Figure 4).

[51] Comb shop, dams, garden

The comb shop was owned and occupied by Robert Hartle in 1848

The remnants of the mill building survive and the track, which linked the site to the road, remains visible.

FIGURE 3
Part of the Bonsall Tithe Map, 1848.

Note the boundary of the civil parish of Bonsall with Matlock to the north (marked in orange) and with Cromford to the south (marked in red along the course of the brook).

The notation W, X, Y and Z on the ponds is a modern addition.

Reproduced with permission of Derbyshire County Council Record Office, reference D2360/3/173a.

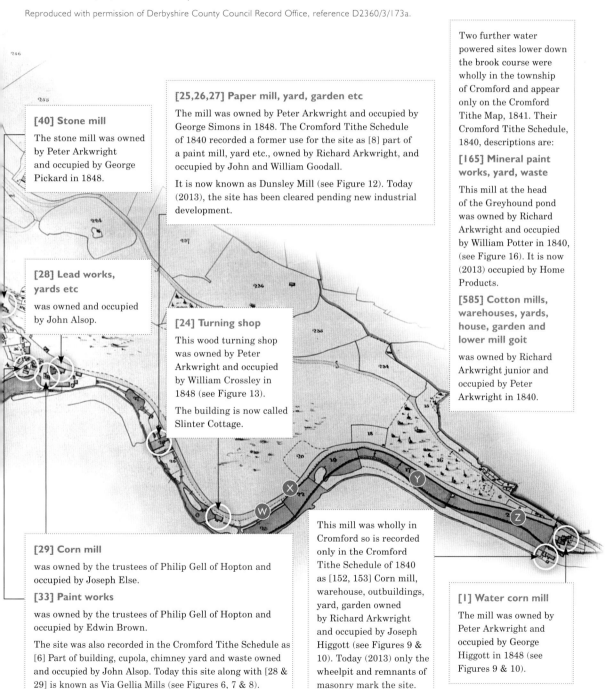

[40] Stone mill

The stone mill was owned by Peter Arkwright and occupied by George Pickard in 1848.

[25,26,27] Paper mill, yard, garden etc

The mill was owned by Peter Arkwright and occupied by George Simons in 1848. The Cromford Tithe Schedule of 1840 recorded a former use for the site as [8] part of a paint mill, yard etc., owned by Richard Arkwright, and occupied by John and William Goodall.

It is now known as Dunsley Mill (see Figure 12). Today (2013), the site has been cleared pending new industrial development.

Two further water powered sites lower down the brook course were wholly in the township of Cromford and appear only on the Cromford Tithe Map, 1841. Their Cromford Tithe Schedule, 1840, descriptions are:

[165] Mineral paint works, yard, waste

This mill at the head of the Greyhound pond was owned by Richard Arkwright and occupied by William Potter in 1840, (see Figure 16). It is now (2013) occupied by Home Products.

[585] Cotton mills, warehouses, yards, house, garden and lower mill goit

was owned by Richard Arkwright junior and occupied by Peter Arkwright in 1840.

[28] Lead works, yards etc

was owned and occupied by John Alsop.

[24] Turning shop

This wood turning shop was owned by Peter Arkwright and occupied by William Crossley in 1848 (see Figure 13).

The building is now called Slinter Cottage.

[29] Corn mill

was owned by the trustees of Philip Gell of Hopton and occupied by Joseph Else.

[33] Paint works

was owned by the trustees of Philip Gell of Hopton and occupied by Edwin Brown.

The site was also recorded in the Cromford Tithe Schedule as [6] Part of building, cupola, chimney yard and waste owned and occupied by John Alsop. Today this site along with [28 & 29] is known as Via Gellia Mills (see Figures 6, 7 & 8).

This mill was wholly in Cromford so is recorded only in the Cromford Tithe Schedule of 1840 as [152, 153] Corn mill, warehouse, outbuildings, yard, garden owned by Richard Arkwright and occupied by Joseph Higgott (see Figures 9 & 10). Today (2013) only the wheelpit and remnants of masonry mark the site.

[1] Water corn mill

The mill was owned by Peter Arkwright and occupied by George Higgott in 1848 (see Figures 9 & 10).

FIGURE 4. **A mill in Bonsall Dale, Derbyshire, watercolour, John Glover (1767-1849).**

The watercolour is not dated but must have been painted, or at least sketched, before 1831 when Glover emigrated to Australia. It shows a mill in the 'succession' described by Jewitt in 1832 and recorded in 1846 as William Thomisson's paint mill (see Figure 3 [52]). Although attributed to Bonsall Dale, and sometimes thought to represent the mill which stood at Mill Pinch in Bonsall Dale, it is considered more likely that the building stood on the site now forming the parking area for Hollowbrook on Clatterway. The buildings in the centre foreground have not survived but that on the right appears to be incorporated into what is now, 2013, Hollowbrook Cottage. The term Bonsall Dale is used ambiguously in several historical accounts.

DERBYSHIRE.

PARTICULARS OF SALE OF THE "FLOWER OF LILLIES" INN, VIA GELLIA, WATER POWER CORN MILL, AND CAPITAL FREEHOLD LAND.

TO BE SOLD BY AUCTION,
By GEO. MARSDEN,

At the house of Mr. John Watson (the owner, who is retiring from business), "FLOWER OF LILLIES" INN, Via Gellia, near Matlock, on THURSDAY, the 25th of February, 1869, at six o'clock in the evening, in one or more lots, and subject to conditions to be then produced;

ALL that substantially erected and exceedingly well accustomed OLD LICENSED INN, known by the name of the "FLOWER OF LILLIES" INN, in Ible, near Matlock, in the county of Derby, together with the yard, garden, stables for six horses, cow houses, cart hovels and chambers over, piggeries, and other appurtenances thereto belonging and occupied therewith.

Also all that well accustomed WATER-POWER CORN MILL, situate near to the above described premises, with powerful water wheel, 60 feet circumference, nearly new, two pairs grey stones and mill gearing, together with drying kiln, store chamber, coke house, and other appurtenances.

And also all those very fertile PIECES OF PARCELS of freehold MEADOW and PASTURE LAND, and land covered with water, known by the name of the Top Edge, Mill Dam, Dam Meadow, Lower Edge, and Meadow, comprising (together with the sites of the "Flower of Lillies," garden, and corn mill and yard), by recent admeasurement 9 acres or thereabouts, more or less.

The owner and occupier Mr. John Watson will shew the property.

The property is bounded by lands belonging the Trustees of the late Philip Gell, Esq., John Sandars, Esq., Mr. George Travis, and the Cromford and Newhaven Turnpike Road. It is within a short drive of Matlock Bath through Via Gellia, and a place of great resort to Tourists and others. An enterprising landlord at the "Lillies" would be sure to attain a speedy competence. The property is suitable for occupation or investment.

For further particulars apply to Mr. J. RAINS, Radbourn, Derby; Mr. WATSON; or the AUCTIONEER, Market-place, Wirksworth.

Derby Mercury,
February 17th, 1869

CHAPTER TWO

George Evans' mills on the Bonsall Brook

The principal investors in the industrial development of the Cromford area in the eighteenth century were George Evans, Peter Nightingale and Richard Arkwright. In this chapter we consider the contribution of George Evans.

George Evans transformed the Bonsall Brook. He was not the first to have found new uses for the stream's power. That achievement belongs to the Cheadle Calamine Company which used the brook in processing calamine from local mines for the brass industry. The company had mills in Bonsall Dale from at least 1753 but Evans was to make more significant and lasting changes. Over a period of 25 years he acquired land along the course of the Bonsall Brook from Clatterway to the edge of Cromford village and having procured the water rights on the brook, he exploited an increasing demand for water powered mills, using his money and entrepreneurial flair to adapt the stream to meet this new market. His or his millwrights' engineering skills enabled him to develop the full potential of a site, on occasion creating two or three mills where only one had stood before.

George Evans' cupola and calamine mill

In 1752 George Evans bought Bonsall's manorial corn mill, from the miller, Joseph Greatorex. It stood at the bottom of Clatterway in about an acre of land and was described in the abstract of title as 'a water corn mill

George Evans

George Evans (1726-1808) was the youngest of the three sons of Edmund Evans (1690-1746) of Bonsall. In the eighteenth century the family were involved in the lead industry as mine owners, lead smelters and merchants and developed a wide range of other business interests. George's brother, Thomas (1723-1814) moved to Derby, where he was first described as an ironmonger. He established a bank, later run in partnership with Samuel Crompton and known as Crompton and Evans Bank. This eventually became part of the Westminster, now NatWest. Thomas and his eldest brother Edmund (1721-1791), vicar of Mayfield, bought mills and land at Darley Abbey and began the development of the Evans' Cotton Mills and the community associated with them.

George Evans stayed closer to home, moving only from Bonsall to Senior Field House near Cromford bridge when he married Ann, daughter of another influential lead merchant, Peter Nightingale of Lea. The house, which in its present form is known as Cromford Bridge House, was purchased by Nightingale in 1757 and settled on his daughter on her marriage. George and Ann's unmarried daughter Elizabeth lived there until her death in 1852.

FIGURE 5. **White Tor, Via Gellia, lithograph, 1822, from a drawing by Eliza Rawlinson.**

This view shows the road along Bonsall Hollow from Cromford, now the A5012, approaching the junction with Clatterway, the turn to Bonsall which is hidden behind Ball Ley or Ball Eye, the hill slope on the right in this picture.

The property on the left of the picture includes the Bonsall manorial corn mill which George Evans purchased in 1752. By 1774 he had added a lead smelting cupola, the building with the tall chimney shown here, a slag mill, an ore house and calamine houses. Johnson Grant commented on passing the site in 1797 'It was dusk as we passed this, and the red furnace had an effect amid the romantic scenery, worthy of the pencil of de Loutherbourg'.

The land in the centre background, called White Tor in this view, was allotted to George Evans at the Enclosure of Bonsall Leys and Green in 1774. On it he built an inn, the Pig of Lead shown here on the right, (a private dwelling since 1995) and the two houses beside it (demolished now). Beyond the cluster of buildings on the left, his development of the 1774 allotment was completed by the construction of a calamine mill.

Private collection

FIGURE 6. **Cromford Bridge House, hand-coloured stereocard, S. Poulton, late 1850s.**

Stereocards such as the one shown here were sold in millions in the second half of the nineteenth century. They provided popular photographic souvenirs of places long before postcards took on that role at the end of the century. They were produced by commercial photographers whose numbers grew to meet the demand. For example in the ten years between the national censuses of 1851 and 1861 the number recorded grew from 51 to 2079, 204 of whom were women.

and kiln with outhouses etc fishings ponds pools streams wheels stanks etc' and 'commonly called Bonsall Mill'. By 1774 Evans had built a lead smelting 'cupola and slagg mill with ore house and calamine houses' on the site (see Figure 5). The actual date of this development is not known but it may have been in or soon after 1759 when George arranged a loan from his brother Thomas secured against Bonsall Mill. The date corresponds approximately with the expiry of the brothers' seven year lease from Philip Gell of a lead smelter, the Middle Mill, at Wirksworth. The cupola was not dependent on water power, its chimney provided the necessary draught for its reverberatory furnace; power for the slag mill bellows would have been generated by a wheel fed from the existing corn mill ponds.

Evans' other mills on the Bonsall Brook, lower in the valley, were new creations not based on earlier mill sites. For them control of the water rights was essential. By 1772 he was renting 'Free Fishery in Bonsall' for £2-2s-0d a year from Anne, Dowager Countess Massareene, second wife and widow of Clotworthy Skeffington, first Earl of Massereene. She was the only child and heir of Henry Eyre of Rampton, Yorkshire who had inherited land in mid-Derbyshire from his distant cousin Thomas Eyre of Rowtor near Winster. In 1777, Evans purchased the water rights on the brook in Bonsall manor from her for £35-15s-0d.

FIGURE 7. **The Pig of Lead Inn, Via Gellia, photograph, 1892.**

The photograph confirms some features of Rawlinson's drawing and also shows, as a dark line, the aqueduct spanning the Via Gellia road, part of the system Evans mentions in 1789 by which water taken from the Bonsall Brook higher up Clatterway was supplied to his calamine mill. In his *Picturesque Excursions from Derby to Matlock Bath*, 1818, Henry Moore describes it as a small wooden aqueduct to an overshot wheel. He gives no detail of the mill's purpose but it was probably producing red lead for paint.

Reproduced by permission of Matlock Local Studies Library

Evans acquired most of the land for his developments through the local Enclosure process. When the common land of Bonsall Leys and Green was divided and enclosed in 1774, in lieu of his right to graze 23 beasts there, Evans was awarded two allotments of land. These included number 29, which was immediately adjacent to his corn mill site (note that the Via Gellia road had not been built at this time) where he built a calamine mill, an inn and two cottages (see Figures 5 and 7). The precise building dates are unknown. Evans supplied water for his calamine mill 'in a cut or aqueduct' taken off the Bonsall Brook near Clatterway Gate, which was close to what is now called Bonsall Green. Today it is difficult to follow the course of this diversion from the stream because part of it has been destroyed by later quarrying behind the former Pig of Lead inn. However it seems likely that the watercourse passed under Clatterway more or less where Millrace House is now, to run below the site where Bonsall Lodge was later built and to join the aqueduct which is shown in Figure 7. By 1809 the calamine mill was in use as a leather mill and later, and for the greater part of the nineteenth century, a colour or paint mill (see Figure 3 [33]). In

1898 when William Hollins & Company took a 99 year lease from Henry Chandos Pole Gell of property which included the 'Old Colour Mill' it was out of use and Hollins had permission to 'take it down'. At that date Hollins already occupied 'the Old Corn Mill' and two ponds previously in the hands of Messrs Bidduph who were corn millers. It is not clear when corn milling ceased; the Biddulphs were paying Poor Rates on the site during the 1870s.

Later uses of the site

After Evans' death in 1808 John Alsop of Lea bought the cupola (see Figure 3 [28]) and in 1821 the remaining property became part of Philip Gell of Hopton's landholding, an addition to his estate which lay higher up the valley.

By the 1850s lead mining in the area was in decline and by 1857 the cupola had closed. In January, 1866 Stone and Wildgoose of Bonsall began to demolish the building for Thomas Elce, (sometimes Else) by then of Manchester, but by birth a local man and a former employee of John Smedley at Lea Mills. Elce built 'a Cotton Mill, an Engine House and all other buildings connected therewith' which opened in April 1867 'with a complement of about 30 hands' (see Fig.8). The local papers reported that the 'building had been put up by an enterprising Manchester cotton spinner as an experiment, in order to try if he cannot compete with his brother cotton merchants more favourably by manufacturing in this remote district'. Later in the year the *London Gazette* reported 'Patent 2244 to John Elce of the City of Manchester and Thomas Elce, the younger of Via Gellia near Matlock, Cotton Spinner for the invention of 'improvements to machinery for spinning and doubling'. Elce was not successful. He failed to deliver the optimistic newspaper forecast of 150 jobs to relieve Bonsall's depressed labour market and in 1870 he was declared bankrupt. The mill was sold to James Carlton, a Manchester cotton merchant who ran it as The Via Gellia Spinning Co. The Company's advertisement in the Manchester Guardian of March 1875 for 'a MULE MINDER, with piecer preferred, for Parr's mules, spinning 28's to 40's' indicates the mill was producing a coarse yarn. After five years Carlton sold it at a loss to Thomas Hill, a director of I & R Morley of Nottingham, the well known hosiery manufacturers. Subsequently it prospered in the hands of his son Charles, spinning merino wool.

By 1882 Charles Hill was also renting a mill on the Arkwright's Cromford cotton mill site where his yarn was reeled and spooled into hanks and by 1888 he had leased part of Strutt's mills lower down the Derwent Valley at Milford. Hill's success made him a serious competitor to William Hollins and Company of Pleasley and Nottingham in

FIGURE 8. **Via Gellia Mill, photograph, about 1890.**

The picture is taken from the steep slope of Ball Eye and looks up and across the valley to the main building of Elce's cotton mill when it was in the ownership of William Hollins and Co and before Hollins built a roadside extension in 1891.

Reproduced from Supplement to the Warehouseman and Draper, March 31st, 1900 'the merino hosiery' market. In May 1890 Henry Ernest Hollins, the company's managing director, agreed the purchase of Hill's business to restrict the competition Hill becoming a member of the Hollins' company board and acting managing director at Via Gellia Mill. He lived at Cromford Bridge House. The company gave up the rented mill at Cromford in 1891. It had been seriously damaged by fire in November 1890 (see Figure 38) when still in use for spooling and as warehousing. It provided employment for about 50 or 60 workers who were mostly girls. The mill was not rebuilt. In the same year a large extension was added at Via Gellia Mill; this also was destroyed by fire in March 1929 and was replaced by the red brick

Cromford Road and the Via Gellia

A letter from Edmund Evans' of Bonsall to Mrs Turnor, a Bonsall landowner, recorded by Adam Wolley, makes clear that the road in the foreground of Figure 8 was constructed in 1736 on the Ball Ley or Ball Eye land 'chiefly by miners who have no wage', the gunpowder - and their ale - being paid for by donations. It was an improvement on the existing Bonsall to Cromford route which ran at a higher level over the flank of the hill from Town End, Bonsall to Stoney Way Road, now called Chapel Hill, Cromford, one of the notoriously hazardous ways into the Derwent valley at this time. Recognising the potential advantage of the new road for travellers wishing to patronise her business, the bath at Matlockwood (later known as Matlock Bath), Mrs Hallam donated a guinea to the construction project. At the enclosure of Ball Eye in 1776 the Enclosure Commissioners formally adopted the route describing the road as 'from Bonsall Green at a place called Clatterway Gate...to Cromford Liberty' and designated it the Cromford Road. Nowadays this length of road is often referred to as part of the Via Gellia but strictly that name refers to the road which runs further up the valley beyond the turn to Bonsall. It was built by Philip Gell on his land in 1792-3 and described as the 'beautiful private road' with 'way-boards inscribed Via Gellia'. The name was chosen in tribute to the family's claim to have Roman ancestry. Gell's road linked Hopton to 'the Cromford Road' so creating a through route from his stone quarries at Hopton to the canal at Cromford and, as John Gell foresaw in his letter to his brother Philip in 1789, giving the Gells the advantage of 'carrying coals back to supply upper country' on the return journey.

In 1804, the whole length of road, from Cromford to Five Lane Ends on Hopton Moor was turnpiked. Only four lanes meet there now, the fifth, Tiremare Lane from Kirk Ireton, is no longer in use. Its closure was approved at Derby Quarter Sessions in August 1890. The Turnpike Act required two new roads to be made branching from it, one 'up the valley between the Griffe and Ible by Grange Mill to Newhaven House', the other 'to the town of Wirksworth'. When the branch towards Newhaven was constructed, it joined the older Nottingham to Newhaven turnpike as it ran between Winster and Pikehall and for some time the trusts shared the remainder of the route to Newhaven. The first toll-gates were at Cromford and Pikehall and Gregory's Gate 'near Joshua Gregory's house at Middleton' on the spur to Middleton which is still called New Road. This gate was later called Kid Lane Gate but the name does not appear in the records after 1835 when the Turnpike Trustees were considering moving it to Rider (now Ryder) Point. Rider Point Gate was listed when the tolls were let in 1836 and it was noted by William Adam in *Gem of the Peak,* 1838, as a 'toll-bar, erected lately, where two roads meet, one to Hopton, the other to Middleton and Wirksworth'. In 1831 it was announced that a gate was 'about to be immediately erected' called Middle Peak Gate. *The Ordnance Survey map* published in 1880 shows a toll house labelled Gregorys T.P. on the Middleton to Wirksworth road which, if it was standing today, would be a little way above the modern entrance to Middle Peak Quarry.

The 1804 turnpike development resulted in travellers bypassing the 'old Manchester road' through the village of Bonsall. Bonsall became isolated. Disgruntled Bonsall residents calculated that now they were required to pay a toll at the Cromford gate (see Figure 88) to use only 1230 yards of highway, a road which had been built by volunteer labour and used without charge for many years and for which the Turnpike Trustees had paid no compensation. The charges were a shilling per horse for narrow wheel carts and fourpence per horse for broad wheel carts. Narrow wheels were usually used by Bonsall people owing to the steepness of the road from the Pig of Lead to the village. In 1850 they succeeded in having the shilling charge reduced to eightpence but not abolished.

mill which now, 2013, borders the road. From 1889 to 1891 William Hollins and Company was experimenting with the production of a yarn combining merino and cotton fibres which could be woven into cloth. The successful product although not woven at Via Gellia Mill took its famous brand name Viyella, registered as a trade mark in 1894, from Via Gellia.

The Via Gellia Mill was closed for spinning in 1905 and re-equipped to process waste raw material from the other Hollins' sites. Cromford Garnetters (Via Gellia) Ltd took over the lease in 1949 running the site until about 1971; the company collected woollen rags from which, when shredded and mixed with new yarn, a cloth known as shoddy could be made. For about ten years after that, nylon extrusion products such as garden netting were manufactured there. In 1983 a local company Wildgoose (Bonsall) Ltd bought the site and rescued much of it from dereliction. Now the complex of buildings, including Elce's mill, houses a range of businesses. The corn mill's wheelpit survives as a conspicuous feature beside the footpath which crosses the mill dam.

George Evans' corn mills

Ball Eye is the long tongue of Bonsall land which forms the steep valley side along Bonsall Hollow from Clatterway at Bonsall to the foot of Chapel Hill at Cromford. Quarrying has gouged into the hillside now but William Adam, *Gem of the Peak*, 1838, described it as 'a lofty rugged cliff, the loose rubble and large fragments from which are perpetually tumbling down into the road'. In the valley bottom, the Bonsall Brook formed the Ball Eye boundary and the boundary between Bonsall and Cromford.

In 1776 a further Enclosure Award of the 'Commons and Waste Ground' around Bonsall, awarded George Evans several allotments including most of Ball Eye, number 246. In 1787 he purchased from Adam Simpson the adjoining allotment, number 244, part of which lay alongside Clatterway immediately to the north of allotment 246 and the Bonsall Brook ran through it into 246.

In 1780 George Evans built a corn mill on the eastern extremity of Ball Eye at the edge of Cromford village (see Figure 3 [1] and Figures 9 and 10). Strictly this mill is in Bonsall parish although it has always been known as Cromford corn mill. For reasons which will become clear and to avoid confusion in the description which follows it is referred to as Evans' corn mill. A considerable dam, some twenty feet deep was built across the valley to secure the pond adjacent to the mill. William Bray's *Sketch of a Tour into Derbyshire,* 1783, noted the mill and the ponds above it 'In the way to Bonsal [sic] some pieces of water have been lately formed by dams across the little stream, which runs down the bottom, and on one of them a large corn-mill is built'. The ponds which Bray mentions were built by Evans. They are indicated by the addition of labels W, X, Y and Z on the Tithe map see Figure 3. Evans sold allotments 244 and 246 with the corn mill and three of the ponds X, Y and Z to Sir Richard Arkwright in 1789. But he retained ownership of the highest, most westerly pond W and the important narrow strip of land which lay between the road and the brook beginning at the eastern end of pond W up to Clatterway Gate which was near Bonsall Green. It secured his access to the brook from the road so enabling him to use his water rights higher up the valley.

FIGURE 9. **Mills at Cromford, watercolour, artist unknown, probably about 1840.**

This view as seen from the A5012 road at the edge of Cromford village shows two corn mills. George Evans built the mill on the left. Long known as Cromford corn mill, it actually stands in Bonsall on the eastern extremity of Evans' Ball Eye allotment. It is referred to in this description as Evans' corn mill. The other mill to the right was built into the hillside on the south side of the Bonsall Brook so was located in Cromford and may correctly be referred to as a Cromford mill. The water which powered it was carried from the Bonsall Brook in a long open goit on an embankment along the lower slope of Slinter Wood. The spillway from the goit appears as a cascade at the extreme right in the picture. The arrangement of these two mills demonstrates considerable skill in using the same water supply to power both mills. The outfall from the mill built into the hillside fed into the pond and so was available to be used again by Evans' mill. In 1818 Henry Moore succinctly described this scene 'two mills, one immediately above the other; the upper mill has an overshot wheel, a cascade near it; they are backed by rock and trees, making a pretty subject for sketching'.

Private collection

FIGURE 10. **North West View of a Corn Mill at Cromford, pencil and wash sketch, George Robertson, 1797.**

Arkwright Society collection

It has been claimed that this Evans corn mill site may have been used for slag smelting at some time in its history. So far no documentary evidence has been found to support this view and we suggest that if slag has been found on the site it may have come from the slag mill higher up the valley and have been used on this site as fill for the dam.

The nineteenth century watercolour at Figure 9 confirms some details shown in George Robertson's earlier drawing Figure 10 which was produced when he was working for the Derby China Manufactory. The attributed date, 1797, has been accepted here despite a significant anomaly in that Robertson's sketch does not include the corn mill kiln building shown in the later watercolour although it is clear from documentary evidence that when Evans sold the property to Arkwright in 1789, a kiln and drying house were included in the sale. In the background Robertson shows a lime kiln in use.

Installation of a turbine

Some time in the last twenty years of the nineteenth century the goit supply to the hillside mill was confined to pipes buried in the in-filled goit. One pipe was fed from the pond, (marked X on the Bonsall Tithe map) which had served the original goit and a second from the pond W above; the valves which controlled the flows in this new system survive. This modification was part of the change from water wheel to turbine at Evans' mill. The piped water was delivered at a high level in a cast iron pipe. A remnant of this system, the bracket which held the cast iron feed pipe is still in place on the mill wall. Water from the turbine was returned to the pond. This installation of the turbine would have coincided with the hillside mill ceasing to operate if it had not already done so. The *Ordnance Survey Map* published in 1900 does not show the hillside mill which suggests that it had been demolished by that date though remnants of the wall which supported the water wheel remained into the 1980s. The wheelpit has recently been partly excavated.

The surviving mill accommodated water wheels at each end but it is not clear if the two wheels worked together or if one replaced the other. The water from the brook now generates electricity using a modern turbine located in one of the former wheelpits.

Did Evans build both corn mills?

The hillside corn mill in Cromford manor shown in Figures 9 and 10 was described in 1789 in a legal source as 'a new corn mill in Cromford' with an explanation of its power supply: 'water is turned and conveyed to it by a cut or aqueduct through the wood called Sling-torr Wood', now Slinter Wood. This cut was for many years known as Higgott's canal after Joseph Higgott who is described as 'of Cromford Mill' in 1794. It was filled in when the pipes were installed as described above and today forms the flat footpath along the bottom of Slinter Wood, within recorded memory spoken of as Goat Lane. The name is surely a modified pronunciation of goit, an old word for a channel of water, which enjoyed widespread use in Derbyshire.

That there was a need for a new Cromford corn mill is clear. The terms of the lease for Arkwright's cotton mill site, which were agreed with William and Mary Milnes in 1771, required Arkwright to protect the water supply to Mr Buxton's corn mill which was close by lower down the brook. This condition was met when the first mill was built but his plans for the great second cotton mill in 1776 required engineering which meant the corn mill could not

Derby Mercury, April 12th, 1776

survive. In April of that year Arkwright received permission from Peter Nightingale to pull it down and within a week of this agreement the mill machinery was advertised for sale.

No evidence has been found of compulsion on Richard Arkwright or anyone else to provide a replacement mill though clearly the demolition of Buxton's mill provided a market opportunity for a new corn mill. It is likely George Evans' construction of the mill, described here as Evans' mill in 1780 was such a response.

Our research has been unable to confirm either the date of construction or the name of the builder of the other mill against the bank in Cromford manor. It was probably not Richard Arkwright, he having neither the land nor the water rights at the appropriate time though we cannot rule out the possibility that he could have leased both. In view of his record of mill building on the Bonsall Brook and from 1777, his ownership of the water rights, George Evans is a more likely candidate, though he did not own the land. This belonged to Peter Nightingale who acquired it when he bought the manor of Cromford in 1776. If Nightingale was the builder, then he would have needed to negotiate with Evans for the lease or purchase of the water rights to it but there is no evidence of such a transaction. When Evans sold pond X to Arkwright on April 7th 1789, he sold him the water rights to this mill, pond X being the pond from which the goit to the new Cromford corn mill was fed. The following day, April 8th 1789, Arkwright agreed to buy the manor of Cromford from Nightingale, a purchase which, it is assumed, included the new corn mill in Cromford so bringing the mill and its water rights into Arkwright ownership.

As to the date of this mill in Cromford manor, it is helpful to consider the archaeological evidence. It may have been an easier engineering option, to dig out the goit and build the relatively shallow dam to form the pond from which it was fed, compared with building the twenty foot dam across the valley for Evans' mill, but the relationship of the level of the new Cromford mill's wheel pit to the level of Evans' mill pond indicates that the Evans' mill and pond were already in place when the Cromford manor mill was built. This suggests a date after 1780 and this is consistent with the mill being described as 'new' in 1789.

Detailed questions remain about the development of these two mills but their existence side by side is evidence of the growth of demand for the cereal products they processed as the village continued to expand and new workers' housing was built on North Street and the Hill. Certainly in June 1797 when both mills were in Arkwright ownership and available to let, one immediately 'with 4 pairs of Stones, Bolting Machine, Drying Kiln' and the other later in the year, the lessor's advertisement in the *Derby Mercury* considered the mills might be run together and were 'worth the attention of those who wish to engage in a capital concern'.

This may have been sales talk but by this date the Cromford housing stock had roughly doubled over a period of about thirty years and the growth continued. Britton and Brayley in *The Beauties of England and Wales,* 1802, estimated that the two Cromford cotton mills and Masson cotton mill employed 1150, made up of 150 men, 300 women, and 700 children. Surrounding villages would contribute some of these workers but there would be additional numbers of workers in other occupations and a growing number of visitors accommodated in the area, especially in Matlock Bath, to swell the demand for mill products. The two mills bear witness to the skill of Evans and his millwrights in exploiting the potential of the brook water supply and in recognising market opportunities.

The shell of the surviving corn mill building has been repaired; internally it contains dismantled milling machinery from Miller's Dale corn mill and parts of a waterwheel from Darley Bridge.

FIGURE 11. **The Corn Mill Cottage, photograph, 1930s.**

Archaeological evidence has shown that Evans' corn mill was built to include two matching wings of which the surviving one, the three storey single bay with the Venetian window shown here, was residential, the use made of the other wing is unknown. The plain three storey extension to the left of the cottage was a later addition. When the photograph was taken, the mill office was in the ground floor room on the right, the sitting room was in the extension and the kitchen and scullery in the outbuilding on the extreme left. The building in the right foreground was for stabling. Behind it there was a covered bay where carts were loaded. Directories show members of the Biddulph family as tenants of the mill from 1860 until about 1900 after which they are remembered working for the next tenants Barker and Son. W H Barker who was agent for the Arkwright estate bought the mill in 1924; Samuel Barker sold it to E H Bailey Ltd, millers of Matlock, in 1933 and in their ownership, at the end of its working life, the mill produced animal feed. The last miller, Alec Paterson, was transferred to Bailey's mill at Matlock before 1947 when the Cromford mill was sold.

A large garage occupies the site of the mill garden now and the stabling was demolished in 1995 when the garage was extended and the corn mill's kiln and malt house were repaired and converted by the Arkwright Society for use as a short stay hostel for parties of young people. Known as the Cromford Venture Centre it was opened by HRH the Prince of Wales in January 1996 and used until 2013.

Arkwright Society collection

Dunsley Mill

FIGURE 12. **Dunsley Mill, photographs, October 1992.**

(Above left) This general view from the north-west shows a detached two storey cottage in the foreground. This was probably the first domestic building on the site. The mill building with a single storey extension lies just beyond. Some time in the latter half of the nineteenth century and certainly by 1878, steam power supplemented water power at the mill. From the engine and boiler house which were added beside the wheelhouse at the west end of the mill, a flue ran to a square chimney high on the bank behind the mill. It is just visible at the right edge of this view:

(Above right) Dunsley Mill viewed from the north-west showing the single storey extension to the mill on the left and on the right a two storey cottage which was a later attachment.

(Bottom left) The original mill entrance in the north end gable viewed from the single storey extension.

(Bottom right) Window detail

All the buildings on the Dunsley Mill site (see Figure 3 [25, 26, 27]) were demolished in 1992 and the record of the mill complex included here is from the field work photographs supplied by the Royal Commission on the Historical Monuments of England, which surveyed the site prior to demolition.

To trace the origin of Dunsley Mill it is necessary to return to George Evans and his purchase of land in the manor of Cromford in 1768. The purchase was from William and Mary Milnes and consisted of five closes of land, called the Lees, now part of Dunsley Meadows, where he built a mill. This later became known as Dunsley Mill. It occupied land on both sides of the brook, in Cromford on the Lees and in Bonsall on Ball Eye. As stated earlier Evans sold his

Ball Eye allotment in 1789 but with the exception of the narrow strip of land between the road and the brook. This safeguarded his access to this mill site and to the brook.

The Royal Commission report described the main mill as a seven bay, three-storey building with the potential for an additional attic floor and dating from about 1800, its configuration and size raising the possibility that it may have been conceived as a cotton mill. Documentary evidence reveals that George Evans built it as a corn mill but no record has been found of its use as such or as a cotton mill and by the time Philip Gell of Hopton bought it from the Evans' estate in 1821 it had already undergone several changes of use, see below.

The changing uses of the Dunsley Mill site

By 1809, the year after Evans' death, the mill was being used as a white lead manufactory by Thomas Barber and George Rawlinson and when their partnership was dissolved in 1812, George Wheeldon used the site as a colour works. A note in connection with Wheeldon's tenure states that Evans had never finished the inside of the house. Five years later the lease was again for sale. Now called Cromford Colour Works, near Cromford, the property was described as a mill, with a house, cooper's shop, counting house and other outbuildings and fifteen acres of excellent meadow and pasture land. William Chawner and William Duesbury continued its use as a 'colour mill for grinding colours'. Duesbury, who is best known for his family's involvement in the Derby China Manufactory his grandfather had developed, had sold his interest there to

VIA GELLIA AND BONSALL COLOUR WORKS,
In the County of Derby.
TO BE SOLD BY AUCTION,
By Mr. EYRE,
(FREE FROM AUCTION DUTY,)
By order of the Assignees of Messrs. Chawner and Dewsbury.
At the Colour Works, Via Gellia and Bonsall, on Saturday the 9th of June, 1827, sale to commence at 10 o'clock.
AT this Sale will be offered a Variety of COLOURS, viz. Mineral and Spruce Ochres, Devonshire Browns, Chocolate, English Umber, Unbleached Barytes, two Hogsheads of Lamp Black, two Hogsheads of Logwood, Casks of Peruvian Bark, Lamp Black, Charcoal, Cast Iron Wheels, Upright Rollers, Levigating Pans, &c. - Also a capital Draught Horse, Cart, Gearing, &c. &c.
Catalogues will be ready five days prior to the Sale, and may be had on the premises, and of the Auctioneer, Full Street, Derby.
At the same time will be offered for sale, the unexpired Lease of three years and a half, in the Cromford Colour Works, and thirteen years and a half in the Via Gellia Works.—Further particulars may be known at the Office of Messrs. BALGUY, PORTER, and BARBER, Solicitors, Derby; or of Mr. EYRE, Auctioneer.

Derby Mercury, June 9th, 1827

experiment with paint manufacture. In 1825 he took out patent No 5258 for preparing and manufacturing a white sulphate from impure native sulphate of barites for use in paint in place of white lead. Glover described it as 'an excellent imitation of white lead applicable to most purposes for which the article is used'. But the business did not prosper. In September 1826 the partners, who now were also tenants of the Via Gellia Works site higher up the valley (see page 24), were declared bankrupt and their assets were advertised in a series of sales - of furniture and effects including valuable oil paintings; of Duesbury's books; of the patent and of their stock in trade at Cromford and at Sutton's Wharf in Derby. John and William Goodall (sometimes Goodale), who had a white lead works and tan yard in Derby, became the new tenants of the mill.

In 1836, during the Goodall's tenure, Richard Arkwright junior bought the mill from Philip Gell. The Goodalls remained in occupation of the site into the 1840s but possibly by 1842 and certainly by 1846 the mill had been converted to a paper mill and had acquired the name Dunsley Mill. It was leased to George Simons who also ran the paper mill at Masson in Matlock Bath. White's Sheffield Directory of 1852 describes Simons as a pasteboard manufacturer. The paper mill closed in 1908 and the site was taken over by the United British Basalt Company. The United Steel Companies Ltd purchased the mill from the Arkwright estate in 1924 and for most of the rest of the twentieth century the premises were engaged in reprocessing carbon waste from the steel industry. In 1992 in the ownership of Swann Minerals, the buildings described here were demolished. The most recent industrial use of the site has been for stone-cutting. In 2011 planning permission was granted for its conversion to an industrial estate and the site was cleared. Today, 2013, it awaits redevelopment.

'Slinter Cottage' Mill

Lower down Bonsall Hollow and at the western extremity of the Derwent Valley Mills World Heritage Site is Slinter Mill (see Figure 3 [24]) with its mill pond and water wheel.

It is not known when or by whom this mill was built but such evidence as has been found suggests that the builder was George Evans. A slag mill is listed in his estate in 1809, the year after his death, and while this might refer to the slag mill he had built with the cupola on the Via Gellia Mill site, it is difficult to believe that both mills were not included in the sale when John Alsop bought the cupola site. There is a brief undated entry, 'Slag Mill Bonsall of Evans and Shore', in Richard Arkwright junior's property records. Elizabeth Evans and Mary Shore were George Evans' daughters and beneficiaries and the item implies that Richard Arkwright bought the mill from them.

Here again Evans' retention of the strip of land between the road and the brook secured his access to the site. The mill would have increased or maintained his capacity to work slag when used alongside or in place of the slag mill on the Via Gellia Mill site. The re-smelting of lead slag, a by-product which had often been allowed to accumulate in thousands of tons on cupola sites when lead was plentiful, became more important as lead mines were being worked out and when the price of lead was high. John Farey's *General View of the Agriculture and Minerals of Derbyshire, Vol I,* 1811, written for the Board of Agriculture from surveys made between 1807 and 1810, records that it was the preferred type of lead for making shot and for red lead. The engineering required to incorporate this mill successfully into the series of mills in the valley required the construction of a long tail race separated from the pond adjacent to it by a substantial bank. Much of its length is visible from the roadside footpath below the mill.

Sanderson's map *Mansfield and*

FIGURE 13. **Saw Mill, Via Gellia, photograph, about 1900**

This view of Slinter Mill shows it in or soon after the last phase of its commercial life as a saw mill.

The chimney suggests an earlier industrial use; the depth of slag waste in what is now the garden bears witness to the mill's earliest known function as a lead slag smelter which, it is reasonable to suppose, was worked in association with the cupola further up the valley (see Figure 6). The cupola smelted lead ore using coal as fuel for the reverberatory furnace and produced lead and slag; the slag mill undertook the 'unwholesome process' of re-smelting the slag to extract a further yield of lead. The water wheel drove the bellows for its furnace which, by the time this mill functioned in the nineteenth century, was probably fuelled by coke cinders from the cupola. For a period between its use as a slag mill and ultimately as a saw mill, it was a wood turning mill.

With acknowledgements to Henry Band

20 Miles Around published in 1835 recorded Slinter Mill as a slag mill but by 1846 when it was owned by Peter Arkwright it had been converted to a wood turning mill making pulleys, wheels and bobbins. There is clear internal evidence of a lower gable showing that the height of the building has been raised from one storey to two; this may have been associated with the change of use but the date when this occurred is not known. The Cromford Church registers include names of wood turners from 1813 but they cannot be linked with this site with any certainty until William Crossley who is known to have been the tenant in 1846.

In 1857 it was described briefly as a lace card manufactory and as a saw mill. It remained in use as a saw mill into the twentieth century. For many years the saw millers associated with the site were the Drabbles; George Drabble who died in 1880, George Stendall Drabble and George Henry Drabble who also had a timber business in Matlock Bath, were each involved. George Henry had 10 years of his lease to run when Elsie Maud Batemen bought the mill and the adjacent Slinter Wood from the Arkwright estate in 1928 but in local memory at about this date, the horses hauling out timber along the infilled goit track to be loaded onto drays at the bottom of Pennyford were from Gregorys, the Darley Dale timber merchants. Timber removal by this route came to an end when the hauling began to cause damage to the water pipes buried in the track, which then became used only as a footpath.

The mill building, often still referred to as the bobbin mill, is remembered as already derelict by the early 1920s but used as temporary accommodation for itinerants including rag collectors and their donkey. Sibyl Young converted the building's upper floor to residential use during World War II and for almost fifty years stoutly defended the mill and the adjacent woodland from development.

The Arkwright Society's purchase of the mill and Slinter Wood in 1991 was made possible by grant aid and donations. Since then further grant aid enabled the Society to repair and restore the building, repair the mill's water wheel and tailrace, restore the mill pond and dam and rediscover and repair the spillway. The wheel is important as one of the only two to survive among the water mills of the Bonsall Brook. After use as a holiday cottage with the undercroft housing an exhibition interpreting the industrial history of the valley and the significant ecology of Slinter Wood and the nearby Dunsley Meadows, the mill is now a private residence.

CHAPTER THREE

Mill sites on the Bonsall Brook outside Cromford

The Colour Works, Via Gellia

The modern photograph below and Figures 14 and 15 illustrate another mill site which is not in Cromford. It is included here because of its importance in the local economy, not least in the late nineteenth and for more than half of the twentieth century in the hands of what became known as the Via Gellia Colour Company, see pages 68-71. It is situated higher up the valley less than half a mile beyond the turn to Bonsall and lies across the boundary between Middleton and Bonsall (see Figure 3 [634]). The original mill was powered by the Via Gellia Brook and the course of the goit which carried water to the wheel may still be traced along the bottom of Middleton Wood beside the Via Gellia road. The site remains in an industrial use within the historic footprint created by its earlier users.

The former Colour Works site, (2012), as seen on the left hand side of the A5012 when travelling westwards up the valley.

Philip Gell of Hopton's accounts of 1807 record Thomas Saxelby, gent of Derby, occupying a house and cupola smelting mill which is considered to refer to this site but his tenancy may have begun at least two years earlier when Saxelby bought half an acre of land from George Evans. Evans' nearest landholding was immediately across the road opposite the cupola where Saxelby may have built a house. Cottage property associated with the mill, just visible in Figures 14 and 15, stood there until the mid twentieth century. It seems likely that Saxelby built the mill, certainly he was the first tenant. Farey confirms a cupola in the name of Saxelby and Co at Via Gellia in Bonsall Dale though in November 1809 a Mr Saxelby's 'Farming Stock and Household Furniture etc' were offered for sale at Via Gellia, he being described as a bankrupt. By 1817 William Evetts Sheffield was the tenant, (see Box).

William Evetts Sheffield's tenancy of the Via Gellia Works site

The property was advertised to let in August 1816 as the 'Via Gellia Lead Works' offering 'a large Cupola with a newly built Smelting Furnace and Calcining Furnace, Slag Hearth, with Slag Mill and Blowing Cylinder worked by a powerful Water Wheel, a Furnace for making Litharge... Also a Dwelling House with suitable offices'. William Evetts Sheffield of London signed a lease from Philip Gell for the site 'at the yearly rent of thirty pounds' on 25th September 1817. The terms of the lease included the use of the 'Mill Lead works stables outbuildings Limeworks and Stone Quarry thereto adjoining'. He was to have 'liberty to get stone clay sand and limestone on the said premises...for the use of the works...' and to occupy the premises 'for the purpose of Smelting the Ores of Copper Lead Zinc and other metals, to make sulphuric acid and to perform any other process or processes in Chimistry [sic] as he...shall think fit'. A letter from W E Sheffield in October 1817 confirmed that he was taking over from Saxelby and that his intention was to smelt lead. The lease also mentions the 'Slagg heap' below the mill and confirms the presence of the 'long chimney on the hillside'. The long chimney was a flue which zig-zagged up the hillside to a vertical chimney (see Figure 15). Farey had earlier described the flue as 'for condensing sulphur sublimed from the galena' and such was the scale of the structure that it was possible to climb up inside to recover the condensed products from the walls; the extra material salvaged helped to offset the cost of the flue. The site retains remnants of a slag heap and of the flue to this day.

Sheffield is described in the lease as from Somers Town, London, but he may be the same William Sheffield who, in 1814, was superintendent and agent for Whiston Copper Works, which lay between Cheadle and Ashbourne in the Churnet Valley, Staffordshire where ore from the famous Ecton mine was smelted and who patented an improved method for working copper. This may have given him local knowledge of this site or his attention may have been drawn to it by his son-in-law William Duesbury who, with his partner William Chawner, was in 1826 working two mill sites in the valley, the lower one, now known as Dunsley Mill, and this Via Gellia Works site. It is not known if they took over the latter in 1822 on Sheffield's death or if they were associated with the site during his tenure.

Chawner and Duesbury followed, and, after 1826, the Goodalls. John Goodall paid rent to Philip Gell of Hopton until 1841. In the same year the Middleton Tithe Schedule records the site as Dunsley Paper Mill with George Simons as tenant. Several more relatively short lived tenancies followed, (see overleaf), during which the site changed from a lead works to a colour works.

This was a significant change. It reflected the decline of the lead mining industry which had been such a significant element in the area's economy for hundreds of years and in its place, the exploitation of the minerals, such as barites, ochre, umber, manganese, which occurred alongside lead in local mines. Cupola and slag mill sites were converted to other uses as the supply of lead ore declined. This site, Via Gellia Colour Works, as its name suggests, was converted to the manufacture of pigments from local minerals and from imports such as Gulf Red, a product of interest to local children who followed the carts of soil as they moved from Matlock Bath station to pounce on locust beans falling from the load. Some of the pigment produced was often used, as here, in the manufacture of paints on the same site, the names colour mill and paint mill often being used interchangeably.

Use of the name Dunsley

The Middleton Tithe map dated 1843, labels the Via Gellia Colour Works as Dunsley Mill. George Simons, a papermaker, was the tenant. Dunsley spring issues from high on the valley side above Tufa Cottage some distance to the west of the mill site. It is thought that Simons may have taken a separate supply of clean water from the spring for washing paper while the brook provided power for the paper making process. For whatever reason, it appears that Simons adopted the name Dunsley for his mill and when, soon after, he moved his business to the mill site lower down the valley he took the name with it.

FIGURE 14. Invoice heading, dated June 30th 1905

Henry Wheatcroft's Via Gellia Works is shown on the right, and his High Tor Colour Works at Matlock Bath on the left.

Reproduced by permission of the National Trust, Kedleston Hall

FIGURE 15. Via Gellia near Matlock Bath, print, published 1869

The lead works in the Via Gellia. The top of the flue chimney is shown high up on the hillside on the left.

Private collection

Later tenants of the Via Gellia Colour Works site

By 1846, part of the Via Gellia Mill site is recorded as Alfred Alsop's lead works where he manufactured red lead and, after his premature death in January 1858 - killed when his horse slipped on ice on Cromford Hill - his sister, Catherine Alsop ran the business until January 1859. The trade directories, *Slater's 1862,* and *Harrods 1870* list William Sperrey at first operating a lead works there and later a colour works. His advertisements in the *Manchester Guardian* for a new or second hand conical burr grinding mill in March 1875 and offering the same article for sale - 'cheap' - in 1876 indicate he was still associated with the mill at these dates but in the *Liverpool Mercury* of June 20th, 1878 William Sperrey, lead smelter and colour manufacturer, Via Gellia Works, is listed in the petitions for liquidation. W J S Peach, who may have overlapped with Sperrey on the Via Gellia Mill site for a period in the 1870s was advertising in Kelly's Directory of 1881 as W. J. Stephenson-Peach, the Via Gellia Paint and Colour Works, selling colours and liquid paints and 'Specially Prepared Colours for Oil Cloth Manufacturers, Paper Stainers & others'. The next lessees Messrs Goodall and Buchanan went into receivership leaving the site closed. John Reid re-opened it in 1886. Reid lived at The Cascades in Bonsall while he was associated with the mill but died in Pendleton, Lancashire in 1890.

Henry Wheatcroft

Henry Wheatcroft took over the site in 1889. Already a successful businessman, he was one of the canal Wheatcrofts (see Chapter 12) and had capital to invest. He extended the works and installed a 100 horse power steam engine though he retained the water wheel. His company remained in business there for more than seventy years and expanded widely. In 1898 he took over the barytes works of Messrs Stevens Bros, Matlock at the foot of High Tor at Matlock Bath and converted it to colour grinding. This new site, the High Tor Colour Works, became the company's head office but the company name, the Via Gellia Colour Co., adopted soon after 1900, continued to reflect the firm's origin. A key to the Company's success was its strength in securing sources of raw materials, investing in the right mines and as local sources became scarce, being able to prospect abroad to negotiate for the minerals they needed and to invest in sites there. By 1901 Wheatcroft had colour mills close to mineral sites in Ireland and Belgium. A limited liability company was formed in 1911 with George Henry Key as chairman and Wheatcroft's wife's nephew Colin Clive Willcock as managing director. After Henry Wheatcroft's death in 1912, the enterprise continued to expand in the hands of these business partners. Key continued to invest in mines including, most notably in 1915, the old Golconda lead mine at Hopton where he installed grinding machinery to process a rich source of barites. From 1914 the Company leased part of Cromford Mill where it continued its core business, producing pigments from minerals, until 1921 when the Cromford Colour Company Ltd was formed to make inorganic chemical colours. This business was taken over by Burrell Colours and closed in 1978.

The Stone Mill, Clatterway

The Bonsall Tithe Map shows two mills near the bottom of Clatterway. Both are wholly in Bonsall. Their early history is unclear. Neither mill is listed in Richard Arkwright junior's assets in 1803 although he owned the land at that date. His son Peter inherited the family estate in 1843 and in the Bonsall Tithe Schedule of 1846, he is described as owning the lower one, a stone cutting mill tenanted by George Pickard (see Figure 3 [40]). Farey listed a stone-sawing mill at Bonsall in 1811 so it seems possible that the mill was built some time between 1803 and 1811. Adam in 1838 describes the mill as where 'all the Hopton stone (a dun-coloured limestone) is cut up into flag-stones and for ornamental purposes' and credits the mill with cutting the Hopton stone for the plinthing for the dining room at Chatsworth House. Pickard had taken a seven year lease on the Hopton quarry in 1835. In 1867, it was referred to as 'the old stone mill' and was being repaired. *Harrod & Co's Directory 1870* shows William Hawley there as a barytes and metallic oxide manufacturer. Directories from the 1870s and 80s continue to list William, (and by 1899, John Hawley) as colour manufacturers on the site.

Subsequently Henry Wheatcroft added it to his clutch of mills, manufacturing colour pigments and latterly only black, for dying purposes, before it was owned by the Taylor Colour Company. The site has been modified now to accommodate two houses but archaeological features of the watercourse survive.

The Hawley business interests extended to Moulbourn Mill at Duffield in the 1870s; William bought the mill there in 1888.

The Comb Mill, Clatterway

The other mill, of which little remains, was sited at the top of the 'stone mill' grounds (see Figure 3 [51]). In 1846 it was a comb shop owned and occupied by Robert Hartle. It is not known when or by whom it was built. Several families in Bonsall were involved in comb making with entries in Directories from the late 1820s to the 1880s but why it appears to have been a common occupation in Bonsall is not known. Thomas Martin's description of comb making suggests that it would have lent itself to a small workshop industry and Abraham Rees in *Manufacturing Industry, 1819-20*, adds information about making imitation

Comb Making – extracts from the *Circle of the Mechanical Arts*, Thomas Martin, Second Edition, 1818.

The commoner sorts of combs are generally made of the horns of bullocks; or of elephants and seahorses teeth; some are made of tortoise-shell, and others of box, holly and other hardwoods.

Bullock horns are thus prepared to be manufactured into combs, the tips are to be sawn off, after which they are to be held in the flames of a wood fire, till they become nearly as soft as leather. In this state they are split open on one side and pressed in a machine between two iron plates, then plunged into a trough of water, from which they come out hard and flat. When the horn is cut to the size intended for the required combs, several pieces are laid upon a pair of tongs, adapted to the business, over a fire, made chiefly of joiners shavings, to soften them. They are frequently turned, and when sufficiently soft, are put into a vice and screwed tight to complete the flattening. When this process is finished, the horns are perfectly flat and hard; they are given to a man who shaves, planes, or scrapes off the rough parts with a knife, similar in shape to the one used by Coopers, having two handles, which the comb-maker works from him, across the grain of the horn, from one end of the intended comb to the other. When both sides are perfectly smooth, it is delivered to the person who cuts the teeth.

…The cutting of the teeth is commenced by a double saw, of which each blade is something like the small one with which joiners and cabinet makers cut their fine work, with this he forms the teeth.

[It is assumed that at a later date power was applied to the sawing process and that this was the use Hartle made of the Bonsall Brook at his comb shop on Clatterway in Bonsall.]

tortoiseshell combs from bullock horns patchily stained with litharge [lead oxide], raw materials which would have been available in Bonsall. Evidence for the use of genuine tortoiseshell comes from the *High Peak News* report of a 'lamentable accident on the Cromford and High Peak Railway' in October 1833 which resulted in the death of two brothers, Benjamin and Jacob Rains, who were described as tortoiseshell comb makers from Bonsall. They had been on a trip to Manchester and Liverpool to take orders and to purchase supplies, presumably of turtle shell imported through the port of Liverpool. On the return journey a link in the chain supporting the train broke at the top of Middleton incline. The brothers failed to jump clear as instructed and were killed as the third wagon 'was pitched with dreadful force upon the other two'.

FIGURE 16. **Cromford Mill, watercolour, the Rev Charles Annesley, 1811.**

This is a view across the Greyhound pond from the mill site which is now, 2013, occupied by Home Products. In the middle distance it shows the backs of the The Greyhound and of the row of houses beside it in the Market Place. At the extreme right is the building which stands at the top of the market place area at the junction with Water Lane.

The large building in the left foreground is the end of the calamine mill to which a waterwheel is attached. This appears to have paddles rather than buckets and thus to be an undershot wheel. The picture shows little of the wheel's power supply; Annesley would seem to have scant interest in mill engineering. The archaeological evidence which survives beside the present wheel confirms that there was an earlier wheel or wheels at a lower level than the present one. The Greyhound pond was constructed by 1785 and this picture indicates that the water level in the pond was low enough to permit the undershot wheel or wheels to operate. The evidence that there were later two wheels is contained in an advertisement which appeared in the *Derby Mercury* in June 1835 when the lease of the site, then described as a Mineral Paint Works, was offered for sale. The archaeological evidence shows that the wheels were arranged side by side. At some time later, probably mid to late nineteenth century the two undershot wheels were replaced by a single overshot wheel fed, as now, by water piped underground from the corn mill pond higher up the valley. Only one of the original two pipes survives.

Reproduced by permission of Scarthin Books

Hartle's use of the comb shop in 1848 with its power supply from the brook, indicates that his production was mechanised ensuring a steady output of combs for his sales outlet. This was Hartle's Bazaar, which stood beside the old road to the New Bath Hotel at Matlock Bath, where visitors might choose combs for 'cleaning hair' or to hold hair in place or for ornament. Older residents at Bonsall may recall that the comb shop was later used as a joiner's workshop.

The Calamine Mill, Scarthin

The mill, shown above, stands at the head of the Greyhound pond. In 1773, Isaac North, then described as an Inn holder of Matlock, leased a parcel of land known as the coal yard to a group of men, Thomas Salt, John Ford, Richard Conquest, John Baskerville, Edward

Calamine production locally

Calamine was not subject to the very particular rules which governed lead mining. It belonged to the owner of the land where it was found and terms and conditions for exploiting it were agreed with the land owner. Wolley provides an example - the 21 year lease which Henry Willcock, ironmonger of Bonsall, agreed with Thomas Goodwin of Shottle in 1752. He was to mine calamine in Matlock parish in land in the tenure of John Bowden at a rent of 3 shillings for every ton dug up and to recompense tenants of the land for damage.

Pilkington described how the ore was processed.

'From the mines calamine is carried to the furnace, which is built near a rivulet or small stream of water. Here it is first washed in the current, [buddled] and cleaned from the soil or clay, which adheres to and is mixed with it. It is then in a vessel filled with water, washed again in sieves, and the foreign matters are picked out. These are chiefly cauk, spar, and lead ore, and all excepting the last are thrown away. When by repeated washing and picking the ore seems sufficiently purified, it is calcined in a reverberatory furnace of nearly the same form and construction with the cupola which is used for smelting lead ore. The chief respect in which they differ from each other, is, that the furnace, of which I am speaking, has not a concave but flat roof and bottom. The time required for calcining the calamine is about four or five hours; and during the process the ore is frequently stirred up with iron rakes. When it is taken out of the furnace, it is picked again, and being ground into a fine powder, and washed once more, becomes fit for use'.

Some other accounts of the process include grinding before, as well as after, calcining and in the absence of a furnace, the ore could be burnt layered with fuel in conical heaps. The procedures described here reduced the weight of material to be carried to the brass works in the form of zinc oxide by about 40% compared with the weight of the ore. The manager of the calamine works in Bonsall in 1760 was charged with inefficiency for a year's production of only 500 tons of calcined calamine from 1129 tons of ore. Calamine works in Bonsall had been set up in 1753 by the Cheadle Calamine Company from Staffordshire and in 1828, are still recorded in the Bonsall Land Tax Accounts in the hands of Joseph Ingleby and Company. Ingleby's father William had been a partner in Thomas Patten and Company, proprietors of the Cheadle Brass and Wire Company. The works remained active in Bonsall until about 1830; its two mills were put up for auction in 1831.

Mention has been made already of George Evans in the second half of the eighteenth century building calamine houses where calamine ore would have been collected and stored on his cupola site and later adding a calamine mill nearby though this use had been given up by 1809.

Ruston and William Sawyer, all brassmakers from Birmingham 'with authority to pull down the said building and walls of the coal yard and to build and erect buildings and furnaces and to do every other necessary act ... for the purpose of calcining and preparing lapis calimnaris [calamine] for the making of brass also to make use of the brook or stream of water which runs on the southwardly side of the demised premises for preparing the lapis calimnaris at a rent of three pounds ten shillings'. The tenants were not to build 'any bog house or necessary house within sixteen yards of the brook or stream'. The property was in Scarthin which was in Matlock parish, and the brook was the Bonsall Brook, flowing in its natural course, before the Greyhound pond was created, marking the boundary between Cromford and Matlock. We believe that it was this partnership that erected the first mill on this site.

The calamine industry

The zinc used in the production of brass, an alloy of zinc and copper, was produced from calamine, zinc carbonate, which, in the eighteenth century, was largely mined in Derbyshire, Somerset and Flintshire. Dr Richard Watson *Chemical Essays, Vol. IV,* 1786, reported the yearly output from Derbyshire as not more than 40 tons in the 1720s and by the 1780s as about 1500 tons though James Pilkington *A View of the Present State of Derbyshire,* 1789, thought the latter figure was an over-estimate. At this date Derbyshire ore was regarded as of inferior quality for the production of brass compared with the other sources of supply, bringing in 40 shillings for an undressed ton and about 125 shillings for a dressed ton while the Somerset products could command 65-70 shillings and 160 shillings respectively. W C Aitken *Birmingham and the Midland Hardware District,* 1866, considered that 1500 tons per annum had been the peak output for Derbyshire in the eighteenth century and though by 1859 when Aitken made his comment, brass production had expanded considerably, the county had not increased its calamine production, evidence of the extent to which Derbyshire had been overtaken by its competitors.

The growth of the calamine industry in Derbyshire was closely related to the increase in consumption of brass by the Birmingham industries. Brass was used to make hollow wares – pots and pans referred to in the trade as battery; brass wire from which pins were made; wire used for textile cards and for sieves and later, for the mesh used by papermakers. Brass was also used for a variety of clothing and footwear products such as buttons and buckles and the majority of all these products were made in and around Birmingham though there were certain other areas which specialised in a particular product such as the pin industry in Gloucester. As Birmingham's domestic and export trade grew, the latter fed by the slave trade where brass goods were exchanged for slaves, so the demand for the raw material increased. Traditionally Birmingham had been supplied by the brass makers of the Bristol area who dominated the industry until the last quarter of the eighteenth century. From 1734 brass made near Cheadle (where the Cheadle Copper and Brass Company's first brass mill had been founded in 1719) entered the market and from the 1760s brass was also supplied from the Macclesfield Copper Company which had extended its activities to include the manufacture of brass.

The Birmingham link

In 1773, as described above, a calamine mill was built in Cromford by a group of Birmingham men, though no company name is attributable to them. Britton and Brayley in 1802 reported up to four hundred tons of calamine being prepared annually in the village by a Birmingham company. Stephen Glover's *The History and Gazetteer of the County of Derby,* 1829, is more specific, attributing this mill to the Birmingham Brass Company which had been formed in 1827. There is therefore a clear Birmingham link which runs through the life of the site as a calamine works. The site did not escape Farey's attention. He wrote in his survey of 'a Work in Cromford where Calamine is roasted and buddled &c' adding 'The refuse of roasted and buddled Calamine, mixed with quick-lime, makes a Mortar which sets exceeding hard, and is used by Mr. Arkwright in his Works'. No archaeological evidence for a furnace has been found on the site.

The development which began in 1773 was Cromford's second calamine works. Its first had been set up in the old lead smelting mills by the river Derwent (see cover image) by John Turner of Birmingham who took a 40 year lease of the site in 1761. Later in 1774 'John Turner, merchant of Birmingham', (who may have been the same John Turner but who could also

Jedediah Strutt's house in Cromford

Included in Arkwright's purchase of the calamine mill was a dwelling house with stable and brew house which in 1775 Isaac North had leased to Arkwright's partner Jedediah Strutt, founder of the cotton mills in Belper and Milford, for 80 years at a rent of £30 a year. Arkwright paid £455 for both properties. Nothing is known of Strutt's house but the fact that it was included with the mill site purchase suggests that the properties were close together. Strutt surrendered his lease of the house to Richard Arkwright junior in 1792. The Strutts had remained on friendly terms with the Arkwrights although the business partnership had ended some years earlier.

Samuel Need's House

Another of Richard Arkwright's partners, Samuel Need, also had a local residence in this case with a chapel attached. This was in Matlock Bath and was built in 1777 if the chapel headstone, which is now built into the wall at the side of the road leading to Masson House, is to be believed. It stood between the river and the road close to the site later developed for Masson Mill. Later known as Glenorchy House, it was purchased by the Ministry of Transport in 1957 and was an early casualty of the A6 road widening scheme.

have been a relative) took a seven year lease on the rights to mine calamy stone in Cromford. It is difficult not to associate these developments in Cromford with the activities of a family of the same name who, in 1740, in response to the increasing demand for brass in Birmingham, set up the first brass making works in the town, the Turner Brass House in Coleshill Street. This was the first step in a course which would see Birmingham replace Bristol as the national centre of the brass making industry. A visitor to the works in 1754 noted that they obtained their copper from Wales and their calamine from Derbyshire. It is not known how long the Turners worked the calamine mill site in Cromford but it would have been out of use by the early 1790s at the latest when Sir Richard Arkwright began to build his chapel close by. It is not known whether the two Cromford calamine mills worked together or at any time shared the same owner. Both sites had the legal right to carry out the process of preparing calamine for the brass market and both had Birmingham connections. The possibility of some association between them cannot be ruled out.

Calamine continued to be extracted in Cromford; for example Abraham Mills of Macclesfield took the lease to mine calamy (zinc carbonate) and black jack, (zinc sulphide), in Mr Arkwright's lands in Cromford Liberty in March 1792 paying £250 annually in each year that 400 tons of dressed ore was raised, less if that target was not reached though in that case, Arkwright reserved the right to mine as much as he liked for his own use or sale. The mill in the centre of the village continued to process calamine into the 1820s.

Cromford Mineral Paint Works and the later uses of the calamine mill site

In 1790 Sir Richard Arkwright bought the calamine mill in Cromford village from Isaac North's heirs, John Wright and Mary Hodkin. The mill was converted to the Cromford Mineral Paint Works in about 1830, a use it retained into the twentieth century, producing pigments and paints and with a variety of tenants including in the 1880s James Walter Wheatcroft from Matlock Bath. The *Derby Mercury's* advertisement for the sale of the lease in 1835 credits the proprietors, Potter and Company, with building the principal part of the works since the commencement of the lease about five years ago and claims 'exclusive rights to the whole of the Minerals, except Lead Ore, upon estates in Matlock, Cromford, and Bonsall'. 27 years remained unexpired on the lease of the works and 26 years on the minerals. With the licence that has been a hallmark of advertisers through the ages, the advertisement locates the paint works as within 200 yards of the Cromford Canal and Railroad 'from which goods are forwarded with great expedition to all parts of England, Ireland and Scotland'.

By the time of the Arkwright village estate sale in 1924 the mill site was in use as the Arkwright estate building yard with glass, plumber's, mason's, carpenter's and blacksmith's shops as well as cart shed, stores and stables. Later Thomas Walker, joiner and undertaker, occupied the premises. In the 1930s a Cromford resident recalls his family fetching slaked lime from the lime pit there for whitewashing the pantry. Mr Walker is credited with building the first house in Cromford after the estate sales of the 1920s for his own use; it is now 3 Water Lane. Leonard Stamp's Sunny Bank on Cromford Hill appeared soon after.

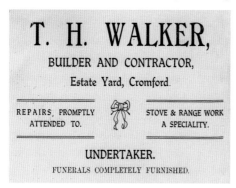

T. H. WALKER,

BUILDER AND CONTRACTOR,

Estate Yard, Cromford.

REPAIRS PROMPTLY ATTENDED TO.

STOVE & RANGE WORK A SPECIALITY.

UNDERTAKER.

FUNERALS COMPLETELY FURNISHED.

Cromford Church Magazine, October 1928

The surviving wheel on the mill site was restored in 1975 by the Arkwright Society as part of the local celebration of European Architectural Heritage Year. The restored wheel was inaugurated by the Duke of Gloucester. The site is owned and occupied now by Home Products.

FIGURE 17. **Tufa Cottage, Via Gellia, photograph.**

This photograph is likely to date from the period 1860 to the 1890s when such large format scenic views (shown reduced here) were popularly produced for displaying in photograph albums. The style changed little in the period so the pictures are difficult to date. The house shown is Tufa or Marl Cottage which was a gamekeeper's cottage. It was built of stone quarried from the hillside and became a feature of interest for tourists on their excursions through the Via Gellia for whom tufa was better known as a garden landscaping stone. In the second half of the nineteenth century John Smedley of Matlock Bath was a tufa merchant at this Via Gellia Quarry and between the two World Wars Cecil Henshall, also from Matlock Bath, used its tufa in his gardening business. William Adam, who drew attention to significant changes in the locality which occurred between editions in his series of guide books, *Gem of the Peak*, noted the local tufa at this site in the first edition of 1838; he does not mention the cottage until the 1843 edition. Grouse and pheasant were still being reared at Tufa Cottage between the two World Wars when the shooting in the valley was rented by Wilson's of Sheffield, manufacturers of Top Mill Menthol Snuff. In 1915 T K Wilson of Sheffield gave the annual supper for the Via Gellia Shooting at the Cheese Factory at Grange Mill with catering by Mr Needham of the Holly Bush Inn. High on the hillside above Tufa Cottage was Dunsley Spring; the flow from it is shown in the bottom right hand corner of the picture. In 1943 William Hollins and Company Ltd at Via Gellia Mill negotiated an agreement with Wirksworth Urban District Council for 'abstraction of water from Dunsley Springs'. The Council was to take a third of the supply for Middleton (by Wirksworth), the Company was to install the necessary machinery.

Private collection

CHAPTER FOUR

Richard Arkwright comes to Cromford

From 1771 until Richard Arkwright's death in 1792 he and George Evans were contemporaries and for most of that time near neighbours, Evans at Cromford Bridge House and Arkwright at Rock House.

George Evans' impact on the local scene was considerable but his industrial investments were of a type with which people were familiar for generations; used technologies which were well established and provided employment for a relatively small workforce. Richard Arkwright's investment in Cromford was on an incomparably greater scale. He had a single-minded aim to mechanise the processes whereby raw cotton could be converted to strong serviceable yarn for supply to weavers and framework knitters. His mills were larger than had been seen in Cromford before; mechanisation and organisation was on a grander scale and they provided work not only for local people but for hundreds who were attracted to the village, most of whom needed housing. The Cromford fashioned by two generations of Arkwrights was, by 1843, scarcely recognisable as the scattered lead mining settlement which Richard Arkwright had chosen for his experiment in water powered cotton spinning in 1771.

On September 2nd 1768, an advertisement in the *Derby Mercury* announced that Cromford Mill was 'To be lett to the best Bidder at the House of Isaac North, in Cromford, on Wednesday, the 21st Day of September'. This referred to Cromford's corn mill and it was the third of a short series of advertisements to let the mill in the period 1766-8. It is not known who placed these advertisements but they reveal something of the condition and importance of the mill site. From them it is clear that the mill was worked by the 'Stream that comes from Bonsall Mill, join'd by Cromford Sough'. In 1766 this mill is described as having one wheel and three pairs of stones though 'if thought necessary, another Wheel will be added on reasonable terms'. In 1768 the mill, is being put 'into thorough repair...and furnished with French Stones...to make it a compleat [sic] Flour Mill'. The introduction of French stones suggests the mill was responding to a demand for a finer product, flour, rather than the meal which the coarser local stones customarily produced. In 1766 it was claimed that advantage might be taken of markets at Wirksworth, Winster, Chesterfield, Alfreton and Higham and in 1768 that 'This mill is situate within a moderate Distance of Derby, Ashbourne, Chesterfield, Alfreton and Wirksworth, [and] is in the Heart of a very considerable Mineral County, where great Quantities of Flour is continually vended'. The prospective tenant of the corn mill was promised that the mill is always supplied with 'plenty of Water from a Stream that never Freezeth, nor is ever troubled with Back Water. There are several other streams as well as the River Derwent within the Manor of Cromford which lie very convenient for the erecting Mills of any Kind, which may be treated and agreed for at the same Time, or afterwards, by applying to Mr Samuel White, of Ashford in the said County.'

In 1768 Richard Arkwright was working in Nottingham. The Derby Mercury was offered for sale in a number of towns though not in Nottingham, and it is possible that one of these advertisements made him aware of Cromford's potential as a site for a mill. Whatever attracted him, in 1771, Arkwright and his partners took a lease on a small parcel of land close to Cromford corn mill on which they planned to build a cotton mill.

The village when Richard Arkwright arrived

Little is known of Arkwright's early years in the village and there is no record of where he lived before Peter Nightingale leased Rock House to him in 1776. The Cromford where his mill building enterprise began appears to have been a scattered community sustained by lead mining and farming. The report, right, from the *Derby Mercury* of May 19th 1769 illustrates that Cromford contributed labour to the woollen hosiery industry which was long established in the area around Wirksworth.

> **D E R B Y, MAY 18.**
>
> We learn from Wirkſworth, that there was laſt Week one of the greateſt Conteſts at Cromford in that Pariſh, ever heard of. Two young Women, (extraordinary Spinners of Soft Jerſey) diſputing about which could earn the moſt Money in a Week, agreed to decide the Matter by a Wager of Five Shillings ; accordingly they ſtarted on Monday Morning the 8th Inſt. at Five o'Clock, for beginning each Day, and to leave off at Eight in the Evening, till Saturday at Three o'Clock, which was to finiſh the Wager ; when one took in 18 Pounds of Worſted at 9d. per Pound, and the other 6 Pounds, at 2s. whereby one earned 13s. 6d. and the other 12s. by their Dexterity at the Jerſey Wheel ; which, it's ſuppoſed, is the moſt extraordinary Performance of the Kind, ever known in the three Kingdoms.

A small number of buildings in Cromford have survived from the pre-Arkwright period; a few examples are illustrated here along with two views which show something of the village before Richard Arkwright made his dramatic alterations.

FIGURE 18. **The Lock-up cottages, Swift's Opening, photograph, early 2000s.**

The row of three cottages shown here at Swift's Opening was built in the early to mid eighteenth century. In 1790 instructions from the Quarter Sessions directed that communities should provide a secure place for alleged felons to be held until they could be transferred to Derby. Cromford's chosen lock-up was the ground floor of the central dwelling here which was modified to contain two small cells though it could be used to house a poor family when not in custodial use. The loom shop window and taking-in doors at first floor level and an outside stair, not visible in this view, are evidence for the industrial use of the upper floor at a later date.

Refurbished by the Arkwright Society, the building now offers office accommodation and storage space, while the lock-up is an attraction for visitors on guided tours of Cromford.

FIGURE 19. **Two storey cottages 78 and 80 The Hill, photograph, 2012.**

These two storey cottages on Cromford Hill, the lower one built of random limestone, interrupt the flow of the three storey gritstone Arkwright housing on the Hill. They are thought to be indicated on the map of Cromford Moor Long Sough dated 1777. An early twentieth century photograph records both in use as shops with earthenware dealer and cycle agent James Young advertising at the bottom house. He was listed in Kelly's Directories from 1908 to 1922.

FIGURE 20. **The Old Cottage at the corner of Alabaster Lane, photograph, date unknown.**

This building dates from the seventeenth century but with a late eighteenth or early nineteenth century extension. It is listed Grade 11. It is understood to contain an early painted ceiling.

Private collection

FIGURE 21. **The bedehouses, photograph, 2010.**

This row of almshouses or bedehouses on Bedehouse Lane was endowed in 1662 by Mary Armyne (sometimes Armine) daughter of Henry Talbot, wife of Sir William Armyne, for the use of six poor widows. The row is now converted into two dwellings and is still managed by the Cromford Almshouses' Trust.

FIGURE 22. **The Old Smithy, Cromford, photograph, about 1904.**

The smithy building, across the road from The Greyhound pre-dates the Arkwright era. The blacksmith was an essential member of the community. Billy Mee, the last of them in Cromford, died in 1997. He had taken over on his father's death in 1921 and with the decline of horse traffic developed the business in other directions including an ironmonger's shop. The blacksmith's workshop shown here was later incorporated into the shop.

Private collection

FIGURE 23. **View of Crumford (sic) near Matlock Bath in Derbyshire, drawn, engraved and published by John Boydell, published 1749.**

This print shows the view from Cromford looking down the road now called Mill Lane. The road was the major route through Cromford at this time, coming from the south, from Wirksworth, and leading to the crossing over the River Derwent at Cromford bridge. The road to Belper, now the A6 south from Cromford, had not been built. The building in the foreground can be located with some precision from its relationship to the dark mouth-like opening in the rock which is still visible at the top of the ramp beside Cromford Community Centre. The road appears to run closer to the rock than it does now and more or less along the line of the present Lime Yard. The Bonsall Brook, swelled by water from the Cromford Moor Long Sough which drained lead mines on Cromford Moor, runs in its natural course to the left of the road. When Richard Arkwright created the market place around 1790, the brook had been culverted and now appears only briefly at the corner of the Lime Yard. In 1817 a new length of road was engineered to pass through the rock barrier on the right of this picture. The road, later to be called Derby Road, was the first section of a new turnpike from Cromford to Belper. The embankment carrying the watercourse to Arkwright's first mill ran at the foot of the rock and across the line of the intended new road so the road level had to be raised considerably to accommodate the watercourse in a culvert beneath it. The embankment survives in the Lime Yard and on the other side of the A6 alongside Mill Lane. To make a satisfactory junction with this new section of road, the road from Wirksworth must have been realigned and its level raised. In the distance there are buildings beside the watercourse; to the right of them above the trees and difficult to see at this magnification, is a double pile building with chimneys which may represent an early form of Rock House.

Private collection

Boydell's early view shows the road now known as Mill Road or Mill Lane. At this date there were two routes towards Matlock Bath on the near side of the River Derwent, neither visible in this view. One from Cromford Bridge lay close to the river and had been made 'passable for a carriage' by Marmaduke Pennell in about 1730, not as a philanthropic gesture but to enable potential clients to reach his thermal bath at Matlock Bath more easily. Church Walk follows part of the route now. The other was the steep road over Scarthin Rock which, despite being turnpiked in 1759 (see Figure 90), continued to be a difficult route for wheeled traffic for many years. It now forms part of the A6 to the north.

It was to be almost sixty years later before there was a public route in the opposite direction to Belper. By the early years of the nineteenth century 'a private Carriage–way' 'belonging to Messrs. Strutts, Charles Hurt and Richard Arkwright Esqrs.' had been constructed from 'Belper (by Alderwasley, through the fine Meadows and Woods, by the Derwent to Cromford-Bridge'). Neither the exact course nor the quality of this road is known. The scant details are from John Farey who was in favour of a good public road being made 'nearly' along the line of the private route. In September 1812 the *Derby Mercury* announced that 'gate-keepers are appointed', the road 'having lately been much trespassed upon, the locks broken and other damage done'; 'no persons whatever can be allowed to pass, unless they are going to or from Willersley, Alderwasley or Bridgehill'. But it was clear that such a route would be 'of great public utility' and by 1817, the Cromford to Belper Turnpike Trust had been formed. The preamble to the Act which empowered the trustees to create the new turnpike road described the inadequacy of the existing situation 'There is no direct road from Cromford to Belper. The present road from Cromford to Bull Bridge is hilly and dangerous'. In June of that year the trustees met at the Greyhound Inn, Cromford 'for the purpose of letting the forming and making of the Road in different lengths'. The plan which they had adopted replaced an earlier proposal, dated 1815, which favoured a route skirting rather

Summary of the sums of money which 'may be demanded and taken as Tolls' on the Cromford to Belper turnpike road, which was built as a consequence of an Act of Parliament in 1817.

For every Horse or other Beast drawing any Coach, Berlin, Landau, Chariot, Chaise, Gig, Curricle, Hearse, Calash, Marine or other such Carriage, the sum of Four Pence Halfpenny;

For every Horse, or other Beast, drawing a Waggon, Cart or other such Carriage, having the sole or bottom of the Fellies [rims] of all the Wheels thereof of the breadth of Nine Inches or upwards, with flat surfaces and not deviating more than One Quarter of an Inch therefrom, and with the Nails countersunk so as not to rise above the Tire, the sum of Two Pence;

[For wheels less than six inches broad the cost increased to three pence and this charge was doubled to six pence if the wheels had nails which were not countersunk].

For every Horse, Mule or Ass laden or unladen and not drawing the sum of One Penny Halfpenny;

For every pair of Millstones, if drawn in pairs, and for every single Millstone, Block of Stone or Piece of Timber drawn by Five Horses or other Beasts of draught, the sum of Two Shillings and Sixpence and if drawn by more than Five...the further sum of one Shilling for each Horse or Beast exceeding that number...;

For every drove of Oxen or Neat Cattle Ten Pence per Score;

For every drove of Calves, Hogs, Sheep or Lambs the sum of Five Pence per Score.

The Lime Yard, Cromford

When and how the Lime Yard got its name is not known. The area is described as Lime Yard, Shed and Weir in the Cromford Tithe Schedule of 1840. It is considered that the cliff face of Allen's Hill above it is natural but at this date there was a stone quarry in Richard Arkwright junior's occupation in the side of the hill facing Derby Road. Had stone been quarried there and burnt at lime kilns in the Lime Yard? This is speculation only. Certainly a trade in burnt lime had been developed at Cromford after the canal opened in 1794. However no other written reference to the name Lime Yard has been found at any date nor has any archaeological evidence been found for kilns at this or the quarry location.

than breaching the rock barrier shown in Figure 23. This was to have been achieved by building a new road branching off Cromford Hill from below North Street (where Victoria Row was later built) and gradually descending across the fields to level off along the valley. In July 1818 the trustees ordered the turnpike to be open to the public with two full tolls being taken at Amber Gate and Meer Brook Gate. Henry Moore remarked on the new route in his guide book published in 1818 and recommended it as 'both delightful and pleasant'.

FIGURE 24. **Near Cromford, Derbyshire, John Webber, pencil and watercolour, (unfinished) July 1789.**

This view from close to Cromford bridge records the area known as Smelting Mill Green and the houses at the foot of Scarthin Rock. The figures in the mid foreground are crossing over the Bonsall Brook on a plank bridge. In the left foreground is waste from the former lead smelting mill, which by this date had been converted for use as a calamine mill. In the background hay makers are at work on Scarthin Rock. Richard Arkwright would dramatically alter this view when the area became part of the park for Willersley Castle. His chapel, now St Mary's Church was built near the smelting mill site and the mill and the houses shown here were demolished.

John Webber (1751-93) was a professional artist who had been the Admiralty's official draughtsman on Captain Cook's last voyage to the South Seas. He had travelled to Derbyshire with his friend William Day, (1764-1807), an amateur artist whose drawing of the same scene from a slightly different vantage point essentially confirms the accuracy of the illustration while showing more of the former smelting mills. William Day's image appears on the cover of this book. Day's particular passion was geology and it may have been that interest which brought them to Derbyshire. He formed one of the earliest private collections of minerals in the country; it was destroyed during World War II while housed in Hampstead Public Library.

CHAPTER FIVE

The Cromford Cotton Mills

It was in Cromford that Richard Arkwright (1732-1792) developed the factory system which revolutionised the cotton spinning industry. Our present knowledge of the 21 years he lived here is based on the scant available documentary evidence, on painstaking work unravelling the clues from the surviving archaeology and on a record bequeathed to us by the artists and writers of the day. The artistic record is still unfolding as works are brought to light, hitherto unrecognised as a source of information and these gradually expand our knowledge. The serious investigation of the history and archaeology of the mill site began in 1967 and while much has been learned, many questions remain. Neither Richard Arkwright's technological developments nor the details of his mill buildings are described here though we do consider some aspects of their impact on Cromford.

In considering Richard Arkwright's choice of Cromford as the site for his mill it is important to understand what in 1770 he and his partners were setting out to achieve. They were embarking on a series of experiments to apply water power to Arkwright's spinning machinery which hitherto, at the mill in Nottingham, had been driven by a horse gin and subsequently to develop machines, also water powered, for the various pre-spinning processes which, in due course, in 1775, were to form the content of the second patent. Their journey from laboratory experiment to factory production of a serviceable yarn was to take several years but at this early stage their requirements for water power were modest and the water of the Cromford Sough was more than sufficient. Visitors to Cromford often ask why the mill was not built on the River Derwent not realising that the partners had neither the need nor the financial resources to establish a site on the river itself. Nor were they free to plant a mill where they might find a convenient spot. Water rights were highly prized and mill sites generally long established and protected by customary and legal rights and though sites might be redeveloped for new uses, landowners were frequently reluctant to introduce new developments on their water for fear of disturbing existing agreements. So when a site became available there was likely to be serious interest. It is not known whether Arkwright and his partners faced competition in their negotiations in 1770-71 for the Cromford site but the career of Arkwright's contemporary, George Evans, the successful developer of so many mills in Cromford and Bonsall, demonstrates the strength of local demand for water powered sites.

What is quite certain is that they made a sound choice. The volume of water from the Cromford Sough was more or less constant throughout the year and emanating from such a depth beneath the hill separating Cromford from Wirksworth, seldom froze. It not only served their immediate purpose but was later adapted to provide power for two mills and a mill/warehouse though some expensive engineering solutions had to be employed to achieve this output. Cromford was also reasonably well linked by road to Nottingham, the hosiery centre with which Arkwright and his partners were familiar and where initially their prospective market lay.

The first Cromford cotton mill

Arranging a lease

On August 1st 1771 the partners who had formed Richard Arkwright and Company in 1770 agreed with Richard Nall, trustee for William and Mary Milnes, to lease land and water rights in Cromford where they planned to build a water powered cotton spinning mill. There are two relevant documents which predate the lease. One, signed on 11th October 1770 agrees that a lease is to be executed before March 25th 1771, for 21 years renewable for successive periods of 21 years up to 84 years at the yearly rent of £10 for the water from the Bonsall Brook and from Cromford Sough and twenty shillings per acre per annum for the land. £200 was to be paid at the first renewal of the lease even if the Cromford Sough water had been taken away.

Then on March 12th 1771, Milnes, Arkwright and Strutt agreed terms which were as in the earlier document except that £200 was now to be paid at every renewal of the lease even if the sough water supply had been lost. Should this happen, the agreement made provision for the partners to take down the mill and erect it upon a piece of waste ground adjoining the river either above or below the place where the Bonsall Brook falls into the Derwent. Mr Milnes was to procure a liberty to erect a weir on the River Derwent and to lease them 'the land the weir and stream of the river' for what remained of the 84 years. The nervousness about loss of the sough supply at this early date was no doubt because the construction of the Meer Brook Sough was about to begin. Its purpose was to drain mines between Cromford and Wirksworth at a level some 29 yards below the level of the Cromford Sough. In the event, there was no dramatic mill rebuilding though nearly seventy years after the signing of the lease, when the completed Meer Brook Sough had the predicted effect of seriously reducing the mills' water supply, attention was again drawn to this option.

There was some delay in executing the lease, contributed to, at least in part, by a legal complication (see below - A legal difficulty) and so it was not until August 1771 that the actual lease was signed by the partners Richard Arkwright, David Thornley, John Smalley, Samuel Need and Jedediah Strutt. All had shares in the company. At first Arkwright and Thornley, the latter later replaced by Smalley, had responsibility for the day to day management of the business and an allowance of £25 annually for 'their personal and constant attendance upon the management and superintendence of the works and servants used and employed in the said business'. Thornley died in 1772; Arkwright bought his share in the business from his widow. In February 1777 terms were agreed whereby Smalley could leave the partnership;

he set up a spinning mill in Wales. When Samuel Need died in 1781, Arkwright and Strutt bought his share from his executors. Strutt had begun building the first of his own cotton spinning mills in Belper in 1776.

In manuscript notes now in Nottinghamshire Archive Office William Stretton claimed that it was his father, Samuel who built a mill for Arkwright at Cromford. He had earlier built Arkwright's horse driven mill at Hockley in Nottingham, the first location where Richard Arkwright had attached a source of power to his machinery.

A legal difficulty

William and Mary Milnes had a legal problem to solve before they could grant a lease to Arkwright and his partners. This arose from the will of William Soresby Mary Milnes' brother. He left half shares in the Manor of Cromford to her and her sister Helen Monroe, their shares being measured as a division of the rental income of the manor. When Helen died William Milnes bought her share from her husband Thomas. This was in 1765 and the following year he filed a bill in Chancery to have the Cromford estate divided in terms of buildings and land, but not the mines, half to be allotted to him and the other half to his wife's trustees and this was duly done. But the terms of William Soresby's will directed that Mary Milnes would have no power over her estate during her husband's life and that her trustees, and by now Richard Nall was her sole trustee, were expressly forbidden to make leases of more than 21 years. So there was a serious dilemma about whether a lease could be executed. Legal opinion was sought from Mr Galliard of Lincoln's Inn, London. The case was presented to him in the following terms 'a set of men have invented a new mill for the spinning of cotton, silk, worsted etc and want a piece of ground near a river to erect a mill...they have made a choice in Mrs Milnes allotment containing about one acre and expect it to be made secure to them by Lease or other use for a term of 84 years'. It was stated that 'this mill will be a prodigious advantage to Mrs Milnes Estate and she is very desirous it should go on'. Several arguments were advanced about how that might be possible along with the view that Soresby 'did not mean to give his sister a naked power but all the estate and interest that he could and the restraint put upon it was merely to prevent her husband from intermeddling with it'. Mr Galliard delivered his opinion on April 12th 1771. Nall could act; the term of 84 years could be covered in renewable 21 year leases.

The water supply for the first mill, SEE FIGURE 25

The lease for the first mill included the right to use water from the Bonsall Brook and the Cromford Moor Long Sough. Map evidence shows that in 1771 the sough water was carried under the turnpike road (the road through Cromford from Wirksworth) and then ran above ground where Cromford Market Place is now to join the Bonsall Brook near 12-14 Market Place, the former chemist's shop. The partners' original plan was to make a new link between the two watercourses via a 'cutt' from higher up the brook course, so that the brook flowed under the turnpike to join the sough 'at the sough mouth'. From there a cut was to be made 'for carrying the united streams to the Mill'. The background details of a dispute between Arkwright and his landlords in 1774 (see Milnes v. Arkwright below) demonstrate that this plan was not implemented. Arkwright chose to use only the sough supply which he directed along the south side of the highway, and 'by several Arches Across the Highway to the mill'. The brook was left unaltered running in its natural course past the north end of the first mill. The sough supply was larger and more reliable than the brook. The Cromford Canal Company minutes in 1791 record the average flow in the sough as 71½ tons per minute and of the Bonsall Brook, $5^3/_5$ tons per minute.

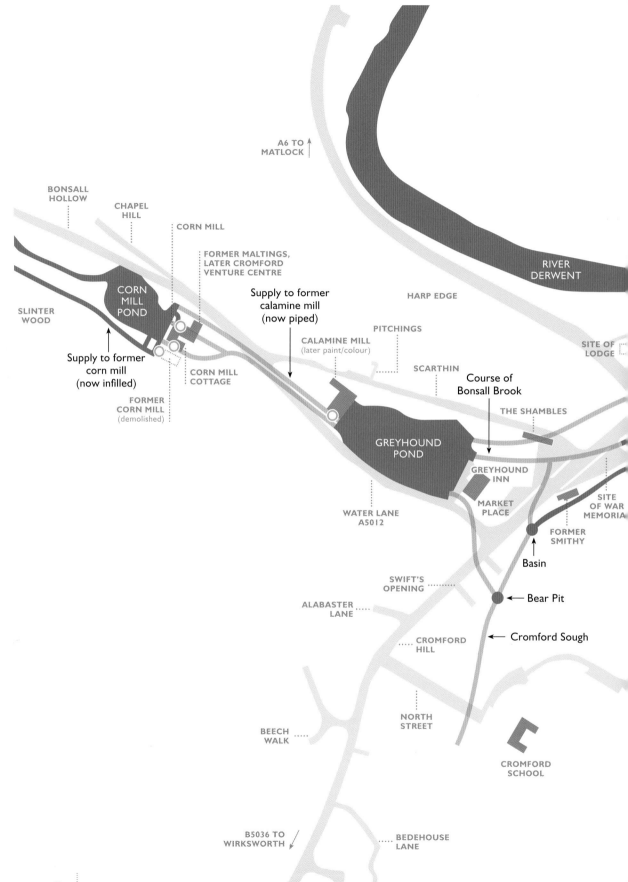

BONSALL
HOLLOW

CHAPEL
HILL

CORN MILL

FORMER MALTINGS,
LATER CROMFORD
VENTURE CENTRE

Supply to former
calamine mill
(now piped)

HARP EDGE

RIVER
DERWENT

SLINTER
WOOD

CORN
MILL
POND

PITCHINGS

CALAMINE MILL
(later paint/colour)

SCARTHIN

SITE OF
LODGE

Supply to former
corn mill
(now infilled)

CORN MILL
COTTAGE

Course of
Bonsall Brook

THE SHAMBLES

FORMER
CORN MILL
(demolished)

GREYHOUND
POND

GREYHOUND
INN

SITE
OF WAR
MEMORIA

WATER LANE
A5012

MARKET
PLACE

FORMER
SMITHY

Basin

SWIFT'S
OPENING

Bear Pit

ALABASTER
LANE

Cromford Sough

CROMFORD
HILL

NORTH
STREET

BEECH
WALK

CROMFORD
SCHOOL

B5036 TO
WIRKSWORTH

BEDEHOUSE
LANE

A6 TO
MATLOCK

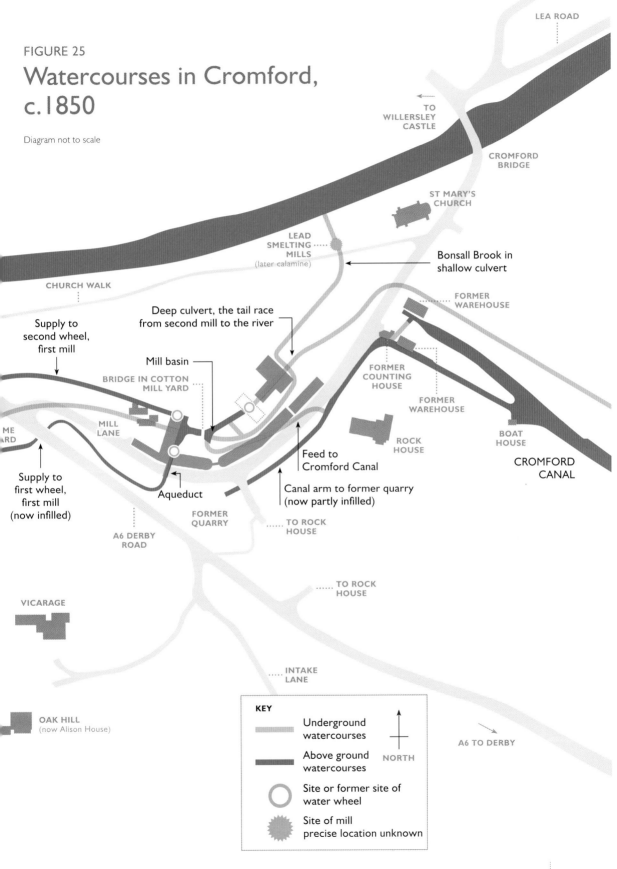

FIGURE 25

Watercourses in Cromford, c.1850

Diagram not to scale

LEA ROAD

TO WILLERSLEY CASTLE

CROMFORD BRIDGE

ST MARY'S CHURCH

LEAD SMELTING MILLS
(later calamine)

Bonsall Brook in shallow culvert

CHURCH WALK

FORMER WAREHOUSE

Supply to second wheel, first mill

Deep culvert, the tail race from second mill to the river

Mill basin

FORMER COUNTING HOUSE

FORMER WAREHOUSE

BRIDGE IN COTTON MILL YARD

BOAT HOUSE

ME RD

MILL LANE

ROCK HOUSE

CROMFORD CANAL

Supply to first wheel, first mill (now infilled)

Aqueduct

Feed to Cromford Canal

Canal arm to former quarry (now partly infilled)

A6 DERBY ROAD

FORMER QUARRY

TO ROCK HOUSE

TO ROCK HOUSE

VICARAGE

INTAKE LANE

KEY

Underground watercourses

Above ground watercourses

NORTH

Site or former site of water wheel

Site of mill precise location unknown

OAK HILL
(now Alison House)

A6 TO DERBY

Milnes v Arkwright

The list of criminal prosecutions for the 1774 Easter Quarter Sessions at Derby includes an entry: 'Richard Arkwright late of the parish of Wirksworth in the County of Derby Gentleman For diverting of an ancient watercourse in the parish aforesaid and thereby overflowing the High Road'. The case against Richard Arkwright was brought by William Milnes. The jury did not find in Milnes' favour. Dissatisfied, he took legal opinion from Mr Boarcroft [Bearcroft] in September 1774 and from Mr Wallace in January 1775, both of Lincoln's Inn. Neither was able to support his case.

The gist of Milnes' grievance was that Arkwright had failed to comply with covenants in the indenture of August 1st 1771 by which he and his partners had leased from Milnes and his wife Mary, the land on which to build 'one or more spinning mills' and the right to use water from the Bonsall Brook and the Cromford Sough. Milnes' deposition explained that Arkwright had used only the sough supply which he channelled in a 'new cut' to the mill. The lease gave Milnes 'a power of putting Fish into the said Brook, Stream, Cut or Mill Dam intended to be made' and 'to take the same out again at pleasure'. Richard Arkwright was not to injure or destroy the fish. Consequently, Milnes was angered when on March 25th 1774, Arkwright's workmen at the mill turned the brook water out of its course and flooded the road to Crich so that for several days 'it was impassable for foot passengers, the water being Knee-deep in the Road'. Milnes pointed out that they could not claim to be turning the water for the benefit of working the mill or to enable them to make a repair as 'no part of that water works the Mill or runs to it'. The following day, it was alleged, Arkwright and Smalley directed their workers to catch fish. George and Francis Roper, Stonehouse and Osborne were mentioned by name taking trout and eels. Arkwright himself was implicated being said to have put some fish in a tub of water, 'of which they made Presents to their Friends and others they dressed Themselves and invited many of their workmen to partake thereof at a feast'. Exercising his position as acting magistrate, Milnes ordered the Surveyor of the Highways of Cromford to 'Stop the Breach made in the side of the Brook to prevent the water running into the Highway'. On March 26th the Overseer and two labourers were deterred from carrying out the order

Cromford corn mill, at that time in the hands of Samuel Buxton, stood somewhere below the proposed cotton mill site and was worked by the combined brook and sough supply. Arkwright's lease required that the quantity of water used or necessary for working Mr Samuel Buxton's corn mill should not be taken away or diminished so the streams must have been reunited below the first mill to provide the corn mill's customary supply.

Extension of the first mill

In 1785 the first mill was extended to the north by the addition of four bays so taking the building over the natural course of the brook which was confined to a culvert beneath it. By this date Peter Nightingale owned the manor of Cromford and by agreement with him, Richard Arkwright had the use of more land both on the mill site and in the village. A new wheel was added in a wheel-pit on the end wall of the extension. This wheel was served by water brought in a new, largely underground watercourse from the pond created for this purpose behind the Greyhound Inn. At the same time and as part of the same development the 'Bear Pit' and its associated culverts was constructed. With the construction of the Greyhound pond where previously there had been only the narrow course of the Bonsall Brook, the future shape of Cromford was irrevocably defined.

The Bear Pit, see overleaf, served Arkwright's purpose well but he had constructed it without consulting the sough proprietors. His action caused problems for the lead miners whose mines the sough drained and resulted in a dispute with the proprietors. The Bagshawe papers describe the case; water backed up the sough, the sough filled with water 'when Mr Arkwright with a Considerable Number of men' threatened them with being thrown in the water. Despite Milnes insistence that the 'intent and meaning of all partys [sic] at the time of Executing the Lease was to reserve 'all the Fish both in the Brook and chose [those?] to be put into the new Cut and Mill Dam (where none cou'd be without being put in)', the court and Milnes' legal advisors accepted Arkwright's defence that the covenant only entitled Milnes to take out the actual fish he had put in, the rest could be taken by the lessees. The deposition offers no explanation for Arkwright's action though Milnes' claimed that it was to provoke him.

Milnes also failed in a second apparently more substantial complaint. He claimed that the lessees had extended some part of their buildings on land which was not included in the lease by building over the brook which formed the northern boundary of the leased land. This is considered to refer to the original weavers' workshop, part of which later became incorporated into the extension of the first mill, and which undoubtedly did intrude into the Milnes' land on the other side of the brook. Again Milnes' claim was not upheld. The legal opinion was that his objection was too late; it should have been made when the building was added; effectual measures could not be taken now.

Milnes' also drew attention to the covenant in the lease requiring the mill partners to indemnify the overseers of the poor should persons employed in the mill and coming to settle in Cromford become a charge on the township by 'Virtue of any Laws… for the Relief and Settlmt of the poor'. Again he was offered no comfort. Should it happen, the Milnes could take action on the covenant but doubt was cast on whether the covenant was 'Good in Law'. The Overseers may act 'as to Certificates & Removals as they would think prudent in Other Cases'.

This colourful account illustrates the conflict between a landowner protecting his traditional rights and Arkwright going about his business with the contempt for other people's interests for which he became notorious. In 1785 a similar action was to set him at odds with local lead miners when he sank the 'Bear Pit' into Cromford Sough.

Information from the Barmasters' Derbyshire Lead Mining Records, belonging to the Duchy of Lancaster which have been arranged and described by Roger Flindall.

and, it is alleged, parts of it collapsed. Several mines which it was designed to unwater were flooded. The case went to arbitration where Arkwright offered no evidence. He was required to pay the proprietors £300 for repairs to the sough and expenses incurred and an annual rent of £20 for the privilege of taking water for his mills.

From the Bear Pit, the water ran in the two underground culverts (shown to the right in the Bear Pit dam) and appeared above ground in what Ebeneezer Rhodes, *Derbyshire Tourist Guide*, 1837, described as 'a deep basin of contracted dimensions, at the foot of the hill by the road-side, nearly opposite the Greyhound Inn'.

FIGURE 26. **Location of shuttle, Greyhound pond, 1990s.**

The photograph shows the site where a wooden shuttle controlled the flow from the Greyhound pond to the water wheel on the extension to the first mill. Parts were removed for safe keeping by the District Council when conservation work was done on the dam in the 1970s and not restored on completion of the work. The position of the sluice is now largely overgrown below the railings in the corner of the 'square' to the right of the Boat Inn.

James Croston, in the first edition of *On Foot through the Peak*, 1862, calls it a 'large reservoir or dam opposite the Greyhound Inn in the market place'. From the basin water ran to the mill in an open channel on an embankment hugging the side of the valley but by the time of Rhodes' description part of its course had been culverted beneath the Derby Road. Much of the embankment either side of the Derby Road survives but the upper section and the basin have been built over; 25-27 Market Place marks the site today. Before this property was built the area is remembered as a boggy patch known as 'the sough brook' with a corroded shuttle in the wall against the road. Children climbed around the shuttle and across makeshift stepping stones in the mud to reach Allen's Hill to play. Now what remains of the basin is to be found beneath a metal plate in front of the garage adjacent to 25-27 Market Place.

The original function of 'Rhodes' basin' may require some explanation. Though described as a basin it was in fact a weir, constructed at the point where the new watercourse to the first mill diverted

FIGURE 27. **The 'Bear Pit', photograph, 2001.**

The photograph shows the short section of the Cromford Sough which Richard Arkwright exposed in 1785 so that he could build a dam and a shuttle to control the water flow. The feature is known locally as the Bear Pit. William Street, described being 'employed in driving the level to turn the water coming out of the Cromford Sough into the present Dam behind the Greyhound Inn and shortly afterwards the Shuttles were put in for the purpose of raising the Water into the Sough and to force it into the Dam'. With the shuttle closed, water backed up the sough to the new culvert Street described and so flowed to the recently built Greyhound pond. This ingenious engineering enabled Arkwright to move water from the sough to top up the water in the pond. This was done each Sunday to ensure that there was an adequate supply of water in the pond for the new wheel when work began again on Monday morning. Alternatively water could be taken from the pond to drain via the Bear Pit. In this way he gained a far greater control over his two water supplies and supplemented the source of power for his new wheel. From the Bear Pit a second culvert was added to increase the capacity of the sough, (the two culvert entrances are shown on the right here). It ran parallel to the existing sough but only as far as the basin described on pages 45-46. The Bear Pit survives beside the path which runs from between the shops at the foot of The Hill up 'the wilderness', as it was known to many twentieth century Cromford schoolchildren, to the school. Its first restoration was undertaken in 1971 by volunteers, including pupils from Bilborough School under the direction of the Arkwright Festival Committee.

from the sough. It permitted surplus water to run within the original course of the sough, join the Bonsall Brook and find its way to the river Derwent. This engineering feature lay at the heart of Arkwright's utilisation of the water power at his disposal and was a vital component of the mill development from the day powered use of the mill began.

Sough water no longer goes to the mill; it flows in its original course to join the brook. Both are in culverts and inaccessible. William Weston, who was born in 1756, recalled as 'a little boy, being in the habit of going to wade or bathe in the Cromford Sough – the water was warm and with other children [we] used to go up as far as we dare as it got dark beyond a certain distance. The Water would not be deep – we had our breeches off should say two feet in depth was the outside.'

It is not known when the streams were confined to culverts but it must have been before 1790 when the market was inaugurated; perhaps it was done in association with the alterations when the Greyhound pond was commissioned or maybe as early as 1778-79 when the Greyhound was built.

The new taller aqueduct referred to at Figure 28 overleaf would have been an important modification. It supplied water to a larger and more powerful wheel. The extension of the first mill, confirmed in a Law Report to have taken place in 1785; the construction of the five storey mill/warehouse which stands at right angles to the first mill believed to have been structurally complete by December 1783 and which ultimately had a power supply to its four upper floors; and the alteration to the aqueduct are known to have occurred before 1786 and are considered to be related developments. These investments in enhanced water power and increased production space indicate that despite the construction of Masson Mill in 1783-4, Arkwright continued to regard his two mills at Cromford as capable of further profitable growth.

The gateway and yard shown in Boreman's view, Figure 28, appear to mark the entrance to the mill, but despite the detailed exploration of the building as set out in the *Cromford Mills' Conservation Statement,* 2007, no evidence has been found for an entrance door in this western side of the building at this date. The most recent archaeological investigations by Dr Patrick Strange have shown that in its earliest form the ground floor of the mill to the north of the service area (offices, staircase, etc) housed the power transmission system only and was not a working floor. Entry to the first mill for the workforce was from the road through a door in the south gable to the service area which gave immediate access to a stairway to all floors, an arrangement which would leave the working floors completely clear to accommodate the optimum number of spinning frames and other machinery. In architectural terms the door on the east side of the mill was the main entrance door, the 'First Door', as Arkwright named it. Certainly it is a door designed to be seen yet it is overshadowed by the aqueduct and both documentary and archaeological investigations confirm that this was always the case. From 1783 it became accessible only via the five storey adjacent building. The first mill had taking-in doors on upper floor levels in the roadside gable and before the building was extended, there was a further door opening in the north wall on the bank of the Bonsall Brook.

The function of the west yard is not clear. Visually it bears the attributes of a stylish entrance, an image which is enhanced by the setting forward of the four central bays of the first mill's façade but, without providing a way into the mill, it had no practical value. We conclude that it served as the public face of the enterprise. The railings and gate would have provided some security. Along with the curious arrangement of the aqueduct concealing the architectural features of the main door, the blindness of the mill's western elevation in relation to the yard suggests the development of the first mill was to a degree haphazard rather than planned.

FIGURE 28. **The west face of the extended first mill, watercolour, Zachariah Boreman, 1786.**

The size of Boreman's picture is about 3x4½ inches and shows the west face of Arkwright's first mill some fifteen years after the first eleven bay section had been built in 1771 and after1785 when Arkwright had extended it by four bays at its north end (to the left side in this view). The extension took the building over the Bonsall Brook and the pit for the new water wheel had to be carved out of the bedrock between the end of the building and Scarthin Rock. The water wheel required a new water supply which came in a largely culverted channel from the Greyhound pond; a substantial engineering undertaking. The last length of the watercourse was above ground on an embankment still visible today behind the buildings on the left of the yard. How much of it ran above ground is not known.

Some time before 1774 Arkwright had built a weavers' workshop close to the north end of the first mill straddling the Bonsall Brook which was culverted to run beneath it. When the mill was extended the workshop was demolished except for a piece of its wall which was incorporated into the west wall of the mill extension. The colour and style of the workshop's random limestone wall still contrasts clearly with the gritstone fabric of the rest of the mill. The building with the dark gable end shown in the left foreground in this view is thought to be the weavers' workshop, which occupies the site today.

In front of the mill 'Grace Cottage' on the right and a double-pile brick building left, both shown here with gabled roofs, flank a yard with a railing topped wall and gateway. Originally a matching pair, the building on the left is shown here, as now, with an extra pile built over the culverted Bonsall Brook. The buildings provided residential accommodation, perhaps for a gatekeeper and others who were required to live on the site; now they offer residential and office space.

The first mill is shown with five storeys and an attic, lit by dormer windows set in a pitched roof. There is a bell cupola and chimneys which internal evidence indicates were associated with hearths which heated the service end of the mill. The new watercourse to the 1785 wheel is visible at the foot of the slope on the left. To the right of Mill Lane is the 'new Cut', the watercourse which carried water from the Cromford Moor Long Sough and directed it at a raised level alongside Mill Lane and across an aqueduct spanning the road to drive the water wheel on the east side of this mill. Later this scheme was modified and it is Boreman's dated watercolour which provides evidence that the alteration was made in 1786. It appears to show a new taller aqueduct under construction. The watercourse running to it is depicted at a lower level than the aqueduct and to be awaiting or undergoing reconstruction.

Reproduced by permission of the Derbyshire Archaeological Society

FIGURE 29. **Derby porcelain dessert plate, inscribed on the reverse 'View of Sir Rd Arkwright's Cotton works at Cromford'.**

The view on the plate is hand painted and based on a small watercolour by Zachariah Boreman in the ownership of the Derbyshire Archaeological Society (see left) which is described in a typewritten label 'Mr Arkwright's Cotton Works, Cromford - taken on the Rocks near the Grey Hound Inn. 1786'. Boreman worked for the Derby China Manufactory from 1784 to 1794. Derby Museums date the plate to about 1790 and attribute the gilding to John Yates. A factory scene seems an unlikely subject for the decoration of high quality dessert ware but its use here illustrates Georgian society's interest in the modern industrial developments of the day.

FIGURE 30. **The cast iron aqueduct, photographs, 1999 and 2002.**

This aqueduct replaced a wooden structure in 1821. An essential component of Richard Arkwright's water power system, it carried water from the Cromford Sough across Mill Lane to drive the water wheel on the east side of the first cotton mill. It was demolished by a lorry in 2002 and is stored awaiting restoration and return to the site. It is listed Grade 1.

FIGURE 31. **View of Cromford Mills , watercolour, artist unknown, second half of the 1780s?**

This watercolour did not come to light until 2004, a hitherto unknown early view of Richard Arkwright's mills at Cromford. At full size compared with previously known views of the extended first mill, it confirms some architectural details in particular the form of the roof, the dormers and the position of a chimney. The ancillary building with a pyramidal roof at the left hand side is a new feature not seen in other images. The buildings either side of the yard are now shown with hipped roofs. Although poorly placed in the picture in relation to the mill, Rock House is quite carefully depicted with a single wide gable and the asymmetrical arrangement of windows it still has today.

The striking feature, hitherto never seen, is 'the sign of the Hound' the greyhound on its decorative arch at the entrance to the yard of the inn sometimes known as the Black Greyhound or the Black Dog. It is impossible to recreate this view now because the level of the valley floor has been raised during road alterations but the image suggests that the fenced 'yard' was extensive and that the road from Wirksworth ran nearer to the embankment along the valley side compared with its present course and as the earlier Boydell view appears to show. The finger post against the distant fence is as on the earlier Joseph Wright painting 'Arkwright's Cotton Mills by Night' indicating the way to Matlock Bath as it rises to wind over Scarthin Rock.

The lady framed in the archway and, more clearly seen in the original picture, is carrying a tray on her head; it is reasonable to suppose that she is taking dinner to her family working at the mill.

Arkwright Society collection

FIGURE 32. **Richard Arkwright's Cotton Mill, Cromford, from Scarthin Rocks above Cromford, watercolour, William Day, 1789.**

This view also shows the west face of Richard Arkwright's extended first mill. Day confirms features as described before but shows another three storey building just visible immediately to the left of the mill. This was the bow-fronted building, 'the Barracks'. Behind it is the second mill built in 1776-7.

Along the right-hand side of Mill Lane the water supply from the Cromford Sough and the aqueduct are shown clearly. In 1821 this wooden aqueduct was replaced by one made of cast iron.

Behind the aqueduct, are three-storey cottages which were modified to stables probably when the mill manager's house was built in 1796. The mill manager Mr Watson was still stabling a horse there in the mid twentieth century. Cromford Colour Company converted the building to a laboratory in about 1965; it is now in use as offices. At a higher level is Richard Arkwright's Cromford residence, Rock House. Here, as in Figure 31, it is shown with a single wide gable. Beside it to the right, the Mews building with its bell cupola is surely the building which still stands at Rock House today.

Reproduced by permission of Derby Museum and Art Gallery

FIGURE 33. **The fire in the bow-fronted building, photographs, May 8th, 1961.**

The *Derby Mercury* of April 2nd, 1789 referred to this building as the semi-circular building when describing celebrations on the mill site held to mark King George III's recovery after illness. On that occasion 'During the day a large bonfire blazed, and the populace had a great quantity of ale distributed amongst them. At night a transparency was exhibited, the whole length of the building, with this motto, in large characters – Rejoice all men for the King liveth'.

Well into the twentieth century it was known as the Barracks a term which denotes its function to provide accommodation for unmarried male workers living too far from home to travel to work

each day and not, as local tradition would have it, to house soldiers needed to keep order in the mills. By 1890 it was leased to Matthew Hill for use as a brewery and in 1912, two years after Matthew Hill's death, it was taken over by Offilers' Brewery. The building was destroyed by fire in 1961 when it was occupied by the Cromford Colour Company. An onlooker recalls sparks, flying in through open windows of the laundry lower down the site, setting the ironing on fire. The view shows the external open frame lift shaft used by the Colour Company. The building's foundations are preserved against the rock face in the mill yard.

Private collection

FIGURE 35. **Arkwright's Mill 1878, drawing on paper, Ford Madox Brown.**

This overshot wheel on the east side of the first mill was driven by water from a wooden pentrough at the end of the cast iron aqueduct. The trough spread the water over the width of the wheel and made it possible to employ a wheel that was wider than the aqueduct. This is thought to be the wheel installed in 1821 and to be part of the significant investment in the water power system made at that time, the wooden aqueduct being replaced by a cast iron one. Over the course of its life, three wheels powered the mill, each more or less in this position on the east side; the first about 1771; the second about 1786; the third 1821. They delivered power to the mill at the middle point of the mill's production floor. The axle hole for the first wheel and probably for the second became for the third wheel the location for the spur wheel seen here to the right of the waterwheel. This transferred power from the geared rim of the 1821 wheel. It is not known who the Arkwrights employed to design and update the water power system though the Arkwright Toplis bank ledger for 1807 records Hewes and Day being paid £200 and £66 in 1808. We assume the reference is to Thomas Cheek Hewes (1768-1832), engineer and textile machine manufacturer. It is not clear what he was employed to do. The tailrace returned water to the Bonsall Brook to provide power for the second mill lower down the site.

The building on the left was multi functional. It is believed to have combined mill, watchouse, picking room and perhaps dinner room uses with the wheel supplying power to the four upper floors. On the ground floor an area is thought to have been used for opening the bales of cotton and next door, the picking room was where raw cotton was prepared for processing by beating out weeds and other detritus. The dinner room also is believed to have been on this floor. Workers' wives or children brought hot food to the mill for their meal breaks. This area has a door which opens to the street which is suggestive of such a use. The building had a warm air heating system and lavatories on each floor.

FIGURE 34. **Sir Richard Arkwright's Mill, photograph, about 1905.**

This view of the five-storey first mill and its associated buildings is immediately comparable with the earlier views though this shows the mill with a hipped roof without dormers, a form adopted about 1790, and a curtain wall across the yard. The tall structure against the mill, crowned by a chimney, housed a warm air heating system and a column of lavatories, innovations also dating from about 1790. The features are shown in Joseph Wright's painting of the 1790s 'Cromford Cotton Mills by Day'. In 1914 and in a further lease a year later Frederic Charles Arkwright leased the building along with others on the site and including the aqueduct to the Via Gellia Colour Company. The top two storeys of the building were destroyed by fire in 1929 when it was being used by the Cromford Colour Works. The lavatory column and the curtain wall have been demolished as has the single storey building on the left of the picture.

The buildings at either side of the yard and the former weavers' workshop to the left survive. The workshop was in use as a laundry around the turn of the nineteenth century and was later acquired by the Colour Works. In 1937 the manager, Mr Watson, had the building remodelled to provide a well lit colour matching laboratory on the top floor. The roof was raised and the old windows torn out to be replaced by modern ones though within the original window openings. The roof of Grace Cottage, on the right, is altered now though the timbers of the hipped roof shown here remain inside the more modern structure.

The Second Cromford Cotton Mill

Arkwright's first patent which he obtained in 1769 covered only the final spinning process and not the many different preparatory stages which lay between the initial opening of the generally extremely dirty cotton bales and the production of rovings of suitable quality and consistency to feed the spinning frames. It is reasonable to suppose that even as Arkwright was perfecting the operation of the frame he was considering how he might achieve a more mechanised system. By 1775 he had sufficient confidence to bring together a number of separate devices in a single patent application. This was awarded on December 16th, 1775. Arkwright was now ready to put his system into production and for this he required new and larger premises.

He began to construct his second mill in 1776 using money, not provided by his surviving partners, but by his neighbour, Peter Nightingale of Lea.

Richard Arkwright's agreement with William and Mary Milnes

To build a second mill Arkwright needed both capital and an enlarged land holding. The land included in the lease of 1771 barely permitted the construction of the first mill, wedged between the road and the brook, and would not support a second. There were therefore negotiations with the land owners, William and Mary Milnes, and their trustee Richard Nall and with Peter Nightingale.

In the Articles of Agreement dated September 27th 1775, between Richard Nall and Richard Arkwright, Nall agreed to convey the manor of Cromford to Richard Arkwright for £20,000 payable on or before April 5th 1776. Part of the payment, £12,000, was to be paid at the end of the year following the date of the conveyance of the property, for which no date was fixed, but which was to be within the six months from September 1775 to April 1776. Interest was to be paid on the £12,000 at the rate of 4% per annum, effectively a short-term mortgage arrangement. The remaining £8,000 was to be paid on or before April 5th 1776 'at or upon the execution by the said Richard Nall William Milnes and Mary his

Peter Nightingale

Peter Nightingale (1736-1803), Richard Arkwright's financier and landlord at Cromford, was a prosperous lead smelting merchant and landowner living at Lea Hall, until he moved to Woodend, the house he built for himself between Cromford and Lea Bridge, in 1795. He built his own cotton spinning mill on the Lea Brook at Lea in 1783, insuring it for £700, and his machinery and stock for £1,000, in December of that year. He was to cross swords with Arkwright for poaching one of Arkwright's trusted employees, Benjamin Pearson junior, to run the mill for him and for using Arkwright's machinery without authorisation. Arkwright pursued him through the courts. The co-partnership which Nightingale and Pearson had formed in August 1783 was dissolved in March 1785. Pearson moved on and set up the first of his own mills at Brough, near Bradwell.

Lea is the only place in the Derwent valley where a first generation Arkwright style mill survives on a site where there has been continuous cotton spinning or textile production since the eighteenth century. Nightingale's mill was taken over by the Smedley family in 1818 and remains embedded in the Smedley's Mill complex at Lea Bridge where it plays a part in the production of the high quality knitwear created from fine yarns which the Company now markets world wide.

Peter Nightingale was a promoter of the Cromford Canal Company and at his own expense built the Lea Bridge arm of the canal to link his lead smelting and cotton mills at Lea to the canal system.

FIGURE 36. **The Second Cotton Mill,**
Cromford, watercolour from Derby China Manufactory patterns, artist unknown, about 1780.

This massive mill, built in 1776-7 was 129 feet long and 30 feet wide, with seven well lit storeys. Note the imposing bell cupola housing the bell which was such an essential feature of the factory day. John James Audubon taking an early morning walk to Cromford in 1826 was made aware of its significance when 'a bell [struck] upon our ear, and we soon saw the long files of little girls, sisters and mothers moving in a procession towards the mills of Arkwright'. Audubon was in England to find a publisher for what would be his famous book *The Birds of America:* his experiences have been transcribed in *The 1826 Journal of John James Audubon.* Also prominent in views of the second mill is the wide chimney stack which appears to accommodate a number of flues. The mill was built tight up against Scarthin Rock so that it blocked the road from Matlock Bath which passed close round the foot of the Rock to cross the Bonsall Brook over the bridge which survives in the mill yard (see Figure 90).

This view from the direction of Cromford bridge shows buildings close to the mill. Their purpose is not known. It is likely that they were used for ancillary and non-mechanised processes. A watercolour by Zachariah Boreman from a similar viewpoint, dated 1787, confirms similar buildings and shows a frame on which bleached yarn might be hung to dry standing in front of them. Some archaeological evidence for buildings at this end of the site survives in the present mill yard. Neither image helps to identify the route of the watercourse from the site to the river at this date.

wife of the proper conveyances and assurances'. Richard Arkwright would 'truly pay or cause to be paid...the Sum of Eight Thousand Pounds the remainder of the said Sum of Twenty Thousand Pounds thereby agreed to be paid for the purchase of the said Premises'.

Richard Arkwright's agreement with Peter Nightingale

Two days before the April 5th deadline, Nightingale and Arkwright signed their own agreement whereby Nightingale took over the purchase Arkwright had agreed. The agreement is a detailed and complete document. After reference to the terms of the earlier scheme between Arkwright and Nall, Nightingale 'contracted and agreed' with Richard Arkwright for 'the absolute purchase of all and Singular the said premises comprised in the said Recited Articles of Agreement at and for the price of Twenty Thousand Pounds and which are hereby agreed and intended to be Conveyed Transferred and Assigned by the said Richard Nall William Milnes and Mary his wife...unto the said Peter Nightingale...'. All the Milnes' conditions listed in the earlier Nall to Arkwright agreement were to be honoured including how certain tenants were to be treated; for example Joseph Britland was to pay 'no rent for the term of his natural life'and before April 5th 1776, the Milnes could take away 'all the young forest trees or plants standing or growing in the Nursery Beds in the Garden, Orchard Filbert piece and Anthony Cotterill's garden'.

But of greater significance for Cromford's development were the new terms agreed by Arkwright and Nightingale. From April 5th 1776, Nightingale leased Arkwright the water corn mill (which stood between Arkwright's first cotton mill and the river) and some houses and land for which Arkwright was to pay an annual rent of £116-3s-7d, a capital messuage or mansion house, the house later to be known as Rock House, at an annual rent of £35 and some further cottages and land associated with the house at an annual rental of £119-1s-2d all for a term of 21 years.

Arkwright was directed to expend £2,000 on 'building or erecting a Mill or Mills for the Spinning and Manufacturing of Wool Cotton Flax and other Materials and also a further £1000 in erecting such and so many dwelling Houses for the workmen or Manufacturers to be employed by the said Richard Arkwright in such places within Cromford and in such manner or form as Richard Arkwright shall direct'. Nightingale agreed to fund these developments, making payments in six £500 monthly instalments from May to October. The lease was for 21 years at an annual rent of £180 and interest on the capital was to be paid at 6% per annum. Arkwright had the right to pull down the corn mill and such old cottages or dwelling houses as would interfere with the plan; the materials were to be used for new buildings in Cromford. The mill built under these terms was the second cotton mill and the first housing to be built by Arkwright under these terms was North Street. In 1780 the £3,000 was declared 'not sufficient' and Nightingale advanced a further £750, on the same terms.

Arkwright could now expand his industrial operations. He had the land and the money to build his second Cromford mill and permission to pull down the corn mill which would no longer be able to work once the second mill was in place. It is not known how soon he demolished the mill building but within a week of the agreement he advertised its machinery for sale. In Rock House he had a substantial house in which to live. He also acquired some of the existing village housing, such as it was; and the land on which he might build more housing.

The terms of this arrangement refine our understanding of Arkwright's role in the creation of Cromford as an industrial community and confirm his significance. For as long as Cromford has been written about it was regarded as the Arkwright village and this was not challenged until 1971 when, as part of the preparations for the bicentenary exhibition, Joan Sinar, then the Derbyshire county archivist, circulated a typescript in which she expressed the view that Cromford was in reality Nightingale's creation. It was a persuasive case. Had he not provided the capital? It can now be seen that the terms of the agreement between Arkwright and Nightingale explicitly awarded control to Richard Arkwright. Cromford was indeed an Arkwright creation though it was funded by Peter Nightingale. It is not known what passed between Arkwright and his original partners, which made him turn to funding from outside the partnership. However, it is clear from the insurance arrangements, see below, that Samuel Need and Jedediah Strutt retained a financial interest in Arkwrights new mill at Cromford and in his Bakewell mill.

For Peter Nightingale this was a business deal with good returns and he more than recovered his capital when he sold the manor to Sir Richard Arkwright and his trustee Robert Mason in April 1789. The sale also included allotment, No 365, the riverside land incorporating what is now called Church Walk, which Nightingale had been awarded from the Matlock Enclosure Act in 1784. The total purchase price was £30,000, of which Sir Richard paid £15,000 immediately, he and his son Richard signing a bond agreeing to pay the remaining £15,000 on March 25th 1790. Arkwright could build on the manor without delay provided that the 'Rents and profits' from the manor for the year to March 25th 1790 which Nightingale was to collect and keep were not 'injured or lessened thereby'. At the end of the year Arkwright was to pay the year's rent on the property which he occupied as Nightingale's tenant and Peter Nightingale was to pay to Arkwright the interest, amounting to £721-3s-0d, on the £15,000 which Arkwright had paid to him in 1789.

Further finance from Peter Nightingale

Adam Wolley, (1758-1827) the respected local lawyer and antiquarian noted that Nightingale spent upwards of £7,000 on buildings on his Cromford estate. Our record so far accounts for only £3,750 of that total but there are hints of further payments. He is known to have insured the Greyhound for £700 in 1779. He has been credited with building the inn but the terms of the 1776 agreement suggest that it is more likely to have been part of Arkwright's development of Cromford and that Nightingale's insurance was protection for his investment in Arkwright's enterprise. It is also known that on December 25th, 1783 Nightingale wrote a memo to remind himself he should not only insure his new Lea Cotton Mill and stock but also the new Mill at Cromford for £1800, the smiths' and joiners' shops on the north side of the Basin for £100 and a building called the picking room and dinner house lying on the south side of the Basin. The memo clearly indicates a need to safeguard a financial interest and it is reasonable to conclude that Wolley's estimate may be correct. This concern to protect individual financial interests is also demonstrated by earlier policies dated 18th

February 1779 in which Samuel Need and Jedediah Strutt, both described as of Cromford, insured 'goods in trade in their new cotton mill situated in Cromford and on the mills and running tackle therein' for £200. The same policy included insurance cover for the cotton mill at Bakewell also 'in the value of £200'. On the same date Richard Arkwright took out a Royal Exchange fire policy for his new cotton mill 'turned by waters situated in Cromford' and his cotton mill in Bakewell for £1000 each.

Significance of Peter Nightingale's Memo

Nightingale's memo is of considerable value for the light it casts on developments at Cromford. The use of the term Mill indicates he was referring to a powered building. This is likely to have been the five storey mill and picking room building close to the first mill, which had powered machinery on the four upper floors. Archaeological evidence today clearly locates on the ground floor of that building a bale opening space with a large picking room beside it where the cotton was batted and cleaned and, beside the bale opening room, what is considered to have been the dinner house. Were the rooms mentioned separately with respect to insurance because fine dust in the picking room, known by this date to be a fire hazard, and the presence of 'hot plates or stoves', as later described by Richard Arkwright junior, in the dinner room represented the greatest risks for fire damage to the building? If this interpretation is correct then it confirms that the five storey mill/warehouse was built by December 1783 though the absence of insurance values for stock and machinery suggests that only the picking room and the dinner house were in use. The building may not have begun operation as a mill until 1786 when the new wheel and heightened aqueduct were in place. The smiths' and joiners' shop must have occupied the area where later the Barracks stood. These would be essential components of the site as this new mill was being built and later equipped, to be followed soon after by the construction of the extension to the first mill with its new machinery, new water wheel and the replacement of its original wheel.

The peaceful image, Figure 36, shows a more open site compared with a view from the same vantage point today with a lower boundary wall for the cart to skirt as it approaches from Cromford bridge along the line of Mill Lane. The mill site was considered to be seriously at risk when there were concerns about possible attack after Arkwright's mill at Birkacre in Lancashire was destroyed by rioters in 1779. The attackers were supporting the cause of hand workers who, at a time when the cotton trade was disrupted by international unrest, feared for their living in the face of competition from machine production. Robert Fitton, *The Arkwrights, Spinners of Fortune,* 1989, records details from a letter written in October 1779 in which Richard Arkwright described his preparation to defend the mill and the village. He had in readiness 1500 small arms and a battery of cannon with ammunition as well as 500 spears and claimed that '5 or 6000 Men, Miners &c. can be assembled in less than an Hour, by Signals agreed upon, who are determined to defend to the last Extremity, the Works, by which many hundreds of their Wives and Children get a decent and comfortable Livelihood'. No rioters reached Cromford but the experience may have been in mind, as, over the next ten years, Arkwright added buildings along the boundary of the site so providing an almost complete enclosure. The shortage of ground floor windows in their outer walls has been considered to represent a concern for security but it is more likely to reflect the functions of the buildings which, for the most part, at least at ground level, were for cotton preparation, warehousing or stabling. Cannon have since been fired in Cromford, not in anger but in salvoes from Willersley Castle in celebration of some national events.

There are accounts of Richard Arkwright's reluctance to let people into his mills when their interest was in the new technology rather than its destruction but an anonymous manuscript journal dated August 1782 summarises one such visit. 'Their appearance from the greater variety of Machines is more interesting than the silk mills at Derby. Upwards of one thousand persons are daily employed in this manufacture which was here created and brought to perfection by Mr Arkwright, who has seen his labour blessed by an affluent fortune.'

FIGURE 37. **The 5-storey mill/warehouse building seen from Mill Lane (top) and from across the bridge in the mill yard (above), photographs 2007.**

What proved to be a greater risk to these early mills than saboteurs was fire. The second mill was destroyed by fire in November1890 when in use by Messrs William Hollins and Co (see Figure 38). The L-shaped four storey building which had been linked to the second mill at first floor level in about 1789 suffered some damage in the fire but the main wing survived intact and is the largest building nearest the camera in Figure 46. In the 1920s Cromford Colour Company built a filtration plant across the cleared site of the second mill. Removal of the plant in 1996-8 revealed the foundations of the second mill and the 20 feet deep wheel-pit sunk underneath the building. The wheel utilised the combined water supplies of the Cromford Sough and the Bonsall Brook. So deep was the wheel-pit that in order to discharge water from it to the river, a culvert was driven several hundred yards into Cromford Meadows to an open channel which joined the Derwent at a point about half a mile downstream from the mill.

FIGURE 38. Ilustration from The Manchester Guardian, November 15th, 1890.

This illustration entitled ARKWRIGHT'S MILLS AT CROMFORD. AFTER THE FIRE. NOV 8. 1890. appeared in the Manchester Guardian, November 15th 1890. It shows three separate sketches - in the top left hand corner is the extension to the first mill, top right is the gable end of the bow fronted building and along the bottom the burnt-out second mill. The first mill, here called The Oldest Mill, is shown with band courses and a hint of the water wheel at the north end which the accompanying account describes as being 'red with rust'; this was in the position occupied by the 1785 wheel. Clearly it was out of use or in the eloquent words of the *Manchester Guardian* 'still and dead for many a year', not so the wheel served by the aqueduct (not shown in the drawing) which is described as [doing] 'the work of the establishment'. The account describes the five storey building attached to the first mill (not shown in this drawing) being 'devoted to carpentry work on the ground floor, whilst in the upper floors will be found stowed away many ancient and curious cotton machines, stranded relics of the early days of manufacture'. The second sketch shows part of the west gable end of the bow fronted building with a flight of external steps close to the rock face. Across the bottom of the drawing the burnt out second mill building stretches the width of the yard with its fire damaged annexe in the background. The end walls of the second mill are still standing to five storey height and a pedimented entrance doorway survives at the south west corner of the building. This sketch also shows the connection between the second mill and the nearby roadside mill perimeter building at this date. The patching of the stone work of the perimeter building visible today and the scorched condition of the surviving joinery discovered when the window frames were repaired confirms that the link was at first floor level. The detailed description of the fire in the *High Peak News* of November 15th comments that once it was clear that the second mill was 'doomed' Frederic Charles Arkwright 'directed the concentration of the whole of the [water] supplies' to this 'corridor' to stop the fire crossing to the roadside buildings. 'Had it obtained a grip there the damage would have been immense'. The crowd lining the street responded 'heartily' to the call for volunteers and the fire fighters from many local districts worked strenuously to stop the spread. This account also reports that the mill was of red brick and makes the distinction that the rest of the structures on the Cromford Mills' site were composed of stone. This is the only known reference to the fabric of this mill; neither the study of the archaeological evidence from the excavation of the site nor the available images of the building have enabled this description to be confirmed but it is clear that the second mill had a stone plinth, the end wall sections of which still stand, and may have been stone above or may have been surmounted by brick upper storeys similar to Haarlem Mill at Wirksworth which Arkwright built at about the same time.

© The Manchester Guardian 1890

FIGURE 39. **Portrait of Richard Arkwright, Joseph Wright, oil on canvas, circa 1783-1785.**

This portrait of Richard Arkwright was purchased jointly by the National Portrait Gallery, London and the Harris Museum and Art Gallery, Preston in 2008. It is recorded in Joseph Wright's account book as 'Mr Arkwright half length £26.5'. It was last seen in public in 1883 and prior to that was exhibited in the National Portrait Exhibition at the South Kensington Museum in 1867. The picture has been dated as mid 1780s 'when Joseph Wright was at the height of his powers'. David Berry, Director of the Art Fund, comments 'it was considered by his children to be the best portrait ever painted of their father. It perfectly captures the private side of a formidable character who helped shape modern Britain'.

Where was Cromford's Corn Mill – and its pond?

The plan which accompanies the lease for the first cotton mill does not indicate the site of the nearby corn mill. This is surprising as it was a condition of the lease that the new mill Richard Arkwright and his partners were to build should not disturb the operation of the existing corn mill. Little is known of the mill though some details emerge from the newspaper advertisements when it was to let in 1766 and 1768, see page 33 and when its machinery was for sale in 1776, see page 17. Arkwright's lease of the manor of Cromford from Peter Nightingale in that year gave him permission to build his second cotton mill and to demolish the corn mill which could not be worked once the new cotton mill was in place.

The undershot wheel advertised in the machinery sale indicates that any pond associated with the corn mill served as a reservoir collecting water to drive the wheel rather than providing a head of water such as would have been the case had the wheel been of the breast or overshot type. In theory such a reservoir could have been located at a distance from the mill even to the west of Arkwright's first mill but the absence of such a feature on the 1771 lease plan would appear to rule this out. The existence of such a pond is known from two witness statements offered in the case between Richard Arkwright and the Proprietors of the Meerbrook Sough heard in the Exchequer in 1839. The two witnesses, William Weston and William Street, were both old men. They were asked to cast their minds back more than sixty years; but there was nothing tentative about their recollections. Weston remembered the cotton mills being built and his testimony refers to a reservoir or in his own words ' The Bonsall Brook and Sough Water were not together sufficient to turn the Corn Mill Wheel a Dam was made to save the Water'. Street confirmed the presence of a dam though he believed it had been removed before the first cotton mill was built. Thus though there is evidence for the existence of a reservoir, these eye witnesses are as unhelpful as the lease plan in determining its location.

The only other known references to a mill dam in relation to the first mill site is in the terms of Arkwright's lease - the cut or mill dam 'intended to be made', and William Milnes claim to ownership of the fish 'to be put into the new Cut and Mill Dam... where none coul'd be without being put in' (see Milnes v Arkwright). There is no difficulty in identifying the new cut. This was the water course which Arkwright created to bring the sough water to the water wheel on the east side of the first mill as described earlier. As to the dam, both references suggest a new structure and with the condition 'where none [no fish] cou'd be without being put in' it appears Milnes is referring to the basin, the structure associated with Arkwright's new cut. Whatever our interpretation, neither reference sheds any light on the whereabouts of a pond associated with the corn mill.

The location of the corn mill building itself is equally uncertain. Arkwright's permission to pull the mill down in 1776 allowed him to use the materials for his second cotton mill but the building or part of it may have survived until 1789. It was only then when Sir Richard purchased the manor of Cromford, if the Law Report of the 1839 case is to be believed, that 'very considerable additions' were made 'to the cotton mill...part of which was erected upon the site of the ancient corn mill'. This information reduces the search area to within the curtilage of the Cromford Mills' site. If the description 'cotton mill' is taken literally it suggests the corn mill may have stood somewhere within the footprint of the second mill annexe; a more general reading places it somewhere within the eastern yard and its perimeter buildings.

The search should not be abandoned. Whereas all of the central area of the site has been excavated, most of the eastern yard is undisturbed and careful examination may yet reveal further information. A watercourse, now dry, has been traced part way under the brick paved area of the yard running roughly from west to east towards the grilled opening at the foot of the perimeter wall in the south east corner of the yard - which has no current function. The remains of a building have been found below present ground level between the south end of the second mill annexe and the building now, in 2013, housing lavatories and while there is no suggestion that this is the ancient corn mill, its existence offers encouragement that excavation may one day answer this and other questions.

CHAPTER SIX

Later uses of the Arkwright mills' site

In 1839 Richard Arkwright junior lost his battle to retain an adequate water supply to the Cromford mills' site. The Meerbrook Sough which had been under construction since 1772 was draining water to the Derwent at Whatstandwell from lead mines on Wirksworth Moor at a lower level than the Cromford Long Sough. An agreement dated July 1825 between Richard Arkwright and Francis Hurt and his partners who were driving the Meerbrook Sough had provided for the erection of wooden 'floodgates or doors', in 1807 or 1808 in a branch level of the sough which would 'press back the water' and 'cause it to find its original channels and ultimately flow into and down the Cromford Moor Sough, thereby supplying the said mills with more water than was used previous to the said branch level of the said Meerbrook Sough having been driven'. William Frost testified that 'In June 1820 I assisted in taking up the Old Gates – they were then losing a deal of water' and 'it was the beginning of 1821 the New Gates were set down…they were Cast Iron and made at the Butterley Works'. He was of the opinion that the doors 'shut out the water as completely as can be' and raised the water to the level of the Cromford Sough. The 1825 agreement stated that the doors would be kept closed but the agreement could be set aside at 3 months notice. The three months notice expired in October 1836. The gates were opened in May 1837 but closed the following month when Peter Arkwright and William Melville who rented the mills 'from year to year' threatened action for loss of water. The case was referred from Derby Assizes in 1838 to the Court of the Exchequer where in 1839 judgement was found for the Meerbrook Sough proprietors. In 1840 the sough proprietors agreed to let a certain amount of water through to Cromford but only subject to pursuing their own interests, an arrangement which provided Richard Arkwright with little comfort that he would continue to enjoy an adequate water supply for the mills.

The loss of the sough water supply damaged the Cromford site irretrievably though it remained in limited use. However when it was valued in 1872 it is clear that there was little industrial activity there. Cromford, in respect of the machinery etc in use, was valued at £221.11s.0d. and Masson Mill at £5874.0s.0d. I P Clark & Co of King Street Mills, Leicester expressed interest in buying Masson Mill and the useable parts of Cromford Mill, and their letter of enquiry dated May 1872 commented 'we quite understand in our interview with Mr Arkwright [Frederic Arkwright] that the mills do not pay now, but still, at a modest rent, we have every confidence that we could make them pay'. No sale or lease was agreed.

Gradually and at different times the Cromford buildings or parts of buildings were taken over for other uses. These included textile production as an adjunct to Via Gellia Mill for Charles Hill and briefly for William Hollins and Co; brewing and bottling for Matthew Hill's Cromford Brewery; warehousing for Messrs Wheatcroft and Sons where cheese from local producers was stored, the cheeses awaiting transport to market. Later Wheatcrofts had a corn store in the five storey roadside building adjacent to the first mill which they vacated in June 1910 and the Arkwright estate stored wood on the site. Two laundries were also established; one, later known as the Troy Laundry, in the East Yard, (see Figure 41), the other near the first mill in the West Yard. In 1914 the Cromford Colour Company occupied buildings at the west end of the site and when the Troy Laundry closed in 1966 it spread into the laundry's space (see Figure 42) to complete its occupation of all the Cromford Mills' buildings apart from the two cottages in the West Yard, Grace Cottage and the red brick building, which was then in use as a single dwelling.

Matthew Hill's Cromford Brewery

An account book survives for a brewery in Cromford for the period July 1825 to June 1837 but gives no indication of its whereabouts or its proprietor. Both Daniel Gell at the Bell and George Higgott at the Greyhound appear in Directories as maltsters at some time in this period. Later there was a brew-house associated with the Boat. In living memory a large building behind the inn was called the old malthouse (see Figure 86).

FIGURE 40. **Matthew Hill, (1844-1910), photograph, High Peak News, October 8th, 1910. Cromford Brewery labels. Note Hill's Brewery bottled and sold Bass.**

Private collection

What became well known as the Cromford Brewery was founded by Matthew Hill. Hill, who had previously worked for the Midland Railway at Longstone was the tenant of the Greyhound from 1876 to 1895; a period during which it was, so his obituary in the *High Peak News* claimed, the commercial house of the Matlock District. Described as 'a good citizen' who had been 'first and foremost in looking after the welfare of the people', Hill had served on Cromford Parish Council, had been a Cromford Poor Law Guardian for many years and held high offices in the Matlock District Licensed Victuallers Association. He was a founder member of the Arkwright Lodge of Freemasons.

His brewing business was begun at the Greyhound but there is evidence to suggest that he learned commercial brewing from a member of the Hanson family of Kimberley in Nottinghamshire. The 1881 census records Hill as a Hotel Proprietor resident in R. Hanson's household. His obituary explained that 'gradually he acquired licensed trade by purchasing properties, in various districts from Holloway and the Via Gellia to Matlock Bath, Winster, Longstone, etc etc'. By 1890 the brewery was housed in the bow-fronted building (the Barracks) on the Cromford Mills' site which Hill leased from Frederic Charles Arkwright; in 1895 he was paying £30 per annum for the premises. On July 4th 1896 the brewery became a limited company 'to carry on the trade or business of Cromford Brewery' with Directors, Matthew Hill, Thomas Tyack, then proprietor of the New Bath Hotel at Matlock Bath, John Willn of Cromford and George Lee Morrall of Derby. The company advertised 'Hill's Chain Ales in cask and bottle'. In 1904 new legislation known as the Compensation Act empowered the police to close some public houses. Owners were compensated from a levy charged on all licensed premises. Along with many other breweries Hill's suffered the loss of some tied houses, the Crown at Parwich for example in 1907.

Matthew Hill died in 1910 at his home, 'The Shrubbery' (the former mill manager's house on Mill Lane) to which he had moved soon after his wife's death in 1895.

In 1912 Offilers' Brewery of Derby took over Hill's Brewery as a going concern and agreed a lease from F C Arkwright although settlement with Hill's debenture holders was not completed until early 1914. In March of that year Offilers circulated Hill's customers informing them of the take–over and drawing their attention to its Nut Brown Ales 'being well known in Derby and the neighbourhood'. In the same year the Via Gellia Colour Company began negotiations with Arkwright to lease the western end of the Cromford Mills' site with an option on Offilers' premises. Offilers meanwhile had found Hill's plant to be in poor condition and had decided not to replace it. The company surrendered its own lease in 1915 and subsequently sub-leased space from the colour company for use as a beer store and distribution depot. Offilers was later taken over by Bass & Co.

Troy Laundry

Many local people will have memories of the Troy Laundry which occupied the extension to the second mill at the east end of the Cromford Mills' site. Some damage had been done to the building as a result of the fire in the second mill in 1890 but in 1895 Frederic Charles Arkwright leased buildings to Messrs Armstrong and Sproul who established the Matlock Bath (Troy) Laundry in the premises. The *Belper News* of August 14th, 1896 reminded readers of the event, explaining that the 'machinery is of the latest construction, all manufactured at Troy, U.S.A.'. The comment that 'Troy is as famous for laundry work in America as Matlock Bath is for health and fine water in England' may explain why the business, though based at Cromford, associated itself with Matlock Bath. At the time the area, and particularly Matlock and Matlock Bath, were well known and attracted many visitors. The expectation of trade from the hotels, restaurants, guest houses and bed and breakfast establishments which catered for them may have encouraged the laundry venture in Cromford. The terms of the lease included 'using the most approved methods by precipitating tanks or otherwise to render the suds waste water and refuse which shall be discharged from the works as little noxious as possible before allowing the same to run into the river Derwent'.

In 1899 James N. Sproul & Co took over the business which then included a laundry at Eccles. A Miss A M May was the tenant at the laundry when it was offered for sale in the Arkwright estate sales of 1924 and 1927. She had taken a 21 year lease on the property in 1911. The lease covered the building shown in the early view at Figure 41 and all the other buildings in the east yard to the east of the entrance from Mill Lane along with a supply of water 'through a pipe of one inch diameter, but the supply shall not necessarily be a continuance one'. At the estate sale the three storey building to the west of the yard entrance was included as part of the laundry premises. It is assumed that the property did not sell in 1924 and that Miss May purchased it in 1927 though some property which had been sold already appears erroneously in the 1927 catalogue. About 1936 or 1937 she sold Troy Laundry to the Chorley Hygienic Laundry Company, based in Chorley, Lancashire. For a period before January 1940 when Thomas Bibby was appointed as resident manager, affairs at Cromford were run from a distance by directors of the company.

TROY LAUNDRY,

CROMFORD.

Permanent Regular Employment offered to

Superior Local Girls, at Progressive Wages.

Girls of School leaving age will be given Expert Training which will be a Guarantee against Unemployment.

Cromford Church Magazine, November, 1936

During Miss May's ownership a large two bay three storey extension had been added to the south side of the old four storey mill building and the two storey east-west wing had been remodelled to a single storey block which housed the laundry's offices. Largely hidden behind these buildings was a boiler house and an engine house. The steam engine and coal fired boiler according to oral evidence drove a generator which provided electricity for some of the machines and steam from the boiler fed the washers, calenders (flat bed pressing machines), and presses. The calenders were housed in a glass roofed extension behind the one storey wing. A worker there in the 1960s remembers 'we pulled a sheet from a trolley, and with a partner took a corner each and put the end into a pressing machine. Two more people took the sheet out at the other end and three others folded it. It was hot in this room and my feet did ache by the end of the day'.

Dirty laundry was delivered in bundles or hampers to the ground floor of the three storey extension for sorting and checking against the enclosed laundry list and to make sure all pieces had the owner's mark on them; if not a mark was added; then conveyors and wooden trolleys carried the laundry to the appropriate washing machines arranged down either side of the ground floor of the old mill building. The machines used water from the Bonsall Brook which had been passed through a purification and filtration plant. After being spun in the hydro-extractors, some clean laundry – bedding and table linen – was pressed in the calenders at ground floor level; other items such as towels went on to the driers. All items were lifted on wooden trays to the ironing room on the first floor and from there, when finished, by conveyor to the top floor of the extension for checking against the laundry book and packing. Small packed bundles, boxes and hampers were sent down a chute to the

FIGURE 41. **Troy Laundry, photographs, on the left, Lot 55 from the Arkwright estate sale catalogue, 1924, on the right, the same buildings, about 1970.**

On the left, the picture shows the extension to Arkwright's second cotton mill after it had been in use as a laundry for over thirty years. The link to the second mill was taken down to two storeys before the building was let to the laundry. Note the boiler house chimney visible behind the mill. The view on the right shows the same building in about 1970 and as it was when the Arkwright Society took over the site. The link is now single storey height, the large three storey extension was added to the laundry some time before 1936. As part of the Arkwright Society's restoration of the mill site, the three storey extension was demolished and the gable end of the original building restored.

Arkwright Society collection

despatch floor below to be sorted into hampers for delivery down the outside chute to the appropriate delivery van, a route also taken by new young workers as part of their 'introduction' to laundry work. The workforce was drawn from Cromford and surrounding villages; some, from Lea and Starkholmes for example walked in, some came by bus from Matlock, Bonsall, Middleton and Wirksworth.

Troy Laundry vans collected and delivered washing and dry cleaning from the area around Matlock, Bakewell, Chesterfield, Ashbourne, Wirksworth and Duffield. Later there was a depot in Derby. Two vans ran back and forth to the company's depot in Macclesfield and collected from Macclesfield, Leek and the villages of East Cheshire and North Staffordshire. Dry cleaning was gathered together in Macclesfield and sent to Chorley for processing.

The Second World War had a marked impact on the laundry's work. The change began with the arrival in the village in the summer of 1940 of an Army Driving School which had its offices in unused Colour Works buildings and its lorries parked on the hard standing in Cromford Meadows. The soldiers who were billeted in the village and the officers who were accommodated in local hotels sent their washing to the laundry. As the war progressed, the amount of work increased significantly. Laundry - personal items, bed linen, towels, overalls - began to be delivered by military transport from about eight camps and bases in locations undisclosed to the laundry though most were probably in north Nottinghamshire and Lincolnshire. By 1943 an American Army Air Force base in Lincolnshire was delivering a huge load twice a week. No doubt laundries more local to them were overwhelmed with work when there were so many bases in the east of the country and especially in 1943-44 when the United States Third Army was based in Norfolk There were also laundry collections from guest houses in various parts of Derbyshire, Parwich and Bakewell for example, which

Heavy snow disrupted train services so badly in January 1940 that laundry manager Thomas Bibby's arrival in Cromford from North Wales was delayed by 10 days. Snow had also prevented any director reaching Cromford to sign the wages cheques so Mr Bibby arrived to find two weeks' wages were owing and when he finally sought to collect the wages cash from the local branch of the bank he was refused the money he needed. Despite telephoned requests from the laundry directors, the bank refused to pay out on the unsigned wages cheques. The vicar, Canon Hazlehurst presented himself at the laundry and arranged to go to the bank to introduce Thomas Bibby and on the way enlisted the company of the local policeman PC Shorthose, known to many as 'Socks'. The bank remained unmoved. Canon Hazlehurst remained unmoved and declared that the three would stay in the bank until the money was paid. Head Office at Wirksworth directed the Cromford clerk to call the police for help. The clerk explained that 'the police' were already 'sitting in'. Canon Hazlehurst arranged that the headmaster of Cromford School Mr Routledge and three senior pupils would arrive at lunchtime to join the occupation. Order was only restored when a director deposited sufficient cash in the Macclesfield branch of the bank and Wirksworth released the money to Cromford.

had been taken over as recovery centres for wounded personnel and twice daily a collection or delivery was made to one or more of the three big hydros in Matlock, Smedley's, Rockside and Chatsworth, which had been requisitioned by the government for military purposes. An unlikely wartime contract involved nappies, which arrived at 7.45am to be washed, dried and returned by lunch-time to Willersley Castle, where it is said an estimated 6000 babies were born between 1940 and 1946 while a mater-nity hospital from London was relocated there.

As a result of these developments the number of employees at the laundry rose from about 75 to 100 by the end of the war. Laundry work became a reserved occupation which meant that young men working there could not be called up for military service. Nevertheless some volunteered and numbers were main-tained by women who were required to do war work including about six who came to Cromford from Northern Ireland. At the same time the civilian laundry collection was reduced from a weekly to a fortnightly service in most areas.

After the war the civilian business recovered and the company expanded. The dry cleaning business at Chorley became a separate undertaking as the Pennine Cleaners. Laundries were bought at Preston and Swinton and some failing laundries, including those at Dron-field, Buxton, Blackpool, Burnley, Stoke and Derby were bought and closed and their work absorbed by the company's active sites. But from the late 1950s, business declined. The growth of the domestic washing machine industry and the spread of laundrettes affected laundry businesses and many closed. Cromford's Troy Laundry survived until late 1966, largely due to concentrating on business customers such as the hotels and restaurants.

The Cromford Colour Works

The Via Gellia Colour Company, which produced mineral colours, signed a draft lease for buildings on the Arkwright Mills' site in 1914 and purchased them in June 1923. In 1921, in response to a recognised demand for chrome colours, the Cromford Colour Company Limited was formed to make inorganic chemical colours based on lead chromate. These were specifically chrome yellow and chrome green. Prussian blue, which was iron based, was also made.

Ronald Wood's account of production at the Cromford Colour Works while he worked there in various capacities from 1935 until 1958 (with a gap from 1941-46 for service in World War II) follows.

The ingredients used at Cromford for colour production were mainly inorganic chemicals including acids, dichromates, alkalis and iron compounds which were bought in from a wide range of suppliers around the country. From them the company manufactured chrome yellow in shades progressing from 'Pale Primrose, through Lemon, Middle and Orange to a Deep Orange'. Chrome greens were produced by blending chrome yellows with Prussian blue. These pigments were supplied to the customer in the form of dry powders for use primarily in the manufacture of paint though some was used in the production of printing inks. The finished products were packed in 5 ply paper sacks for home consumption or in plywood kegs or hardwood casks for export to destinations which included Egypt, South Africa, Pakistan and India.

Producing a colour was called striking. For colours other than blue, the process began on the upper floors of the former five storey mill/warehouse adjacent to the first mill. The multi-storey layout permitted gravity feed of constituents, which were prepared in mixing vats on the upper floors, to the striking vats on the lower floors and allowed a more convenient means of dispersal of the acid fumes which were generated in the preparation of certain constituents at the higher levels. For example lead nitrate was prepared from canary litharge (lead oxide) and nitric acid on the top floor so that the unpleasant acrid fumes given off by nitric acid could be vented from the top of the building. The appropriate prepared constituents were run into a large striking vat with water and continuously agitated by belt-driven mechanical paddles. There were ten such vats arranged along the length of the building supported from the ground floor so that the lip of each vat stood about a foot or so above the level of the first floor for ease of visual control and for addition of ingredients if required (see Figure 45). Eventually the colour was allowed to precipitate out. Water was decanted off and replaced with clean water, stirred, re-settled and tested as many times as necessary to ensure the colour was free from unwanted by-products before it was allowed to run into trough filters at ground level. Here water drained off to a settling tank lower down the site leaving the colour as a paste capable of being shovelled out into trolleys - a heavy, messy job. More efficient filter presses which forced water out under pressure were also used. The paste or cake produced from either process was moved in trolleys to trays in long tunnel-shaped ovens on the first floor of the former first cotton mill. Air was blown through the tunnel over a long radiator which was heated from a boiler housed in the yard behind the mill. The dried lumps of colour were emptied from the trays to be stored in carefully labelled casks.

When a colour was needed for an order it was brought from store and dry ground to a powder in enclosed mills in the ground floor of the first mill using edge runner rollers which were later superseded by more efficient Torrance mills. A finer particle size could be produced in a machine known as a disintegrator.

FIGURE 42. **Cromford Mill site, overview from the south, photograph, 1975.**

This aerial view illustrates the conglomeration of additional building squeezed into the site during the years it was occupied by the colour works. Watercourses were covered; new openings were created in existing buildings; extensions to buildings, lift shafts and lean-to sheds were added.

Arkwright Society collection

Prussian blue pigment was made in the bow fronted building (the Barracks) on the other side of the brook in the mill yard - 'on the blue side'. It was struck from a chemical reaction using iron based ingredients and the precipitate was steam boiled to hasten full development of the colour. The dried colour was ground finely in a Raymond mill housed behind the bow fronted building; the finer particle size made blending with chrome yellow easier. Dry Prussian blue was readily combustible, a property it conveyed to green pigments in blending.

Pigments were also blended to match a specific shade requested by a customer. Often this required some additional substance such as a mineral colour not produced on the premises. The ingredients needed to make up a bespoke order were decided in the colour matching laboratory which at first was housed in a building below the bridge in the mill yard (subsequently used as a shop called Country Colours but now demolished) and later in this period in the top floor of the former weavers' workshop (see Figure 34). Here, in the simplest terms, a Cromford sample of dry colour of known composition and batch number was chosen by the colour matcher to compare against the customer's sample. A small weighed amount was ground in a pestle and mortar, mixed smoothly into linseed oil, spread onto a glass plate and checked against the customer's similarly treated sample. The colour matcher would make a series of carefully recorded balancing additions and re-tests to achieve a good match, the number of additions needed being a reflection of the skill of the matcher. There was also testing for other qualities including the covering power of the pigment. When the

customer approved the product, quantities of pigment were reserved in the proportions used in the test so that the order could be made up in bulk. This was done on the ground floor of the first mill where there was further testing and, if necessary, adjustment as the grinding and blending proceeded, supervised by production control which was housed in a laboratory with a large window on the upper floor.

During World War II the company supplied not only pigments for the more mundane requirements of the Armed Forces but also pigments for pyrotechnic devices and highly specialised chemical products essential to aircraft construction.

FIGURE 43. **The burnt beams of the fourth floor of the first mill, snapshot, 1929.**

In 1929 during the Colour Company's ownership the first mill building was severely damaged by fire. The two topmost storeys were not rebuilt and of the remaining three storeys only the ground floor and a new upper floor were retained.

Private collection

FIGURE 44. **Snapshot, 1929.**

Cromford Colour Company workmen pose in front of the first mill after the fire.

Private collection

FIGURE 45(a)

FIGURE 45(b)

FIGURE 45(e)

FIGURE 45(c)

FIGURE 45(d)

FIGURE 45(f)

FIGURE 45(g)

FIGURE 45. **Some images from the last 40 years.**

FIGURE 45(a). An overview of the site from the south east, 1971.

FIGURE 45(b). The five story/mill warehouse, 1979.

FIGURE 45(c&d). The east side of the second mill extension, 1979 - and in 1988 with the derelict Trout Farm fish tanks.

FIGURE 45(e). The first mill, right, and the 5 storey mill/warehouse, left, when the Arkwright Society took over the site in 1979 after the scrap men had removed all that they wanted.

FIGURE 45(f). The second mill's tail race in 1978, twenty years before the removal of the lead chromate waste. The culvert at this point is large enough to garage a small car.

FIGURE 45(g). The Colour Works filtration plant, 1979. The remains of the second mill lie beneath.

FIGURE 45(h). The west face of the first mill extension incorporating the wall of the weavers' workshop before restoration.

FIGURE 45(i). The damaged aqueduct being loaded for removal off site to safe storage.

FIGURE 45(j). Ten holes along the length of the first floor of the 5 storey mill/warehouse building which housed the Cromford Colour Company's colour vats c.2000. This building is in the final stage of repair and in 2014 will open for modern use including a gateway to the Derwent Valley Mills World Heritage Site.

Arkwright Society collection

FIGURE 45(h)

FIGURE 45(i)

FIGURE 45(j)

FIGURE 46. **Overview of the site from the east, photograph, 2004.**

This view shows the effects of the gradual clearance and decontamination of the site since the complex was purchased by the Arkwright Society in 1979 to reveal the early layout and form of buildings and to enable restoration to begin. Here the site is shown before a first stage of work was undertaken on the first mill extension which is shown, top right, scaffolded and screened. A temporary new roof has been added and the structure of the building has been strengthened by the introduction of an internal steel frame.

Arkwright Society collection

The Arkwright Society's intervention

When the Colour Company offered its premises for sale in 1979, there seemed to be little likelihood of the Cromford Mills surviving as a single entity. Having failed to rouse any interest in the official bodies which might have been expected to be concerned about its future, the Arkwright Society successfully funded the purchase of most of the mill site in September that year. The Society had grown out of the committee which had been formed in 1969 to organise the Arkwright Festival celebrating the two hundredth anniversary of Richard Arkwright's arrival in Cromford in 1771. The rescue included the colour production buildings but the East Yard and associated buildings were retained by the company by now known as Burrell Arkwright and put to use as a Trout Farm. The Bonsall Brook water proved unsuitable and the fish farm failed. In 1988 the National Heritage Memorial Fund and English Heritage enabled the Society to purchase the area which had housed the fish farm and, soon after, the National Heritage Memorial Fund enabled the Society to acquire the land surrounding the mills including Scarthin Rock.

CHAPTER SEVEN

Working for the Arkwrights

The principal elements of Arkwright's factory system were his new technology, a source of consistent power and a disciplined workforce.

His first concerns when he came to Cromford were to build his mill and to perfect and construct the machinery needed to run it. No doubt the skilled machine builders, the clock-makers, joiners and turners were imported from outside the area but the first mill labour force seems to have been brought together from Cromford and nearby settlements such as Bonsall. The Arkwright machinery was simple to use and was designed to be operated by children recognised at this time to be an under utilised economic resource, but once the new project expanded and the second mill was in prospect, an enlarged workforce had to be recruited. He might have used parish apprentices as some of the later rural mill owners chose to do, instead he placed the family unit at the heart of his operation, a choice copied by all the lower Derwent valley mill owners, the Strutts at Belper, the Evans at Darley Abbey and Peter Nightingale at Lea Bridge.

The migrant families attracted by the promise of work at Cromford needed to be housed and employment had to be found for their adult members, particularly the men who were not required in the mills. Arkwright's solution to this problem was to provide jobs for framework knitters and hand loom weavers, both traditionally men's occupations. These solutions are reflected in the advertisements Arkwright placed in the Derby Mercury.

The early years

These dated advertisements illustrate the change in Arkwright's position over his first ten years in Cromford. The emphasis in December, 1771, just over four months after the first lease was signed, is to

Cotton Mill, Cromford, 10th Dec. 1771.

WANTED immediately, two Journeymen Clock-Makers, or others that underſtands Tooth and Pinion well: Alſo a Smith that can forge and file.—Likewiſe two Wood Turners that have been accuſtomed to Wheel-making, Spole-turning, &c. Weavers reſiding in this Neighbourhood, by applying at the Mill, may have good Work. There is Employment at the above Place, for Women, Children, &c. and good Wages.

N. B. A Quantity of Box Wood is wanted: Any Perſons whom the above may ſuit, will be treated with by Meſſrs. Arkwright and Co. at the Mill, or Mr. Strutt, in Derby.

Derby Mercury, December 10th, 1771

attract men who have the skills to construct the mill machinery. Ten years later he is recruiting staff for what is by this time a going concern, recently enlarged by the opening of the second mill.

Arkwright's early offer of work for weavers 'in this neighbourhood' was confined to those who lived nearby because he was not able to provide housing in Cromford yet. So much is clear but it remains a mystery that he should

be seeking to employ weavers at all when the mill is so far from completion. To speed the construction process Arkwright had acquired cut stone from a house which he had bought and demolished at Steeple Grange between Cromford and Wirksworth and, for comparison, a few years later we are told that five to six months were required for 200 men to build the much larger second mill. Yet it is clear from Arkwright's letter to Strutt in March 1772 that seven months after taking on the lease he is still engaged in experimenting with yarn production and in fitting out the mill building. Thus the opportunities for employment must have remained limited. This was to change by the end of the year. A letter which appeared in *Creswell's Nottingham Journal* in January 1773 describes 'mills at Nottingham and Cromford...that go by water and horses, that employ a number of industrious people in spinning of cotton yarn...of excellent quality'. This evidence that the Cromford mill was in production by the beginning of 1773 is supplemented in March 1774 by the details which emerge from Milnes' statement to his legal advisors. He records that families had been moving to the village and 'more will be coming'. We do not know how or where these families were accommodated at this time.

By 1781 Arkwright is still recruiting ready-trained men and their families but by then his appeal was not confined to the neighbourhood. He had been building houses and could provide accommodation in Cromford for workers moving from further afield. And he was in a position to take on unskilled labour and offer training with the positive inducement that it would be worthwhile. Simeon Cundy's experience recorded by the *Factories Inquiry Commission* of 1833 is an example of the opportunities available. He started work in 1782 at the age of six at the younger Arkwright's Bakewell mill, and four years later began his seven year apprenticeship to learn 'turning, filing, and fitting up of wood, brass, iron, steel, and every branch of machinery'. By 1793 he was a manager at William Young's mill in Manchester. Abraham Rees reflected early in the 1800s that he considered the mills to be 'schools for mechanics in almost every department of that science; and good ones too'. Arkwright needed other skills by 1781; 'men who can write a good hand'. He had more ledgers and accounts to keep now and other mills and property outside Cromford generating more correspondence, and as Francis Staley later found, (see below), it was not good enough to write slowly.

Richard Arkwright, like his partners Jedediah Strutt and Peter Nightingale, employed weavers to work up his yarn making calicoes and muslins. In Cromford they were based in workshops at the mills and in the village notably in the top storey rooms of the houses on North Street.

Local use of the mills' products by knitters continued in Cromford through to at least the first half of the nineteenth century. 20 narrow knitting frames making cotton goods are recorded as late as 1844. Bonsall was a larger centre of framework knitting, there being 143 knitters in 1844 and the industry continued in the village well into the twentieth century when many knitters worked for the Smedley business at Lea.

Dr Stanley Chapman has drawn attention to the weaving business in Cromford developed by James Longsdon of Little Longstone. He

FIGURE 47. **Clock face, photograph, 1999.**

This clock was made in Cromford in the 1770s and certainly not later than 1780 by J. Jeffryes. Nothing is known of this man but it is possible that he was a member of the group of skilled craftsmen that Arkwright brought to Cromford to build his machinery. Arkwright advertised in the *Derby Mercury* for clockmakers. It is not known how successful he was in recruiting them but a man of the name of Jeffries entered his employment at about this time. This is confirmed in a further newspaper entry which appeared on November 14th 1777 'committed to the House of Correction at Derby, one John Jeffries, a Gunsmith, of Cromford, for the space of one Calendar Month and to be kept to hard Labour and corrected; he being charged by Mr Arkwright, Cotton Merchant, with having absented himself from his Master's Business without Leave, (being a hired Servant for a Year) and likewise being guilty of divers Misdemeanors and Misbehaviours'. The British Horological Institute comments that it was not unusual in rural areas for gunsmiths to make clocks and vice versa and both would have skills which Arkwright needed. Perhaps clockmaker and miscreant were one in this case or at least members of the same family drawn to Cromford in response to the promise of work

Arkwright Society collection

identifies Longsdon as a significant purchaser of Arkwright's yarn with a rented depot in Cromford 'for distributing yarn among rural weavers and collecting finished fustians and checks'. In 1783 his credit with Arkwright stood at more than £2000. The location of his depot is not known but it would be wrong to rule out that he rented space in one of the ancillary buildings on the Cromford Mills' site. It is thought likely that Longsdon's business in Cromford came to an end when he built new premises at Great Longstone in 1786.

The labour force at the mills consisted largely of children and a much smaller number of adults. For most we have no evidence of any formal contract to define their terms of employment. But there were 'boys and young men' who came for a number of years to learn a trade and others, already skilled in some trade, who were bound to Richard Arkwright. Some of the bonds from these transactions have survived and reproduced below are the terms agreed with Adam Pearson of Matlock Wood in June 1777 for a period of 14 years. A similar bond exists for Richard Mansfield of Cromford from June 1777 also for 14 years, as a joiner; a third bond from November 1786 bound Henry Boam of Matlock for 5 years.

Know all men by these presents that I Adam Pearson of Matlock Wood in the Parish of Matlock in the County of Derby I am miner held and firmly bound to Richard Arkwright of Cromford in the said County cotton merchant; in the sum of ten thousand pounds of lawful money of Great Britain, to be paid unto the said Richard Arkwright or his certain attorney, executors, administrators, or assignees; for which payment to be made and faithfully made; I bind myself, my heirs, executors and administrators firmly and by these presents, sealed with my seal, dated this twelfth day of June in the seventeenth year of the reign of our sovereign Lord George the Third by the Grace of God of great Britain France and Ireland; King Defender of the Faith etc and in the year of our Lord one thousand seven hundred and seventy-seven.

Whereas the above named Richard Arkwright hath lately invented some pieces of machinery, for the more expeditious, and better preparing of cotton wool silk or flax; and hath obtained his Majesty's letters patent, for the sole use and benefit thereof; and he the said Richard Arkwright having the occasion to employ several artists, or workmen for repairing and improving the same, and for making other machinery of the like nature, hath hereby agreed with the said Adam Pearson to work with him in this or any branch of art which the said Richard Arkwright shall think proper to employ him, for the term of fourteen years from the day of the date hereof and the said Adam Pearson doth hereby agree to work with the said Richard Arkwright, in such branch or art as he shall think proper to employ him for the said term of fourteen years, in any part of Great Britain as he the said Richard Arkwright shall appoint or direct and at all times during the said term of fourteen years; and to work six days in every week, reckoning thirteen hours to each day's work, at the rate or wages of seven shillings and sixpence for the first and second year; eight shillings and sixpence for the third and fourth year; ten shillings a week for the fifth and sixth year; twelve shillings a week for the seventh and eighth year; and fourteen shillings a week for the last six years the remaining part of the said term of fourteen years; for such time as he shall work for the said master.

Now the conditions of the above written obligation is such that if the above bounden Adam Pearson shall and do, from time to time during the said term of fourteen years, faithfully and diligently to the utmost of his power serve the said Richard Arkwright, in working for him to the best of his skill and judgement, in the art or business in which he shall think proper to employ him; and willingly obey his commands and orders, and shall and do from time to time and at all times during the continuance of the said patent or patents, he the said Richard Arkwright may obtain during the said term of fourteen years and so long as the same shall be enforced, keep secret, and not on any occasion whatever directly or indirectly, disclose or make known to any person or persons whatever, the form, construction use or manner of working any machine or machinery belonging to the said Richard Arkwright, or any matter or thing used in such or the like machinery or engine or instruct any person whatever, how to make construct or use any such of the like machinery or engines (without the consent of the said Richard Arkwright first hand) then the above written obligation to be void or else to be and remain in full force or virtue.

Sealed and delivered by the above

Bounden Adam Pearson
(being first duly stamped)

In the presence of

Richard Arkwright Junr
Benj. Pearson Junr

Adam Pearson

A more personal view of the Arkwrights as masters is afforded by letters written by Francis Staley to Richard Arkwright junior on August 4th 1794 and January 5th, 1795 politely asking for a wage review reminding him that 'the terms of my agreement has been expired some time' and 'if Sir Rich'd your father had not been dead I had great reason to believe I sh'd have had a[n] addition for the time I had served'. He explained that he had worked 4 to 5 years for Sir Richard before returning to mining. 'When Sir Rich'd your father heard of it he sent word he was sorry I had left without letting him know, that if I would come again he would advance my wages handsomely…If I chanced to meet him on the road he frequently asked me if I was not tired of working at the mines, and whether I would not work for him again.'

Eventually Staley signed an agreement drawn up by Thos. Buxton for a further five years at twelve shillings a week. He objected to the wages and 'would not have hired under a shilling per week adve. [advance] every year if he had not said he sh'd make me a better alowe. [allowance] than that if I behaved well; I did not seem to countenance that so well as he could have wished I suppose, as he ask'd me whether I disputed his word, he said he'd had a liking to me from the first time I came to work for him and all the Family; and that he meant to do me good else he sh'd not have been at so much trouble about me. From these and more promises and persuasions I consented.' Staley refers Richard Arkwright junior to Mr Barton, Mr Fletcher, Mr Harrison or Mr Nuttall for an account of his behaviour and character.

In his second letter, the description of his periods of work makes clear that he had worked in other Arkwright mills, at Maston [sic] almost certainly in the first period of his employment, Wirksworth at the beginning of the second and finally at Cromford. At Masson he claimed 'that it had not been found so neat if I had not led them to it by first setting the example'. In the year and a half that he was at Wirksworth he commented that 'there was nearly a sixth part more work done than had ever been done before with less wages' and that a year after he left Wirksworth Sir Richard had told him more than once that he 'should have been more than a thousand pounds better in that mill if he had kept me there'. This would have been at what is now called Haarlem Mill before it was leased to Robert Heptinstall and Robert Sykes in 1792. Staley was moved from Wirksworth to take Mr Fletcher's place to keep the ledger and accounts but was too slow at writing and was asked to superintend the Cromford mills when Mr Condon left. His self assessment is rather touching when he explains that he did it 'for a month or two but things being but in an Indft [indifferent] loose way and I was young and had been used to work amongst them so that I could not manage to my mind so I ask'd your father several times to let me be of[f] that but he kept encouraging me till I was taken ill and was of[f] work 3 or 4 weeks, and when I came again he said if I had rather be in the Counting house where I have been since …'.

How Richard Arkwright junior honoured his father's promised 'better allowance' is not known though it is clear that he did consider the matter as Staley writes 'you asked me what wages I should expect, to which I did not give a direct answer, knowing that it all depends on what you are pleased to give me'.

Richard Arkwright junior, the Factory Master

More detail is provided about the conditions of employment at the mills under Richard Arkwright junior's management from evidence he gave to Sir Robert Peel's enquiry on the *State of Children employed in Manufactories* on 7th June 1816.

He stated that no children under 10 years of age had been employed at Cromford for the past ten years though formerly they were taken in at seven or eight, 'probably seven'. He explained the principal reason for the change being 'that they might learn to read before they came' though he conceded that the pressure from parents trying to push their children into employment had resulted in 'a lowering of standards'. He considered that boys might better be taken in at nine: 'I see them often running about and in mischief' while 'girls have to nurse their younger brothers and sisters or they work at home; or they do something; but boys have nothing to do unless they go to school'. He confirmed that there were two Sunday schools in Cromford which he provided free attended by 225 and of these 131 were in Cromford. It is reasonable to suppose that these schools had continued from February 1785 when the *Manchester Mercury* reported Richard Arkwright [senior] had set up a school in Cromford which 'already consists of two hundred children'.

Two years after Sir Robert Peel's enquiry, the Select Committee on the Education of the Poor received more information. The inspector of schooling in Cromford reported a day school for 55 children; three schools kept by women containing 62; an evening school consisting of 25 or 30 children and a Sunday school of 80 boys and 35 girls. The report does not identify where these schools were in the village but an announcement of a meeting of the Cromford Old Sick Club in the School Room, Cromford on June 25th 1825 shows there was a designated place.

The school Richard Arkwright junior opened in 1832 and which, in an extended form, remains in use 180 years later, was built in anticipation of the provisions of the forthcoming factory legislation. The 1833 Act, in addition to its regulation of the hours of work for young people in cotton mills and the prohibition of the employment of children under 9, authorised factory inspectors to 'establish or procure the establishment' of factory schools though it did not suggest how this might be done. It was left to enlightened employers to take up the challenge of creating a system which combined mill work with effective exposure to education however limited that might be; in Cromford it was three hours a day. It is evident from the inspection of the Cromford schools made in about 1837 that Arkwright adopted what was first known as the Relay System, later the Half Time System, whereby children divided each working day between the mill and the school. The inspector who visited Messrs Arkwright and Melville's cotton mills in Cromford, whose findings were reported in the 1839 report on the educational provisions of the 1833 Act, notes that the school was established about 5 years ago. It describes a boys' school under the charge of a master and a girls' school under a mistress, 'both very efficient teachers', having the assistance of one principal monitor and one to each class. 40 boys and 28 girls attend in two sets, three hours each. The children are taught writing and ciphering and the females are taught to sew and knit and to mend their own clothes two days a week. The school is also open in the evening for young people who work at the mill and on Sunday 'when the attendance is very large'. The report states that

Henry Daniel

Henry Daniel was the Headmaster at Cromford School from 1891 to 1929. On his retirement in late November 1929, the High Peak News reported Daniel recalling his period of service there: 'Mr Arkwright [Frederic Charles Arkwright] used to own the school and was the manager for eleven years. Then free education came in and was a great relief to the parents. In 1902 they came under the County Education Committee and things got better still'. He reminded his audience that 'Cromford School was a half-time school when he came there, and children of ten years of age could go to work at the mill'.

In front of the packed school, a former scholar, Dr R H Chapman, then the headmaster at the Ernest Bailey Secondary School in Matlock made the retirement presentation 'of a gold watch and a wallet of notes' gladly acknowledging that 'No one owed more to Mr Daniel than he did'. Attention was drawn to such a small country school's extraordinary record in gaining scholarships, an achievement qualified by Daniel as 'every year since they were first offered' and that the school 'would have got more but, with families big and wages small, parents had to take their children away from school to go to work'. Tributes were paid to Daniel as being a man twenty to thirty years ahead of his time. He was one of the first headmasters in England to start a school garden, he had introduced nature study and geology and it was entirely his initiative to teach alabaster stone sculpture using foot treadle lathes. Over ten years specimens of the children's work were exhibited and won prizes in London. Twelve pieces were given a permanent home by the Save the Children Fund and exhibited in Geneva.

factory children do not pay for their schooling. Other children of the neighbourhood, about 120 boys and 70 girls, are admitted on payment of twopence per week, Messr Arkwright paying all remaining expenses. It was observed that the parents were not noticeably glad but they had the advantage of 'the school established here before'. A less generous interpretation of the parent's response might be that they had the disadavantage of reduced wage packets from their children.

The inspector concluded that 'of the various schools visited, this one appeared, on the whole, to be the best conducted' but his summary of achievement was perfunctory. The master's conclusion was that the children who attend the school from the mill only half a day make very frequently as much progress as others. More than fifty years later, Henry Daniel, the headmaster of Cromford School was not so positive. He identified one of the several disadvantages of the system. 'It was', he said 'difficult to teach children who had worked in the mill from 6am to noon and then came to school for the rest of the day. Very often they fell asleep at their desks'.

Working in the mills

The mills, Richard Arkwright explained in 1816, employed 725 people and a greater proportion of them were adult now, only 269 being between 10 and 18. Of those there were 4 under 11, 22 under 12, 25 under 13, 39 under 14, 49 under 15, 58 under 16, 32 under 17 and 40 under18. He reported 7 out of the total number being on the sick list at this time and that when they were on the list they received half wages. The provision of half wages for sick children was not always so but was introduced he said 'a very long time ago'. The working day was 13 hours including meal times, from six to seven in the summer and from seven to eight in the winter. Richard Arkwright's detailed response to the question 'What time do you allow for meals?' is printed in full. 'An hour for dinner. As to breakfast, it is very irregular. In the summer-time the bell rings for breakfast at half past eight; those who go to breakfast which includes the workmen, but not the spinners, go and stay half an hour. There is a room called the dinner-house, in which there is a range of hot plates or stoves, much the same as in gentlemens kitchens; the mothers, or the younger sisters of the hands employed, bring the breakfasts into this room; they bring them probably a quarter of an hour before the bell rings. As soon as the bell rings, a number of boys, perhaps eight, carry those breakfasts into the different rooms in the factory; those who come first may receive their breakfasts probably in two minutes; those who come later may not receive it for a quarter of an hour; so that possibly some of the hands may have eight and twenty minutes at breakfast, others may not have more than fifteen, they cannot have less. In the afternoon the bell rings at four, and they are served in like manner; but very few have their refreshment, probably not one in five, I should think.'

Further questions established that the machinery driven entirely by water was never stopped during working hours except at the dinner-hour. The suggestion that employees might go home to eat, which he considered would be inconvenient, led him to the calculation that the 373 hands from Cromford lived an average of 970 yards from the mill while the remaining 352 workers who came from different townships, lived on average a mile and a quarter from the mill.

Seventeen years later, an inspection of Masson Mill, presented in evidence to the enquiry on *Employment of Children in Factories*, 1833-34, added further details. The total number of people employed there of all ages was 350 of whom about 110 were below 18. They were provided with free medical assistance and their holidays for the year, for which they were not paid, were Christmas Day, Good Friday, Shrove Tuesday, half days each for Whit Monday, 12th May and Bonsall Wakes and 4 days for Cromford Wakes.

In Robert Fitton's *The Arkwrights, Spinners of Fortune* the comparison of this regime with working conditions in the Manchester mills emphasises the liberality of Richard Arkwright's management. Most mills worked longer than a 13 hour day and offered less than an a full hour for dinner during which their spinning machinery was kept running; provision of a dinner-house was not the norm but considered an unusual benefit. Paying half wages for sick children was a further sign of the relatively benign nature of the Arkwright regime. No reference is given to holidays in other mills. Does this reflect a different attitude to allowing time off for traditional festivals for workers at a mill in a rural setting? The Strutt accounts for Belper record workers being fined for 'Off without leave at a wakes' or 'Going to Derby fair' or 'Going without leave to a Shearring [sic]'. Was the fixing of official time off recognition by Arkwright that he might as well close down for celebrations of this kind or was it further evidence of benign paternalism?

A member of Richard Arkwright junior's staff from a quite different sphere of the family's life was his gamekeeper, Stagalls. Mrs Gell of Hopton wrote to Mr Arkwright in 1795 asking that he would 'restrain his gamekeeper from shooting the woodcocks and wild ducks in the Via Gellia as 'the firing of guns there disturbs their pheasants which are with great pains, & care, foddered there, & become very tame'. She reminded him that 'the whole of the Via Gellia is the peculiar plaything of Mr & Mrs Gell, and the ornamenting of it , & rendering the game happy there, their most agreeable amusement'. It seems that Stagalls was directed to reply though, since the rather less than penitent version, right, remains in the Arkwright's archive, it is probable that this was not the approved final draft.

It seems no permanent damage was done to neighbourly relations as later in the year, when it appears Mr Gell had been unwell, Mrs Gell writes again to thank Mr Arkwright for 'the finest trout they ever saw. They are really concerned at the greatness of the donation as half the quantity would have made a banquet'. And Stagalls remained

Sir

I am very sorry and humbly ask your pardon for taking the liberty coming a little way upon your manor upon the Turnpike Road, and never was ten yards out of it. I happened upon some snipes and shot four of them and one mallard which you may have if you will exept [sic] of them. Woodcocks I never shot one neither was it my intention to seek after any, though we keepers in general take liberty one with another with such things that are not Game for of such we have plenty at home, I once more humbly beg your Pardon, but desire that Mr Ishman be very careful how he shoots without Licence.

I am your very humble servant
Jas Stagalls
Cromford Jan'y 24th 1795

in employment - to be the subject of complaint again in 1798, 'shooting up the Via Gellia Wednesday and Thursday as far as Dunsley Spring'.

Richard Arkwright's information about his workers casts light on the extent to which the mills dominated the local economy and even whether Cromford can be described as a factory village at this time. It is not possible to draw consistent conclusions from the early published census material. In 1801 about half the population were engaged 'chiefly in trades, manufactures or handicraft' and this would include work at the mills as well as framework knitting and weaving but also many other occupations such as bakers, smiths, joiners. It would seem reasonable to conclude that this pattern continued until the mills suffered setbacks which appears to have been the case between 1821 and 1831 when the number of families engaged in the same categories dropped from 262 to 125. Later in the century employment at the mills was certainly in decline. In March 1851 the census enumerators commented on a drop in population 'Decline owing to partial suspension of work at cotton factory' and again in April 1861 'Decline due to want of employment'. The cause in 1851 is not clear but in 1861, the cotton famine, the shortage of imported cotton from the southern states of the USA when the northern states blockaded the southern ports during the American Civil War, was beginning to impact on the industry.

The fall in value of the Cromford Mills for textile use once the Arkwrights lost their battle with the proprietors of the Meerbrook Sough in 1839 and the family's reluctance to invest in the modernisation of Masson Mill despite the losses they incurred there, must have contributed to a decline in employment opportunities. The valuation of the business in 1872 revealed how low its value had sunk but it was not until 1880 that Frederic Charles Arkwright recruited John Edward Lawton to turn the business around. The area also suffered from other economic pressures. The Middleton census enumerator's note on falling numbers in 1871 'due to unproductiveness of lead mines causing migration in search of employment' is a reminder that traditional alternative sources of work were no longer to be relied on.

FIGURE 48. **Map of the Willersl(e)y Farm Estate, William Brailsford, 1759.**

Edwin Lascelles acquired the Willersl(e)y Farm Estate and the smelting mills, shown here close to Cromford bridge, when he married Elizabeth Dawes in January 1746. The map shows that the bulk of the estate lay on the east bank of the River Derwent. Willersley Castle now stands there above the riverside 'holm' meadows whose boundaries were swept away to create a park-like setting for the house. The map shows interesting field names, including Up[pe]r Old Hall and Nei[?]r Old Hall for which we have no explanation. The name Old Hall persists on the Matlock Tithe Map of 1848 and corresponds to the open flat land behind the castle which the estate sale catalogue of 1927 identifies as 'Tennis Lawn with space for three courts'; there is a swimming pool and putting green there now. The Rock and Wood shown alongside the

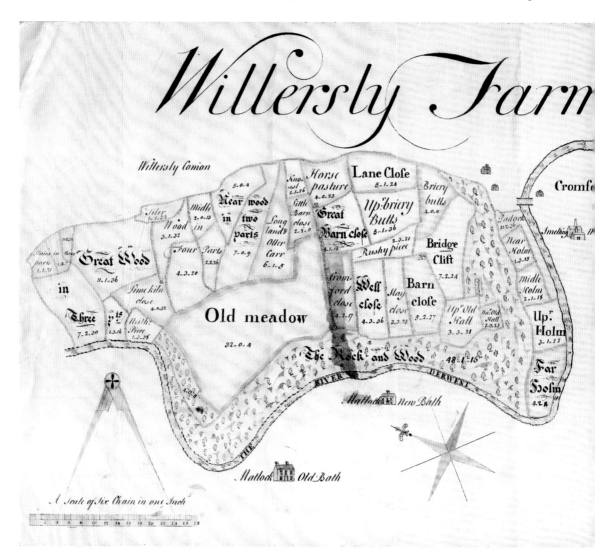

river on this map includes the area already by 1759 leased for Lover's Walk, the pleasure ground at Matlock Bath where visitors to the Old Bath, (demolished) and the New Bath (later known as the New Bath Hotel) could take their leisure.

The furthest point of the meadows on the west side of the river can be located today as the place where the outfall from Arkwright's second cotton mill joins the river.

Arkwright Society collection

CHAPTER EIGHT

The Willersley Estate

Richard Arkwright purchased the estate known as Willersley Farm from Thomas Hallett Hodges and his wife Dorothy. The purchase price in the agreement dated March 7th, 1782 was £14,864 but Hodges was to retain the property until March 1783 for which £300 was to be deducted. The main body of land (see Willersly map opposite) was in Matlock parish lying between the River Derwent and Willersley Lane and stretching from Cromford bridge to the southern slope of High Tor but there was some property on the Cromford side of the river including the old smelting mills, then in use as a calamine mill, close to Cromford bridge. The estate was to form the parkland setting for his intended new house Willersley Castle and his chapel. He died aged 59 in 1792 before the house and chapel were completed. His only son Richard inherited the estate.

Willersley Castle

Willersley Castle was designed for Sir Richard Arkwright by William Thomas (? -1800), a London-based architect, who was influenced by the more famous, and more skilful, Robert Adam. The house is built in what has come to be known as the Robert Adam castle style and shows similarities to Adam's designs for Culzean Castle in Scotland which was roughly contemporary.

Thomas was producing plans for the castle in 1787 and 1788. His final undated designs which are held by the Bodleian Library, Oxford, show the house almost as it was built. A drawing dated March 1787, not included in the Bodleian set, reveals that he toyed with more fanciful features - a two storey high music room for example with 'Orchestra' pencilled into the oval atrium at the upper floor level, a grandiose proposal which Sir Richard clearly rejected.

By March 1788, Thomas was concerned with more practical matters; a working drawing of

FIGURE 49. Photograph of watercolour entitled Cromford nr Matlock Derbyshire, signed E.E.1786.

This watercolour shows the view towards Cromford bridge from Mill Lane. The bridge is shown in its present widened form, the added width supported by rounded arches on the upstream side, in contrast to the pointed arches of the older mediaeval structure on the downstream side. John Farey in Volume II of his survey of Derbyshire, (published in 1813 from surveys made earlier) commented that the bridge was widened 'a few years ago'. If we accept the evidence from the watercolour, ''few' has to be seen as a very loose estimate, representing at least 25 years and maybe more.

The tall chimneys belong to the lead smelting mills which lay either side of the Bonsall Brook near to the bridge. Some time in or soon after 1789 the mills were demolished to make a suitable setting for Sir Richard Arkwright's chapel, now Cromford Church. The mill site looks dilapidated but appears to be in use here although not smelting lead. A lease of the estate in the *Tibbitts Collection*, Sheffield Archives, to Edmund Hodgkinson of Matlock from Edwin Lascelles dated 1761, directs that the four mills, earlier described as 'two smelting mills with each an Ore Hearth and Slagg Hearth' were to have £200 spent on their repair and conversion into a mill or mills for grinding calamine or for some other use. In the same year John Turner of Birmingham took a 40 year lease on the mills from Hodgkinson for use as a 'calamy mill'. From the smoke issuing from one of the chimneys it would appear that calamine is being roasted in a furnace and it may be assumed that once it cooled it was crushed to a fine powder then packed in tubs for dispatch to the Birmingham brass works.

The house in the background to the left, now known as Derwent House, stands on the other side of the river near the bottom of Willersley Castle drive. The estate map does not show this building and it is considered to be the 'one good and sufficient dwelling' on which the 1761 lease directed Hodgkinson to'lay out £300'. When, in 1778, Hodgkinson bought the estate from Lascelles for £6,800 the transaction included Hodgkinson's 'recently erected house'. It came into Arkwright ownership when Richard Arkwright bought the estate in 1782. Perhaps it was from this house that Richard Arkwright junior wrote in January 1788 to remind Georgiana, Duchess of Devonshire about repayment of her debt to him; he used a Willersley address for his letter. To the right of Cromford bridge, the cluster of buildings includes a farm building and the mediaeval bridge chapel. J C Cox, in *Churches of Derbyshire* 1886 quotes Adam Wolley's report that in 1796 Richard Arkwright junior took down the chapel which had for some considerable time been in use as two small dwelling houses, and reduced it to a picturesque ruin. Part of the other building was retained and given the external appearance of a fishing lodge and was used by Arkwright's water bailiff. It continued in use as a cottage well into the twentieth century. By this means the view from the Castle of the lodge, the river and the chapel achieved an elegance befitting the status of a new country seat. The jumble of buildings across the river includes Cromford Bridge House which was known as Senior Field House when it was purchased by George Evans in 1757 using the dowry provided by Peter Nightingale when his daughter Ann married Evans. It is tempting to speculate that the EE with which the picture is signed refers to their daughter, Elizabeth Evans, though there is no other evidence to support this. Elizabeth was Florence Nightingale's great aunt.

The road runs closer to the rocky outcrop on the right than it does now. It was re-aligned when Cromford wharf was developed in 1794. The wall in the left foreground marks the Cromford mill boundary. Traces of it can be seen in the much higher wall which now encloses the site.

Arkwright Society collection

that date directs that 'Great care must be taken with the foundation of the House there is at present a great quantity of rough Stones thrown promiscuously in the foundations and in many places there are large Cavities concealed, that when the weight of the Piers of the Building comes to press on these cavities I am apprehensive the foundations will give way, therefore it is my order that these loose stones be removed untill [sic] you come to the firm Rock & then work a foundation up in a workmanlike …[word missing]'. This evidence that the erection of the walls did not begin until well into 1788 is difficult to reconcile with the established view that the house was built and roofed within the year. If it was, then it was an astounding achievement. Nevertheless Adam Wolley supports such a view. 'In the year 1788 he [Richard Arkwright] erected and covered in the House on the Willersley Estate opposite Scarthin Torr…but tho the house was erected in 1788 yet he had employed a great Number of Labourers for most part of 3 or 4 preceeding [sic] years and at a very considerable Expence in preparing the Ground work etc of the House, the whole of the Ground work being cut out of solid Rock'. Wolley's account also suggests that work had begun on the site before 1786, the date given in numerous accounts. It is unfortunately impossible to ascertain whether Wolley, who as a young lawyer worked for Arkwright in 1788, was writing his account contemporaneously or from memory some years later. His manuscripts and documents bequeathed to the British Museum in 1828, the year after his death, are considered to be a collection made over a period of 50 years.

The White Tor stone quarries between Cromford and Lea were advertising stone for sale in February, 1788. In 1865 the quarry boasted the use of its stone for Arkwright's Castle, a claim since confirmed by geological analysis.

LEA, Feb, 6, 1788.

To be Sold,

AT the White Tar STONE QUARRIES, near Cromford, Derbyshire, S T O N E of any Size, either Blocks for fawing, or Scantling for hewing, Pavers, or Hearths of any Dimenfions.——Apply to SAMUEL SIMES, Stone Mafon at Lea aforefaid, who will execute Orders on the fhorteft Notice.——There is good SLATE to be fold near the fame place, at 7s. per Hundred.

N. B. Wanted 2 er 3 good Stone Mafons, who may have conftant Work; alfo an Apprentice wanted, apply as above.

Thomas's plan for Willersley is of a compact symmetrical three storey house with a centrally placed oval lantern which, on occasion in his drawings, he referred to as the observatory. The plans show small, single storey east and west wings to the back of the central residential block. Flanking the building are detached two storey service wings, connected only by open arcades which are screened by single storey curtain walls to the front.

Since 1934 when *The Torrington Diaries,* 1781-94, were published, so revealing for the first time Torrington's opinion of Sir Richard's intended home, the Castle has become inseparably associated with his condemnation of its architectural qualities and the social pretensions of its owner. It was, for Torrington, who on his second visit to Cromford in June 1790, gained access to the Castle 'the house of an overseer … not of a gentleman' and 'an effort of inconvenient ill taste, built so high as to overlook every beauty…the ceilings are of gew-gaw fret work; the small circular stair-case, like some of the new built houses of Marybone [sic], is so dark and narrow that people cannot pass each other; I ask'd a workman is there a library? –

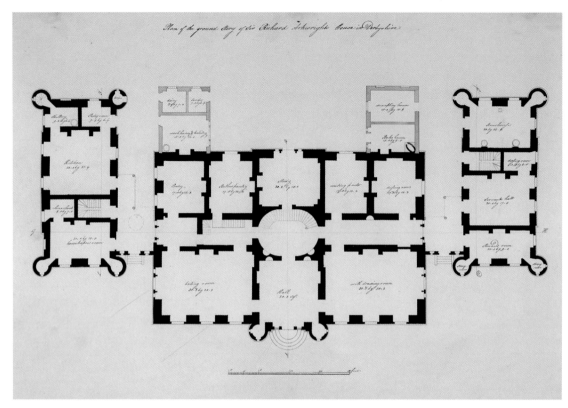

FIGURE 50. **Plan of the ground story [sic] of Sir Richard Arkwright's House in Derbyshire, signed Wm Thomas Architect, undated.**
Reproduced with permission from The Bodleian Libraries, University of Oxford, Gough Maps 41a, fol. 74

Yes answer'd he, at the foot of the stairs. Its dimensions are 15 feet square … it is too dark to read or write without a candle … At Clapham they can produce nothing equal to this, where ground is sold by the yard'.

It is no wonder that Torrington's views have acquired such importance. His is the only known contemporary account which offers any details of the house as it was first built. He held strong views about the new social order of which Sir Richard was a high profile and potent symbol but setting aside the social stigma, how valid were his judgements of William Thomas's design?

It might be argued equally well that the location of the house was inspired. It overlooks splendid nearby views of river and rocks and more distant prospects of Cromford Moor and the valley of the Derwent, and not, as Torrington implied, the mills. The Cromford mills were conveniently near but completely hidden by Scarthin Rock and not visible from the castle; Masson Mill, also nearby, was screened by the shoulder of the hill. At the same time the scale of the shelf on which the house stood was a constraint which could not be entirely overcome. It was cut out of the hillside leaving a rock face behind the building, the closeness of which was the cause for Torrington's justified concern about the darkness of the library. Thomas's principal staircase, see Figure 51 was poorly designed. The central oval was too small to accommodate a staircase successfully and its later removal achieved a visual improvement. It left the most striking internal feature of the house, the central light well with its cantilevered galleries unbroken by the intrusion of a stairway. Subsequently plans were made to incorporate a principal staircase elsewhere but none was considered satisfactory and the Castle survived in use without one until the 1840s.

By 1790 Sir Richard Arkwright was ordering furnishings from Edward Wilson, cabinet makers and upholsterers of 376 Strand, London, some for Cromford and some for the house at 8 Adam Street, London, which he had bought in 1788. Walter Wilson was included in the list of craftsmen employed at Chatsworth House during the alteration and refurbishment of apartments for the fifth Duke of Devonshire and his wife Georgiana in the 1770s to1780s. The Wilson business at the Strand later became well known and both Sir Richard and his son used the firm in furnishing the Castle. Sir Richard later trusted Edward Wilson as an arbitrator in a dispute with William Thomas and in October 1792, Richard Arkwright junior employed the firm to prepare the London house for sale.

Two sets of proposals offered for the decoration of the principal rooms of the Castle survive. One set, dated July 1789, includes Thomas's plasterwork designs and designs for fireplaces and is included in his plans for the Castle. The other set, dated June 1791, is signed RW. It is not known if the signature represents a member of the Wilson firm.

On August 8th, 1791, Willersley Castle was damaged by fire. The *Derby Mercury* of August 11th reported that the mansion was 'greatly damaged' but was happy 'to hear that most of the elegant furniture was preserved'. Adam Wolley explained that a fire had broken out, 'occasioned by a flue's being overheated and communicating with some timber over which it was improperly carried which consumed the Roof and the inside of the Body of the House, except the Stair Cases and the Ground floors; the principal part of the Windows and Doors were saved, as were likewise the two wings... As the House was scarcely finished, so there was little or no furniture in it, except some indifft Pictures which were saved'. No more detail has been found of how much damage the fire did to the building, how much restoration work was subsequently needed, or how much of it was done – if any – in the twelve months before Sir Richard Arkwright died in August 1792. Elements of Thomas's proposals for the decoration of the house referred to above appear to have been implemented before the fire and attracted Torrington's caustic comment but none of the features shown in the designs, with the exception of the plaster frieze around the central lantern, are evident in the house today. There is no evidence of any of R.W.'s proposals having been implemented. It is possible that they were used but were not reinstated after the fire.

Despite the fire, Arkwright continued to order furniture and mirrored French plate glass for the Castle and in July 1792, a month before his death he was invoiced by Wilson's for a year's 'Insurance and Warehouse Room' for Sundry Furniture and Glasses. It seems likely that Arkwright saw none of these purchases at Cromford. Some items were brought from London in December 1792 when Wilsons invoiced £45 for 'a Man with a Waggon and 4 Horses to carry your large Glasses and sundry other furniture to Cromford 141 Miles, about

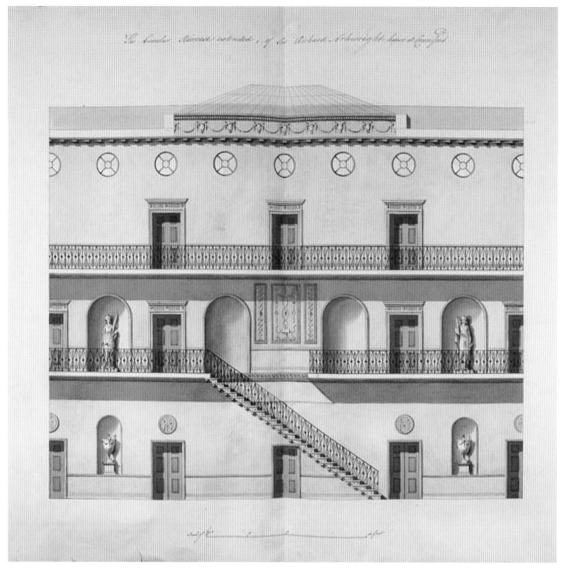

FIGURE 51. The Circular Staircase extended, of Sir Richard Arkwright's House at Cromford, undated.
The drawing of the oval saloon flattened out to show William Thomas's original main staircase, the first and second floor galleries and the lantern with the plaster frieze of ox skulls linked by garlands. Note the central door to the Library is reduced in height to accommodate the staircase.

3 Ton Weight'. This was a spectacular achievement given the appalling state of the roads over which this fragile load had to be conveyed. Only a few years later the canal would have offered a much safer option for such a delivery. The workman's expenses for the fifteen day, 282 miles round trip and 'Unloading Unpacking & fixing up the large Glasses and Sundry other furniture' was £12-18s-6d. Expensive large chimney and pier glasses are reported to have been ordered for the drawing room, the dining parlour and the music room. If, as the account claims, the workman 'fixed' them up, then these principal rooms must have been in good order by December 1792.

Thomas Gardner's modifications for Richard Arkwright junior

Richard Arkwright junior moved from Lumford House at Bakewell to Rock House after his father died and along with settling his father's affairs and taking over management of his estate, he fulfilled the direction in his will to 'complete in a proper manner the Mansion house I have lately erected'. He commissioned some practical modifications to William Thomas's house and completion of the interior from Thomas Gardner of Uttoxeter. Gardner's influence on the building was important but limited to some internal change and some building to the rear. His plans for alterations to the castle are dated 1793; his surviving accounts for his work begin in March 1794, more than two and a half years after the date of the fire. Within the intervening period, it is assumed that the workforce on site set about some restoration of the fabric of the house, at least to safeguard and weatherproof it, though nothing is known of this stage.

The ground floor plan signed by Gardner is believed to show his proposed alterations to Thomas's building or at least to what had been built before the fire. This plan shows one

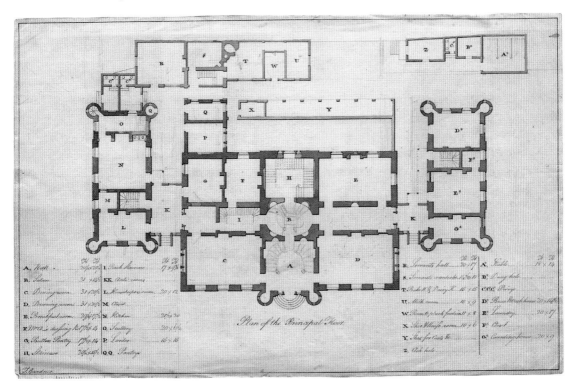

FIGURE 52. Thomas Gardner's signed plan of the ground floor of the castle labelled on the reverse Plan of Alteration at Willersley 1793.

The drawing shows, in black, the plan of the ground floor of the building as Gardner found it after the fire. The 'pink' colour appears to denote Gardner's proposed new building. The scraps of colour elsewhere are interesting. Do they indicate places where fire damage was still to be repaired? Gardner's proposed site for a principal staircase is shown at 'H' behind the central oval 'Salon'. It is not known if the alternative positions of stairs roughly sketched in on this plan are contemporary with it or if the drawing was re-used at a later date. None were built. Only the 'Back Staircase' shown here at 'I' which William Thomas had designed was retained at this time.

particularly significant proposed change within the house. This was Gardner's attempt to relocate the grand staircase which, according to Torrington, Thomas had built in the central oval salon and which Torrington had described with incredulity. The new site offered for the stairs was in the room behind the central oval which Thomas had designated as a study or library. This proposal was not adopted. It appears that no replacement for the principal staircase was built

An alternative Willersley?

A number of Gardner's signed but undated drawings for Willersley Castle, plans and an elevation, offer a radically different design for the building. They show the principal rooms on the first floor; staff and service accommodation on the ground floor and wings at the back. We do not know why Gardner went to such trouble. There is no evidence for his being involved at Willersley before 1793 yet it seems remarkable that he would suggest a complete rebuild after the fire which, though serious, had not threatened the integrity of the structure. Did he really expect Richard Arkwright to demolish what had been built and start again? Alternatively had he submitted plans in competition with William Thomas which Sir Richard had rejected?

and Richard Arkwright junior made do with the more modest, less decorative 'Back Staircase' which both architects placed to the west of the saloon. These stairs are still in use.

Gardner also shows an added range of service accommodation behind the castle close up against the rock face. It is not known how much of this was built and there were later alterations but the area remains in service use and its scale and relationship to the rest of the house retains a sense of Gardner's plan. Richard Arkwright's apparent reluctance to lose rooms to accommodate stairs and the need for more service accommodation perhaps reflected the needs of the larger family unit which was to occupy the castle. Richard and his wife Mary already had nine children when Gardner finished his work on the house. Gardner labels the links between the house and the service wings 'anti rooms' but it is not clear if they differed significantly from Thomas's open arcades. Later building alterations in these areas make it impossible to determine which design was built. At the west end of the central corridor of the house, the impressive door which opened into the house from this link has survived.

Carefully attached to Gardner's plan of the ground floor is an undated pencil- sketched overlay of a small part of the plan. It shows the short north east wing of the residential block which was shown on Thomas's plans but apparently not built by him and some associated rearrangement of the rear service range. It is not known if this overlay was an alternative proposal to Gardner's plan in 1793 and was implemented then or if his plan was re-used to sketch in a modification at a later date. At some stage a north east wing was built and when the house was sold in 1927 it housed the billiard room. The Wilson accounts of 1794-96 for furnishings for the house and for decoration refer to a billiard room but no room is labelled as such on Thomas's or Gardner's plans.

Gardner's accounts show that he visited Willersley fifteen times during the period March 1794 and December 1795 'attending the finishing of Willersley Castle, & the additional Buildings to it'. The work began in April 1794 using a relatively small group of local men under the supervision of John Hewitt who was not local - he was provided with an allowance of five shillings for board. The accounts throw some light on the nature of the work and mention ashlar works, Hopton stone steps, landings, rebates and chimney pieces with hearths, costs for joists and floorboards, folding and double stile [sic] doors, ovolo and bead [mouldings], old dado fixing, run of old frieze, making designs for the plasterer, mentioned as Mr Dugdale, and the joiner William Taylor's charge, £21-9s-7d, for ovolo in mahogany doors at one and ninepence a foot. Compared with the early designs for interior decoration there is less decorative detail in the house today. Nevertheless there are some elaborate plasterwork cornices and doorcases and some good fireplaces.

Richard Arkwright junior continued to order furniture from Wilsons though he had chosen not to take possession of all that Sir Richard had ordered but left some for Wilson's to re-sell, not easily it seems. What might be considered a reliable opinion of his style comes from the Reverend Richard Ward, who was the first and long serving curate of Cromford Chapel and no doubt a regular visitor to the house. He produced several editions of a very useful guide book T*he Matlock, Buxton and Castleton Guide* and in 1814 comments 'The house itself is not shewn, as its furniture has not been selected with a view to splendour of appearance, but rather for the purpose of utility and comfort, which this mansion possesses in an eminent degree.'

Gardner also designed the lodge and gate piers at the foot of the castle drive and in September 1794 produced a set of detailed plans for the stables which stand just above and to the east of the Castle and which were built according to his design. He produced drawings for a farm building but it is not known if they were used. The former farm building, now a private house, which stands just outside the gates to the Castle has some of the features of Gardner's designs but does not fully match his proposals.

In English Heritage's Register of Historic Buildings, Willersley Castle is listed Grade II*.

FIGURE 53. **Pencil and wash portrait of Richard Arkwright junior, signed W Carpenter 1836 and on the reverse, Richard Arkwright Esquire of Willersley done by Mrs Carpenter 1836.**
Arkwright Society collection

Edward Blore's alterations to Willersley Castle for Peter Arkwright

The Castle is known to have undergone further alteration when the architect Edward Blore (1787-1879) who had lately worked on Buckingham Palace, was commissioned by Peter Arkwright, Richard's third son, to make some changes. The only record found for Blore's involvement is his account for a visit made in June 1843 with a Mr Armstrong to consider the 'proposed improvement' and for a further visit in November to inspect the works and make a further plan. Meanwhile it seems Armstrong had visited to oversee the progress of the work. It is understood that the principal change Blore made was the construction of a two storey connection between the eastern service wing and the house. The connection accommodated the main staircase which serves the house today and brought the wing into residential use. The alteration involved raising the height of the curtain wall on the east side of the front elevation from one storey to two. The source of reference closest to 1843 is the Matlock Tithe map,

FIGURE 54. **View of the Dining Room, Willersley Castle, photograph, date unknown.**

The view of the dining room shows the famous Joseph Wright of Derby 'View of Ullswater Lake' hanging on the end wall. The picture was bought by Richard Arkwright junior for 300 guineas in 1801, four years after the artist's death but he had also commissioned a number of paintings from Wright in his lifetime.

He took delivery of 'the picture of the girl looking through a bladder' from Wright's executors Messrs Wright, Holland and Sale in 1798, paying £35 for the picture, frame, packing case and delivery from London 'by Bowmer, the Cromford carrier'.

Arkwright Society collection

FIGURE 55. **Willersley Castle, viewed from Church Walk, stereoscopic photograph, John Clark of Matlock Bath, 1860s.**

dated 1848, which shows enlargement of the western service wing compared with any known earlier plan of the Castle. This may represent Blore's replacement for service space lost from the east wing. It would seem logical that Blore added the presently used main entrance and porch and altered the original, centrally placed principal door from its 'gothic' style to its present form. Figure 55 above and an earlier Samuel Poulton view show these changes.

After 1928 and before 1937 an additional single storey extension was added at the east end of the house. When first built it was shorter and had a separate entrance at the chamfered south east corner; it was extended forwards and assumed its present rectangular form with no separate entrance, in the mid 1950s.

The Park

The relationship of Willersley Castle to its park might reasonably be expected to have been part of William Thomas's concept though there is no documentary evidence to support this view. Robertson's drawing overleaf illustrates the elements of a fashionable picturesque setting in which features such as the bridge, the bridge chapel and the fishing lodge were made points of interest in the view, the new chapel adding to the effect.

The landscaping is attributed to John Webb (1754-1828) an architect and landscape gardener who lived at Lee Hall near Lichfield but it is not known how early he was involved in the planning process. Webb was a pupil of and later worked with William Emes, a local landscape architect and gardener who is believed to have contributed to a phase of the landscaping of Lover's Walk in Matlock Bath. This public walk was laid out on part of the Willersley Farm estate adjacent to Willersley Castle grounds and had been in use for over forty years when Richard Arkwright purchased the estate in 1782. He continued to honour the lease

FIGURE 56. **Willersley Castle, Cromford Church and Scarthin Rock, pencil and wash drawing, George Robertson, late 1790s.**

This drawing is from the period when George Robertson worked for William Duesbury at the Derby China Manufactory. It shows Willersley Castle in a picturesque landscape setting overlooking the curve of the River Derwent and the contrasting features of the rocky eminence of Scarthin Rock and the softer meadow land along the valley. Robertson appears to have drawn the stable block close behind the castle building though it stand some distance above and beyond the house. As part of the design of the park, the smelting mills and the nearby housing were demolished; the chapel, completed in 1797, takes the eye now. The road between the river and Scarthin Rock, once a public route between Matlock Bath and Cromford is firmly fenced off. It became known and used as Church Walk but the Arkwrights closed it one day each year to mark their ownership and exclusive right to use it – should they choose to claim it.

To the right of the chapel is the first warehouse at Cromford wharf, built in 1794. The tower has a castellated parapet which is thought to be an added picturesque feature to distract the viewer from the industrial nature of the building. The practical purpose of Robertson's carefully drawn 'gothic' tower is not known but it is suggested that it may have been to mask or enclose a weighing machine. The Canal Company's brief for Mr Unwin, its clerk at the wharf in 1794, included the construction of a weighing machine. The twentieth century Avery weighbridge visible on the wharf today occupies the site close to the position of the tower. There is no physical evidence of the tower now. In his survey published in 1813, Farey commented on the weighing engine and noted that makers of such machines included the late Mr James Bown of Matlock and the Butterley Company.

The cluster of buildings to the left of the bridge includes Willersley Castle Lodge, farm buildings and Cromford Bridge House. In the distance, beyond the bridge is Woodend, built by Peter Nightingale in 1795. He wrote to William Loxley of Bonsall in October 'I can now take two or three hundred of good floor boards, ash, elm or sycamore delivered at my new house, or at my Cotton mill, desire you will write me whether you can supply me; and at what price'. He moved to Woodend from Lea Hall in Spring 1796 explaining in a letter to Sir Joseph Banks 'I have found my situation at Lea too cold for my constitution'.

of the land for public use, a practice which has survived to the present day making Lover's Walk the oldest public pleasure ground in the country to have remained in continuous use since its creation. Webb's parkland meadows and woodland merged with the existing landscaping of the valley and his paths were laid out leading to viewpoints from which its romantic scenery might be appreciated - 'a diversity of scenery, that can hardly be paralleled within a similar extent in any part of the country'. Richard Arkwright junior's planting was not confined to the park. He is reputed to have planted 350,000 trees over seven years, on his property in Cromford and Willersley.

In the late 1790s Willersley Castle's grounds were open daily to the public, a

SCARTHING NICK . ENTRANCE TO MATLOCK DALE . DERBYSHIRE.
Drawn, Printed & Published by G. Rowe, Lithographer &c, Cheltenham.

FIGURE 57. **Scarthing [sic] Nick, Entrance to Matlock Dale, Derbyshire, drawn, printed &c published by G. Rowe, lithographer &c Cheltenham, about 1830.**

This print was made soon after this gothic lodge at the west entrance to Church Walk was added to the Willersley Estate. Richard Arkwright junior received several sketches and drawings of lodges in 1828 and 1829 one of which was signed 'Rawlinson'. It is not clear who the Rawlinson in question was. George Rawlinson, who designed and built Belle Vue in Matlock Bath, and who had planned a bridge over the river there which was never constructed, had died in 1823. All the other Rawlinsons who have come to our attention were related to him but it is not known that any of them, either his sons James and Joseph or his granddaughter Eliza worked as architects. The elevation and plan reproduced overleaf closely approximate to the structure which was subsequently erected but these drawings are not signed. The lodge was demolished in 1961. The gates have been restored and recently re-hung.

Private collection

privilege which was soon reduced. Lipscomb's *A Description of Matlock Bath*, 1802, offers the explanation that 'some injury having been done to the shrubberies in consequence of this indiscriminate admission – visitors are now shewn the place by a guide, two days every week'. The gardener's tour included a visit to the walled kitchen garden situated some distance behind the house to the north where the glasshouses were famed for the production of melons, peaches, pineapples and a variety of grapes. Richard Arkwright junior, a Fellow of the Horticultural Society, was awarded medals from the Society for his expertise in growing winter grapes. The glasshouses have not survived and the kitchen garden is now in separate ownership. At the end of their tour visitors were guided out through a door in the wall which marked the boundary between the park and Lover's Walk. The grounds of the castle are included in English Heritage's Register of Historic Parks and Gardens.

FIGURE 58. **The Lodge, Willersley Castle, stereograph, Samuel Poulton.**

This hand-coloured stereograph from the late 1850s shows a detail, the break in the rock where a small gothic door opened from the road to the back of the building. It was described by Jewitt in 1832 as the 'rude hermitage-like entrance to Mr Arkwright's lodge'. More than a hundred years later imaginative local children furnished their fairy stories with the same small, pointed door.

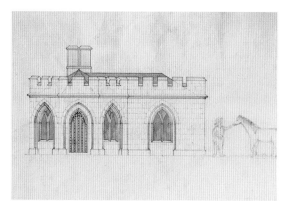 

FIGURE 59. **Elevation and Plan, Design for a Lodge to Willersley Castle, the seat of R.Arkwright Esq., August 8th 1829.**

Arkwright Society collection

CHAPTER NINE

St Mary's Chapel

Cromford Chapel was built close to the site of the former lead smelting mills. Sir Richard Arkwright's will dated 29th July 1792, five days before his death, shows that, like the Castle, it was a project which he had begun but would not see completed. He directed his son to 'compleat and finish the Chappell I have lately built'.

Charles Cox's description of the building tells us that 'It partook of the plain characteristics of the period and was destitute of a chancel...It was lighted by a double tier of five windows, circular headed, and having cast-iron frames'. If indeed the windows had cast iron frames, it would be remarkable at such an early date.

It is not known who designed the chapel. An undated plan and elevation exist produced by the Manchester architect Samuel Hope (1741-1817) who with his brother John worked on the Piece Hall at Halifax. The chapel as built does not relate to Hope's plan except in scale and simplicity. Since the chapel is a significant feature in the landscape setting of the Castle it might be expected to have been part of William Thomas's overall plan. Nicholas Pevsner, the architectural historian, has attributed it to Thomas Gardner. No reference has yet come to light for Thomas's or Gardner's association with the building as early as 1792 but towards the end of 1795 the accounts for Gardner's work on Willersley Castle record that he did just over a month's work on the chapel. It is not known what this work was but an undated Gardner design for the west end gallery survives. It is similar to the present gallery but with round headed arches matching the windows of the chapel at that date. According to Joseph Farington, Gardner's design for a gallery provided seating for children and also neatly accommodated an organ. This represented a departure from an earlier plan,

FIGURE 60. **Cromford Chapel. S.W., sketch by the Revd. Guy Brian, Rector of South Normanton, September 17th 1818.**

The Reverend Guy Brian made drawings of 53 Derbyshire churches between 1816 and 1820. His view of Cromford chapel shows it in its original plain classical form. In the notes at the bottom of the page he draws attention to the 'Blank windows at the west end Hills planted with fir etc Walls on hills where no foliage appears' and faintly in the right hand corner signs the picture off as 'Finished'. The trees in the surrounding park do not form an avenue but are irregularly spaced. The sketch book page has a watermark EDMEADS & Co 1809.

Reproduced by permission of Derby Local Studies Library

the Arkwrights having purchased an organ which, according to Torrington's scathing diary entry for June 19th 1790, was destined for the Castle. He wrote 'There is likewise a music room; this is upstairs, is 18 feet square, and will have a large organ in it: what a scheme!' The inclusion of the instrument in Gardner's drawing suggests that Richard Arkwright had decided to put it in the chapel. Farington confirms that there was an organ there in 1801. It is surprising that he did not find its presence more remarkable. Few churches of this size could afford such a luxury. The instrument was in fact second hand having been purchased from Earl Ferrers and brought to Cromford from Staunton Harold. The present organ dates from Peter Arkwright's remodelling of the church and was supplied by W. Hill and Sons of London in 1859. In 1797 Wilson's were supplying furnishings for the Chapel such as rich crimson velvet for the pulpit vallens [valance], rich crimson silk fringe and 'a Sheep Skin Pillow case fitted with fine White lawn for a pulpit - £18-6s-0d.'

While it had been planned as a private chapel, by the time it came into use in 1797, almost five years after his father's death, Richard Arkwright junior had reached agreement with the Queen Anne's Bounty Commissioners for it to be endowed and used for public worship as a Chapel within the parish of Wirksworth. Queen Anne's Bounty was a charity which supplemented the stipends of clergymen. The Endowment Deed for the chapel dated 20th September 1797 reminds us of Cromford's need for a place of public worship 'that owing to the extensive manufactures the village had become very populous, [and] that it was distant two miles from the Parish Church of Wirksworth'. The chapel opened with a service conducted by the curate appointed by Richard Arkwright, the Reverend Richard Ward, on Whit Sunday, June 4th 1797 and the building was consecrated on September 20th of that year by the Bishop of Lichfield.

By 1837 Ebeneezer Rhodes complained that 'the Chapel is of scant dimensions –

> ## Diary of Joseph Farington, vol.5
>
> Entry for Sunday August 23rd, 1801
>
> *'We went to Church at Cromford where is a Chapel built abt. 3 years and ½ ago by Mr Arkwright. The Revd. Mr Ward, who lives near the Chapel is the Minister and performed the service. It began at Eleven. There is a small neat Organ. - Leedham, of the Old Bath, - Saxton, of the Upper Bath, - and Froggart, of the Hotel each have handsome seats in it, - for the accommodation of their Company, - Mr Ward preached rather less than 15 minutes. His text St. Matthew, Chapt: 13 Verse 13. "Therefore speak I to them in parables: because they seeing, see not: and hearing they Hear not, neither do they understand." - His discourse was well designed, and as far as it went instructive. On each side [of] the organ is a gallery in which about 50 Boys were seated. These Children are employed in Mr Arkwrights works in the week-days, and on Sundays attend a School where they receive education. They came to Chapel in regular order and looked healthy and well & decently cloathed [sic] & clean. They were attended by an Old Man their School Master. - To this School girls also go for the same purpose, and alternately with the Boys go to Church the Boys on one Sunday, - the Girls on the next following, - whichever are not at Chapel are at the School, which they both go to every Sunday both morning and afternoon. - The whole Plan appears to be such as to do Mr Arkwright much credit.'*

not large enough certainly for the population of Cromford' and from an early date the chapel had catered not only for Cromford but also for visitors to Matlock Bath, the 'Company' referred to by Joseph Farington. Their numbers grew as did Cromford's population and in

1838 in response to the pressure for space, side galleries were added to the chapel, see plan right. The arrangement of the windows in two tiers would have been convenient for making the change although the galleries were later described as 'low and inconvenient'. In his diary entry for Sunday 16th June, 1839, Mr Evans of the Temple Hotel, Matlock Bath confirmed 'Cromford Church Chapel of Ease reopened after putting up lofts'.

When Matlock Bath Holy Trinity Church was opened in 1842, the congregation at Cromford declined and, as part of the alterations made to a design by Henry Isaac Stevens (1806-1873) in 1858-59, the galleries were removed. Surviving evidence shows that Stevens offered a series of proposals to Peter Arkwright, who resisted the more ambitious schemes, which would have altered the building beyond recognition, opting instead

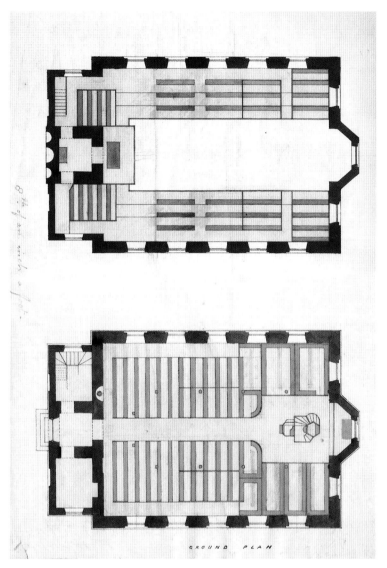

FIGURE 61. **Plan of St Mary's Chapel, 1858.**

The drawing shows the gallery and ground plans of the chapel as it was before Henry Isaac Stevens was asked to make changes in 1858.

Arkwright Society collection

for more modest though substantial change. It is said that the work cost £3000. His alterations included the addition of a chancel with three stained glass windows, improvement to the roof and tower and replacement of the two rows of windows on each side with a single row with the tall Gothic proportions and stone mullions and traceries as seen today. A substantial portico was added to the west front and a new clock face. Inside, the side galleries and the flat ceiling were removed, the organ gallery arches were gothicised and the high back pews were replaced. The *Wirksworth Advertiser* of September 6th, 1861 reported that the Cromford organ was back in use after enlargement by Mr Lloyd of Nottingham. It now had 535 pipes and 16 stops. The chapel became Cromford Parish Church in 1869.

FIGURE 62. **St Mary's Church, Cromford, interior, photograph, about 1900.**

This view shows the interior of St Mary's Church soon after Frederic Charles Arkwright had delivered his major scheme to celebrate the centenary of the church and Queen Victoria's Jubilee. The old chancel arch was replaced with one 'much wider, of a more handsome design'; new choir stalls, new windows over the west gallery and gas lighting were added.

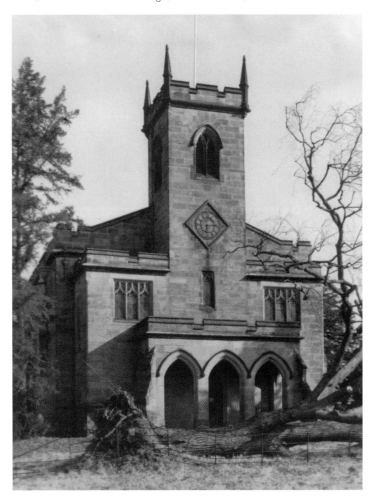

Alterations were made to the vestries and the roof, seating was renovated and in April 1898 a peal of six tubular bells in the tower was heard for the first time. The most dramatic element in the scheme was the redecoration of the church with wall paintings covering the chancel, the chancel arch and the nave and the addition of three stained glass windows in the chancel paid for by members of the family and dedicated to Frederic Arkwright, James C. Arkwright and Fanny J. Galton, and 'to commemorate the centenary of this Church'. Fanny Galton (1817-1894) was Peter Arkwright's daughter.

Private collection

FIGURE 63. **St Mary's Church, Cromford, west front, February 1962.**

This photograph shows the 1858 changes, the remodelled west end and tower and the substantial porch. The clock face is dated 1858. The clock movement was made by John Hacker of Nottingham and is dated 1796.

Private collection

Endowment of St Mary's Chapel

The Reverend Richard Ward recorded in the first Cromford baptism register that the chapel was endowed by Richard Arkwright with a rent charge of £50 p.a. payable from the Cromford Estate to which he subsequently added a further £200 to which as a consequence, Queen Anne's Bounty also contributed £200. In December 1800 the aggregated sum of £400 was invested in land at Woolley in Morton Parish from which the initial rent was £16 p.a. The curate also received the pew rents but these were not part of the endowment.

The chapel's dependence on the Arkwrights was absolute. In 1816 further land was purchased, this time near Darley Bridge, at a cost of £800 which was believed by the Reverend Robert Morgan Jones, Ward's successor, to have been met by Richard Arkwright and to have been supplemented by a further contribution from Queen Anne's Bounty. All the expenses for repairs, the salaries of the organist and clerk and the cost of heating and cleaning and all other charges were covered by him. The Communion plate was kept at Willersley; the wine and bread for the celebration of the Lord's Supper were provided there; the surplices were regularly made and washed there and the grounds were kept in order by the Willersley gardeners.

By the time of Reverend Robert Morgan Jones' appointment as perpetual curate in 1838 the endowment yield was just over £95 per annum and Jones states that Richard Arkwright, shortly before Jones marriage in July 1841, agreed to increase the endowment by £100 per annum and to build a house for Jones' use. For the house Jones was charged a nominal rent of £1 p.a. with Richard Arkwright agreeing to pay for the repairs. Jones did not conceal his dismay when he discovered his benefactor had not made provision in his will for the enhanced payment nor it would seem was there a record of the landlord's responsibility for the upkeep of the house. 'For reasons known only to themselves' Jones records bitterly, Richard Arkwright's trustees, James and Alfred Arkwright reduced the additional funding to £90 p.a. and though the rent remained nominal, Jones had to take responsibility for repairs. He adds that the Trustees also 'in the course of time declined to pay the salary of the organist and the charges for coal and wine ... these three items have since fallen upon the diminished offertories to the somewhat serious injury of the poor'.

While these accusations may be justified they should be seen as no more than a temporary difference of opinion which cannot have lasted long and did not blight the family's concern for the Church which seems to have imbued each generation in turn even after the family left Cromford and continues to the present day.

The artist given the commission to design the murals and stained glass in St Mary's described at Figure 62 was Alfred Octavius Hemming (1843 – 1906). He brought to his work in Derbyshire a reputation fashioned in London and across the United Kingdom as an exponent of mural painting and stained glass. As the *High Peak News* reported with breathless awe, his most recent work had been a large window for the Chapter House of Canterbury Cathedral. In much of his work Hemming employed a cartoonist, George Daniels 1854 - 1940, whose job it was to draught the figures and scenes for Hemming to follow. From the similarity of many of the figures in the Cromford murals to others known to be from Daniels's hand, it is likely that he contributed to the Cromford scheme. The work was completed by April 1898.

In 1922 a report presented to the annual church meeting identified the need to improve the lighting in the church but it was not until 1928 that the elegant gas lights in the nave were converted to electricity and new lights installed in the chancel. The impetus for this large undertaking was the provision of mains electricity down Mill Lane. The work was done by Leonard Stamp for no more than the cost of the materials with help from a team of volunteers. In July of that year the vicar recorded in the parish magazine that 'most evenings there are three or four at work'. The gas standards were sent away to Sheffield to be adapted

FIGURE 64. **Two views of St Mary's Church interior during the restoration of the wall paintings by Wallpainting Workshop of Faversham in 2002.**

Reproduced by permission of St Mary's Church, Cromford

for electrical use and to be re-lacquered. The lights were used for the first time in September on Wakes Sunday to acclaim from the secretary of the Church Council who wrote 'the old standards have gained in beauty by the adjustment of the curved swan-neck pendants, and the lighting of the chancel and particularly the altar exceeds all our expectations'.

In 1978 it was discovered that St Mary's had sustained serious damage from rampant dry rot in the roof timbers, the roof was declared unsafe and the church was closed. The community adopted its traditional response. A meeting was called in the school chaired by the Archdeacon of Derby. He appealed to the village to make common cause with the vicar and the church wardens to save the church. The meeting elected a committee, the Cromford Church Restoration Committee, to handle the task and this brought together local residents, members of the Parochial Church Council and representatives of the Arkwright Society which also agreed to provide administrative services. No one who answered the Archdeacon's call realised it would take twenty years and cost at least £250,000 to put the church in good order.

Not all the money raised was from traditional approaches. There were of course house to house collections, raffles, pie and pea suppers and contributions from donations and from grants but there were also annual chartered train trips to London and sometimes to Blackpool and an annual autumn bulb sale which at its height sold more than one and a half tonnes of bulbs. For many years the committee was also permitted by the Cromford Steam Rally to run the tea tent. Step by step Cromford's church was put back on its feet. At the start of the restoration process and throughout the 1980s the architectural and historical significance of the building was underestimated and the first application for grant aid was turned down on the grounds that the building was of insufficient importance. But opinions change and as the Arkwright story along with the village and the mills came to be seen as worthy of enhanced protection and public funding so too the significance of the Arkwright church was better appreciated.

The damage had been so extensive that much of the plaster in the nave had to be stripped so destroying the upper portion of Hemming's wall paintings. A later outbreak affected the paintings in the chancel. In 2002 the Wallpainting Workshop of Faversham began to restore the murals to their former glory. The paintings were rededicated by the Bishop of Derby on April 20, 2002. The quality of Hemming's work is now recognised and this and the rarity of comprehensive mural schemes which survive from the Victorian period enabled the restoration project to attract funding from national as well as local sources. Throughout the 25 years it took to repair the church and restore the wall paintings,

FIGURE 65. **View of the chancel and the chancel arch from the nave, St Mary's Church, after the restoration of the wall paintings, 2012.**

Ashley Franklin Photography

the branch of the Arkwright family, previously associated with Willersley Castle and Cromford, the late Colonel Peter Arkwright, his wife Marguerite and eldest son Charles supported each phase of the renovation programme.

In 2011 English Heritage which had contributed generously to the wall painting fund upgraded the listing of the church to Grade I citing its association with Richard Arkwright's Cromford Mills, the Arkwright family and the 'very rare and complete scheme of wall paintings of the late nineteenth century, executed by Hemming, integrated with stained glass into a very unusual overall scheme'.

FIGURE 66. **The advertisement forming part of the booking form for a special train trip,1981.**

Special trains were chartered to raise funds for the restoration of Cromford Church and the Arkwright Society every November and in some years more frequently from 1979 until 1992. This advertisement is typical of the early booking forms for the London trips. In July 1985 the name Venture Rail was adopted to brand these fundraising trains and it was in that year this remarkable enterprise enjoyed its greatest financial success twice running a weekend train service from Wirksworth to Derby; a line that had been closed to passenger traffic since 1947.

Private collection

CHAPTER TEN

The growth of the village

Some survey and census information

When William Soresby purchased the manor of Cromford in 1716, the buildings identified in a schedule of property were described as 10 messuages, 80 cottages and 2 corn mills from which it is reasonable to assume that there were 90 habitable dwellings within the settlement.

Fifty one years later in 1767, when William and Mary Milnes owned the manor, following a decision from the Master of the Rolls that an account be made of the Cromford Estate, a further survey indicated that there were 20 messuages, 40 cottages and 2 mills. A third survey in 1776 recorded 30 messuages, 60 cottages, 2 mills and 1 cotton mill, which, though the constituent parts differ brings the number of dwellings back to the level noted sixty years earlier. There is no obvious explanation for this apparent decline and growth in the size of the community or real certainty that the information gathered in 1767 was correct. As a plausible record the last of the three surveys does have the attraction of suggesting a settlement of comparable size to what had been found near the beginning of the century.

The survey of 1776 is too early to be recording growth from Arkwright's first significant investment in housing for his mill workforce. His landlord, William Milnes, commented that soon after the execution of the

> The inclusion of 2 corn mills in the survey of 1716 is of interest but cannot be explained. Only two water powered sites on the Cromford side of the river are known to be in existence before 1771, the corn mill and the smelting mills. Water powered sites from time to time change their function but it is hard to believe in this case that the lead smelting mill came to be used to grind corn. This is an anomaly which remains unresolved.

lease in 1771 the partners erected buildings for mills, warehouses and habitation of employees on the north side of the highway but the space available for housing on this part of the mill site (or to the south of the road where he is believed to have built houses) would have been very limited and most likely provided accommodation only for key workers. Milnes' report in early 1774 that 'Families are now come to Reside in Cromford' offers no information about how they were housed. The evidence for growth is more readily apparent from James Pilkington's survey of the County in 1788, published a year later who attributed 'about 120 houses' to Cromford. By 1788 Arkwright had added North Street and is believed

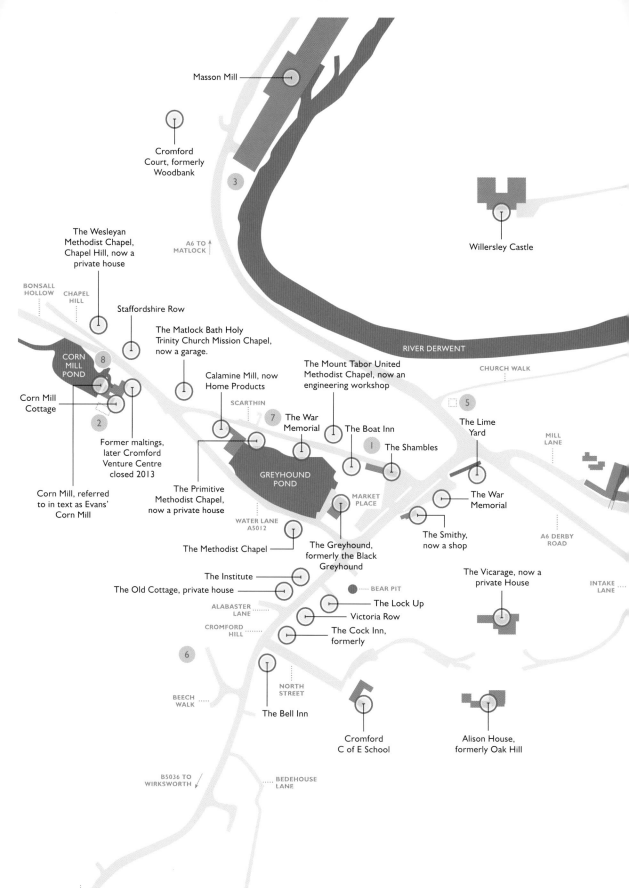

Masson Mill

Cromford Court, formerly Woodbank

3

A6 TO MATLOCK

Willersley Castle

The Wesleyan Methodist Chapel, Chapel Hill, now a private house

BONSALL HOLLOW

CHAPEL HILL

Staffordshire Row

The Matlock Bath Holy Trinity Church Mission Chapel, now a garage.

CORN MILL POND

8

Calamine Mill, now Home Products

SCARTHIN

The Mount Tabor United Methodist Chapel, now an engineering workshop

RIVER DERWENT

CHURCH WALK

5

The Lime Yard

MILL LANE

Corn Mill Cottage

2

Former maltings, later Cromford Venture Centre closed 2013

7

The War Memorial

The Boat Inn

1

The Shambles

Corn Mill, referred to in text as Evans' Corn Mill

The Primitive Methodist Chapel, now a private house

GREYHOUND POND

MARKET PLACE

The War Memorial

A6 DERBY ROAD

The Smithy, now a shop

WATER LANE A5012

The Methodist Chapel

The Greyhound, formerly the Black Greyhound

The Vicarage, now a private House

INTAKE LANE

BEAR PIT

The Institute

The Old Cottage, private house

ALABASTER LANE

The Lock Up

Victoria Row

CROMFORD HILL

The Cock Inn, formerly

6

BEECH WALK

NORTH STREET

The Bell Inn

Cromford C of E School

Alison House, formerly Oak Hill

B5036 TO WIRKSWORTH

BEDEHOUSE LANE

The Bedehouses

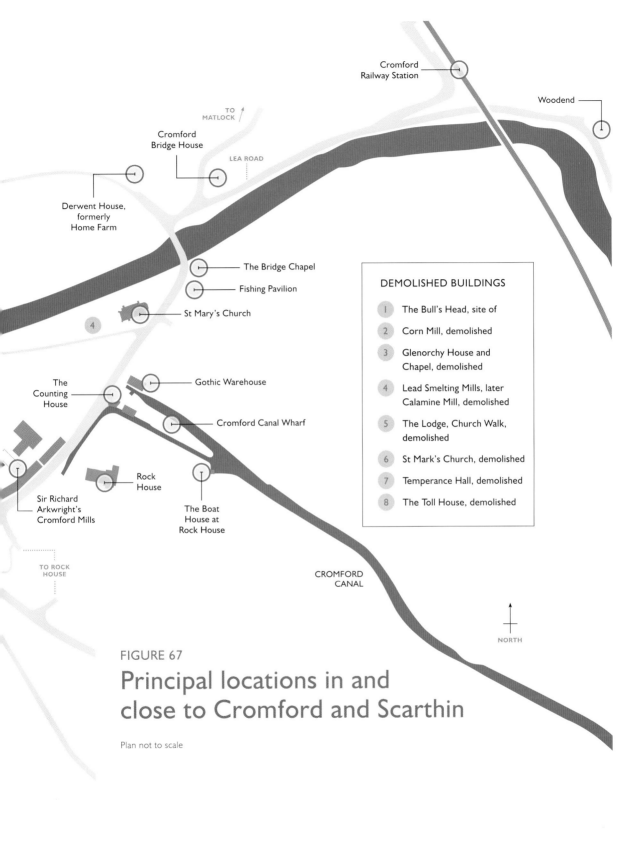

Cromford
Railway Station

Woodend

TO
MATLOCK

Cromford
Bridge House

LEA ROAD

Derwent House,
formerly
Home Farm

The Bridge Chapel

Fishing Pavilion

St Mary's Church

4

The
Counting
House

Gothic Warehouse

Cromford Canal Wharf

Rock
House

Sir Richard
Arkwright's
Cromford Mills

The Boat
House at
Rock House

TO ROCK
HOUSE

CROMFORD
CANAL

NORTH

DEMOLISHED BUILDINGS

1   The Bull's Head, site of

2   Corn Mill, demolished

3   Glenorchy House and
    Chapel, demolished

4   Lead Smelting Mills, later
    Calamine Mill, demolished

5   The Lodge, Church Walk,
    demolished

6   St Mark's Church, demolished

7   Temperance Hall, demolished

8   The Toll House, demolished

FIGURE 67

Principal locations in and close to Cromford and Scarthin

Plan not to scale

to have built the three storey houses on the Hill. If this was so then Pilkington's estimate must be considered low although Arkwright's agreement with Nightingale in 1776 which included his right to demolish such old cottages and dwellings as might interfere with the building of the second mill could have affected the total. Evidence for the growth of Cromford reaches firmer ground with the 1801 census which records 207 houses occupied by 283 families. If Pilkington's figure is accepted the village had seen 13 years of prodigious growth; a 73% increase in the number of houses since 1788. Where all this growth took place is unknown but there are some indications. Sir Richard's purchase of the manor in 1789 led to the development of the market place, the housing around it and on the lower part of the Hill. But it is also during these years that Sir Richard and his son shaped the boundaries of their estate and some of the older housing was lost, for example near Cromford bridge, when Willersley Castle's park was created.

The next decade saw more modest growth, the number of houses increasing to 230 in 1811, an 11% increase. The census records 7 houses were being built. Thereafter the village maintains its size with 232 houses recorded in 1821 and 233 in 1831. This was followed by a marked period of growth when the addition of 29 houses brought the total to 262 by 1841. In terms of population this was the high water mark, the 1407 persons recorded that year falling back each decade until in 1871 the population was below the 1115 recorded in 1801 and in 1891 the figure fell to1052, its lowest point in the nineteenth century.

The umbilical link between mill work and mill housing which was so crucial in the development of the mills in the 1770s, remained in place more than a century later to a significant extent. In 1883 workers at Masson Mill in Matlock Bath occupied 103 of the cottages owned by Frederic Charles Arkwright, Peter's grandson, though not all of them would have been in Cromford.

Land use

The three eighteenth century surveys also describe land use within the manor but the discrepancies in acreages make the information difficult to interpret and there is little evidence of how the land was worked. A more focused picture emerges from the 1801 crop returns submitted by the Reverend Richard Ward in October 1801 as part of the survey of the nation's food supply. He wrote ' Cromford contains about 1270 acres of land a very considerable quantity of which is moor-land and of no use – a very small proportion is tilled, many cows being kept here for the accommodation of the people employed in spinning cotton. The produce in general exceeds an average crop, as is the case throughout the neighbourhood'. The crops he records confirm the general picture he presented. He estimates there were 10 acres of wheat; 2 roods of rye; 1 acre of barley; 33 acres and 3 roods of oats; 12 acres of potatoes; 2 acres 2 roods of peas and no beans, turnips or rape. The report from John Pickering, the Tithe Commissioners' agent in 1839 concluded 'There are a few spots of productive meadow beside the Derwent, but the pasturage among the hills is very inferior, and much broken in upon by mine tips: the arable land is chiefly confined to oats and potatoes … there is no such thing as a flock of sheep, the greatest number kept by any one person being I think about 30'. Like Ward he recognised the considerable consumption of dairy produce and

FIGURE 68. **Working at the Dene, photograph, about 1900.**

The photograph shows a group of workers posing on the Dene, the land to the west of the upper part of Cromford Hill. They were there to cut hay for fodder for the horses working on the Cromford canal. On the right, on horse back, is William Wilkinson who was a horse driver on the canal.

Private collection

that 'this is the staple agricultural production'. The land use figures recorded in the Tithe summary in 1841 reflected his view, 795 acres out of a total of just over 1300 being meadow and pasture, only 80 acres arable. His estimate of population as 'upwards of 2000' is more than generous compared with the 1841 census figure of 1407.

The provision of milk for the industrial communities of the Derwent Valley was a serious issue. The Strutts in Belper and Milford created their own farms and had agreements with local farmers to deliver an agreed quantity of milk. In Darley Abbey the Evans family also contracted with local farmers for the supply of milk particularly through the winter months thus providing an incentive to retain rather than kill cows ahead of the winter. The Arkwrights are known to have encouraged cow keeping, for example the *Derby Mercury* of July 24th 1783 reported that Richard Arkwright had given to 27 workmen '27 fine milch cows worth £8 - £10 pounds each'. It is not known whether other deals were made or if other incentives were offered on a regular basis to secure the vital local milk supply. Britton and Brayley in 1802 draw attention to the existence of a society 'of rather a singular kind' in Cromford formed by the owners of cows to insure against loss. The cows were valued twice a year and the owner made monthly payments into a fund at the rate of one penny for each pound of value of his stock. When the club's fund reached £40, payments were discontinued until its reserves fell below that total. If a cow died, the owner was paid the full value of the beast from the fund.

Further evidence of a strategy to supply the new community with milk may be provided by the large number of 'barns' which were widespread on Bonsall Moor and on the high ground around Elton and Winster many of which survive. These were cowhouses and hay stores, each providing shelter and winter fodder storage for a small number of beasts. Their construction which clearly followed enclosure may have been a response to the new market opportunities created by the burgeoning population. For Arkwright it would have been a means of supplementing the supply of milk for the growing community. Many of the barns are derelict now but they are an important feature of the upland landscape. The Bonsall Barns Project has restored a number of them on Bonsall Moor and returned them to use.

There was no parliamentary enclosure in Cromford and in the absence of the Cromford Manor Court Rolls, it is not known if the Court made any rulings on the matter but there is some evidence for the process. Enclosure is implicit in the name Intake Lane for the wide, well-built track which runs across the hillside below Cromford Moor to join Longway Bank close to the Cromford-Alderwasley boundary. It provides access to fields and plantations and served a quarry known at some time as the Parish Quarry. The lane pre-dates the construction of the Cromford & High Peak Railway which opened in 1831 and which is bridged over it.

Roger Flindall provides references to intakes from the Cromford Barmaster's books, for example, in 1750 'Marts' Intacks' which were 'on the moor' and in 1780, 'Roose's Intakes'. Mart and Roose were local family names, Roose remains so. The purchase of a 'lately erected house and several numbered parcels of enclosed land' by Thomas Hobson, a servant of William Milnes, from George Mather in 1774 for £70, points to a more formal enclosure process. Hobson's property was described as 'in the manor of Cromford at a place called Cromford Intake'; its location is not known.

William Adam recognised Richard Arkwright junior's interest in the landscape of the valley and in 1838 looking towards Cromford Moor from the grounds of Willersley Castle described the transformation he had made there. It is, he said 'judiciously laid out in fields and woods, according to the nature and circumstances of the ground' where 'a few years since this was covered by heath and furze, unsightly mine hillocks and rude cliffs with few or no trees to hide them'.

The village

Richard Arkwright's first significant venture into building workers' housing was North Street in 1776, two terraces of high quality, three-storey, single bay, gritstone houses facing one another across a broad street and with one terrace slightly lower than the other on the slope of the hill. The terraces are not of uniform length, the upper terrace has 16 houses and the lower one 11. The top floors were well-lit with glazed openings front and back to accommodate weavers' work rooms, a feature which was not repeated in any later Arkwright terraces. The lower two floors had a pattern of fixed light and sash windows and pilasters adjoined to the front doorways. Such architectural details as sash windows were, as the advertisements in the pages of the *Derby Mercury* at this time indicated, newly fashionable in Derbyshire in the houses of farmers or the commercial classes. Later the Arkwright estate

FIGURE 69. **North Street, Cromford, photograph, about 1900.**

This photograph shows the two terraces of gritstone houses on North Street which were built in 1776. The pavements and drainage gutter are shown surfaced with limestone pitchings. The school, here seen with its original windows, was built at the end of the street in 1832. The older building, which stands nearby, just out of sight to the right in this view, housed the schoolmaster. Note the single gas light at the end of the street. Cromford was supplied with gas in the 1850s but according to the *Derby and Chesterfield Reporter* complaints about street lights being concentrated in the centre of the village and not in other localities came to a head in 1860. Peter Arkwright offered to 'defray the cost of several lights' and a decision was taken to 'carry it over the whole place, so that all would receive the benefit and all contribute to the expense'. The Matlock Gas Company (which was based at Matlock Bath), was to be approached. The *Wirksworth Advertiser* in April 1861 reported 'the last of the public lamps is finished…It is a handsome lamp containing three burners and is erected on a pillar of white stone placed in the centre of the Market Place'. The tree canopy in the top left corner of the photograph marks the survival of a tree from the row which the 1841 Cromford Tithe Map shows stretched the length of the street.

The crowd are gathered around a decorated cycle. What they were celebrating is not known but local intelligence reports a pre-World War I habit in North Street for dressing bicycles or tricycles prior to assembling in the Market Place and processing to the Venetian Fete in Matlock Bath.

Private collection

blocked the rear windows and two of the four lights at the front on the upper floor. Over time and piecemeal, some owners have chosen to unblock some sections.

Each house had a garden plot allocated to it. The Cromford Tithe Map of 1841 shows plots in orderly rows on the land now occupied by school buildings, the school playgrounds and the area where the road to the houses once known as Oakhill (see Figure 82) would later be built.

Today at the west end of the lower North Street terrace, adjacent to No. 1, are two double fronted houses opening on to the street, one two storey and one three storey, both created from buildings formerly belonging to the Cock Inn (see Figure 72). The Cromford Tithe map of 1841 does not show these houses; the space is still occupied by the Cock Inn. The view which has sometimes been expressed that the three storey house was for a manager of this part of the Arkwright estate seems unlikely given the late date of the conversion; the occupier may have had some managerial status but the need for a person to manage any particular part of the Arkwright housing stock at any time is not recognised.

The single block of school building lying across the line of the street was provided by Richard Arkwright junior in 1832. The OS map surveyed in 1878 shows an additional block at right angles to the first, labelled Infants, and in 1893 the school was extended again by order of the County Education Committee. A new classroom for 50 children was added to the boys' school and improved facilities were provided for the girls and infants increasing the accommodation from 280 pupils to 370. The cost of the work approached £1000 towards which Frederic Charles Arkwright gave £350. His wife raised £250 from a two day bazaar held at Willersley Castle where curiosities exhibited included 'the original spinning frame, Sir Richard's shoe buckle and a bible with his writing inside'.

After the Second World War there was a move to demolish the North Street housing as being unfit for human habitation but this was prevented by the intervention of the late Professor J D Chambers of Nottingham University and subsequently the Ancient Monuments Society which purchased houses in the lower terrace.

The present day heart of the village was not formed until around 1789 when Sir Richard purchased the Cromford estate from Peter Nightingale, and began the construction of a market place where a Saturday market was established in 1790. Apart from the Market Place, Cromford was not built to an overall plan and houses were added from time to time and in a number of different styles. The similarities in style of most of the three storey houses on the Hill above North Street with those on North Street suggest they were built soon after and are given a date of about 1780. They are considered to pre-date the two storey hillside row but its date of construction is not known. With the exception of North Street, almost all the housing was built in terraces flanking the existing routes through the village. The growth of housing must have matched the development of the mills but so little is known of the building dates that it is not possible to associate particular phases of house building with the expansion of the mills at Cromford and Masson. There has been some infilling of buildings since the Arkwright family sold the estate but the historic shape of the village and its contact with its setting remains tangible.

A development which occurred before the Arkwright family left and which was independent of it was the building of Addison Square. Dr Christopher Addison, (1869-1951), formed the first Ministry of Health in 1919 and formulated the Housing and Town Planning Act, the Addison Act, which provided government subsidies for building low rental housing. He appointed architects to draw up model plans but local authorities could use their own architects provided that they observed the spirit of the government's recommendations. John Burnett, *A Social History of Housing, 1815-1985*, describes the Addison houses as 'the best of all inter-war local authority homes in terms of space standards' and quotes the average cost of an Addison house as just about £1000.

Cromford held a public meeting in April 1919 to discuss the National Housing Policy and resolved to ask for 12 houses with 'not less than three bedrooms, parlour and necessary conveniences'. By July 1st a Ministry of Health Inspector had visited Cromford and 'approved of Sheppard's land' for the purpose and by September 1922 the Parish Council was allocating tenants to the eight houses which had been erected.

FIGURE 70. **The Bell Inn, North Street Cromford, photograph, 1897.**

The Bell, formerly the Blue Bell stands at the end of North Street. The date of the building is not known. It is unusual as one of the very few brick-built buildings in Cromford. Was it a rebuilding of an earlier stone building? Could an earlier inn have taken its name from the lead mine in the nearby Hanging Eye close, which in 1769 was named the Blue Bell Mine or was the mine named after the inn? The picture shows the licensees of the inn in 1897, William and Ellen Mee, who were both former employees of the Arkwright family at Willersley Castle - as butler and head cook. They are standing at the front door of the inn; the name W MEE is written beneath the bell on the hanging sign above their heads. The name on the Grocery and Provision Stores next door is Reeds.

Private collection

FIGURE 71. **House on Cromford Hill, photograph.**

The image is of a house on Cromford Hill and is said to be of an earlier date than the evangelical leaflet, *Eagles Wings* dated April 1906, in which it appeared. The photograph shows the early Arkwright housing window pattern, one fixed light and one sash here protected by shutters on the ground floor.

Private collection

FIGURE 72. **Cromford Hill, postcard, early 1900s.**

This view down Cromford Hill from the end of North Street towards the Market Place shows the former Cock Inn on the right hand side. By the time this photograph was taken the building was in use as the Cromford Refreshment Rooms. The inn is thought to lie along the lower side of North Street behind this later remodelled front. The two double fronted houses adjacent to No. 1 North Street have been formed from buildings associated with the Cock; the three storey house is a remodelled and refronted agricultural building. A local resident still refers to the yard, entered from just below the building shown here, as Cock Inn Yard. There are advertisements for the Cock Inn, by name in the *Derby Mercury* in 1763, see opposite and in the *Leicester and Nottingham Journal* of June 1761 as 'at the house of Roger Frost, in Cromford' when 'CUDGELLING' was on offer. Later the important contribution which the Cock made to the Arkwright community was of a more cultural nature. By 1852 the Mechanics' Institute met there. The 1851 *Religious Census* reports that both the Wesleyan Methodist Reformers and the General Baptists met in Mart's Clubroom; a John Mart is listed as the landlord in trade directories from 1820 to 1860 and Mrs Mart in 1867.

From the 1860s, George Statham, and later, his widow, combined a butcher's business with the inn trade at the Cock. In the twentieth century a butcher's shop was housed in the extension with the large sash window shown here on the right. By then, according to the *High Peak News* report of Mrs Statham's death in March 1910, the inn had been closed by Frederic Charles Arkwright. No reason was given but Mrs Maria Statham had requested that the licence be withdrawn in 1893 after which she used the premises to sell refreshments. Ernest Yarwood writing from Minnesota in 1923 but formerly from Nottingham recalled stopping there [the Cock] in his youth when it was kept by Mrs Statham. On hearing that it had been converted into a butcher's shop he wrote 'Well Sir, it might be a good thing for my native land if all the rum shops were turned into butchers' shops'. The dark roof of the Cromford Institute is visible in shadow lower down the Hill on the left. The *High Peak News* described the building as a 'princely gift' from Frederic Charles Arkwright who laid the foundation stone in December 1897 so that it would rank as a benefaction celebrating Queen Victoria's Diamond Jubilee. Built of Stancliffe stone, it was erected as a home for 'the prosperous St Mark's Men's Institute'. When it was opened in October1898, the accommodation included a billiard room and a reading room. The newspaper reported that more than thirty years earlier the Reading Room was in the Greyhound Clubroom in the Greyhound yard. In December 1876 it was housed in a new building which Frederic Charles Arkwright presented to the village but by 1898 this was considered 'too confining' and it was moved to the Institute.

Private collection

This is to inform the Publick,

THAT on *Thursday* the 30th Day of this Inftant *June*, there will be a CUDGELL PLAY for ONE GUINEA, free, at *Roger Froft*'s, being the Sign of the COCK in *Cromford*, near *Matlock Bath*: Eight Men to enter, and one to win the Prize, in the Form of a Welfh Main, or no Prize.

Alfo at the fame Place, on *Friday* the 1ft of *July*, there will be a WRESTLING MATCH for a Silver Laced HAT, Value FIVE SHILLINGS, free: Eight Men to enter, and one to win the Prize, as above-mention'd.

Derby Mercury, June 30th, 1763

Cudgell play was fighting with short stout sticks called cudgells until one combatant was knocked out or otherwise unable to continue. The term Welsh Main comes from cock-fighting where more than 30 birds fought head to head in a series of knock-out rounds. The winner was the last bird standing. Here, at The Cock, the prizes were to be for the last cudgeller and the last wrestler standing.

FIGURE 73. **Cromford Hill, photograph, about 1910.**

The houses illustrated are part of the linear development on Cromford Hill above North Street built about 1780 and financed by Peter Nightingale. Though similar in style to the North Street houses, they provided domestic accommodation on all three floors with no workshop space on the top floor. J.P. Malcom writing in the *Gentleman's Magazine* on the occasion of Sir Richard Arkwright's funeral in 1793 described it as 'a long rough hill, lined by new stone houses' and added 'Much to Sir Richard's credit, those habitations are most comfortable.' Compared with Figure 71 the window glazing pattern has been altered and the shutters removed.

There were 'bridges' across the gullies at the side of the road. The houses had no launders until after World War I so that rainwater ran straight from the roofs and into the gully.

Private collection

FIGURE 74. **Victoria Terrace, Cromford, photograph, early 1900s.**

This row of eight houses lower down Cromford Hill was built for Richard Arkwright junior in 1839. They have a roughcast render and cast-iron window frames with central opening lights for ventilation. Unlike all earlier Arkwright housing, with the exception of the semi-detached housing on Water Lane, this row was set back from the road behind front gardens. The bottom house bears the signboard 'Abel Boden Boot and Shoe Warehouse'. It is not known what prompted Richard Arkwright to build new houses at this time when the battle to save the water supply to the Cromford mills was all but lost. An extension was built at Masson Mill some time in the second quarter of the century; extra housing may have been considered necessary for new workers required there but this is speculation.

The houses below Victoria Terrace are older and are believed to date from about 1790 when the Market Place was developed.

Private collection

The first weekly market day at Cromford

Lord Torrington visiting Cromford in June 1790 commented on 'the much levelling of ground, and increase of buildings for their new market, (for this place is now so populous as not to do without) which has already been held once and will be again tomorrow'. He drew attention to 'Sir Rd's prudence and cunning' in putting in place an incentive scheme – the promise of prizes at the year's end for the vendors 'as shall have best furnish'd the market...for without ready provisions his colony cou'd not prosper'. The agreement which covered Arkwright's purchase of the manor of Cromford from Peter Nightingale in 1789 included permission to build on the manor and the creation of the market place appears to have been an early response to the opportunity. It seems it would not have been Torrington's choice; he commented 'that religion is as necessary as food; and that a chapel might have been built; but trade thought not of this'.

The *Derby Mercury* of June 17th, 1790 described the first market day:

'On Saturday last was held at Cromford, the first Meeting for the supply of that place with provisions, &c. at which an immense concourse of people attended. Very large quantities of different articles were offered for sale. The festivities of the day were also numerous; eight clubs of that town and neighbourhood went in procession, attended by several bands of music, to the place of meeting, where they were regaled with ale, &c. – To the beneficence of Sir Richard Arkwright are the inhabitants of this populous village indebted for this very beneficial institution, which we hope will meet with that encouragement it so justly deserves.'

FIGURE 75. **Market Place, Cromford, photograph, 1920s.**

The Greyhound Hotel, formerly called The Black Greyhound or the Black Dog, shown on the left hand side in this view, was built 1778 – 1779. An entry in a Guardian Exchange ledger dated February 1779 records that 'a house not yet finished intended for an inn' was insured for £700. Still an imposing building, and now listed Grade II*, it must have been a startling sight in its early isolation before the rest of the market place was developed more than ten years later. In 1863 the *Derby Mercury* reported that Peter Arkwright had paid for a clock on the Greyhound, with the inference that it was a new addition rather than a replacement.

The evidence of the market today is to be seen in the surviving single storey permanent market stalls, the Shambles, shown behind the crowd in this view. A second row of such stalls which stood where Cromford Community Centre is now (across the B5036 road to the right) would have contributed definition to the market area. For a period of unknown duration fairs were also held here; the *Derby Mercury* of April 2nd 1818 carried a notice drawing attention to three annual fairs in that year, for 'Horses, Cattle, Sheep, Corn, Grain, Cheese, &c' – in February, May and September - with the September Fair being the principal one for cheese. In 1862 White's *Cromford Directory* noted 'Fairs were formerly held here but are now discontinued'. The creation of the market place and institution of the market there provided the new community with a heart and the Market Place became the social centre of the village. The raised level of the B5036 road and its associated street furniture is a later intrusion in the streetscape but the area would still fulfil those functions were it not for the car parks.

The building seen to the right of the Shambles in this view may be part of the row referred to by Lord Torrington when he stayed at the Black Dog in 1790 and complained that 'The bold rock opposite this house is now disfigur'd by a row of new houses built under it; and the vales are every way block'd up by mills'. It seems that Lord Torrington's concern was not only on aesthetic grounds but that he harboured anxiety about where this trend might lead 'a fear strikes me that this (our over stretch'd) commerce may meet a shock; and then what becomes of our rabble of artisans!!'. The houses on the right behind the Shambles have been demolished; the brick house beside them was built in the last 20 years of the nineteenth century on the site of the Bull's Head inn. For many years the Philanthropy Society met there; its purpose as described in 1832 was 'for raising by voluntary contribution a fund for the relief of each other its said members in sickness, age or infirmity'.

The picture records the crowded motorised charabancs waiting to set off on a Friendly Society outing to Monsal Dale organised by the Cromford branch of the Royal and Ancient Order of Buffaloes.

Private collection

FIGURE 76. **Two views of Kidd's Shop, photographs, dates uncertain, perhaps early 1900s and 1930s.**

These views of the property across the Market Place show the village en fete. Cromford, and Scarthin particularly, had a reputation for 'going to town' to celebrate occasions such as coronations, jubilees and other national events. The relief of Mafeking in the Boer War on May 17th 1900 for example was marked by an extraordinary celebration. The newspapers reported the 'profusion of flags' displayed everywhere and heavy cannon being fired all day from Willersley Rocks 'their sound reverberating with terrible distinctness right through the valley'. The church bells were rung and the bellman was sent round to call a thanksgiving service at St Mark's Church for the evening. Children no doubt held their own celebration when a school holiday was proclaimed. On the earlier photograph the bunting shows names of leaders associated with the Boer War. Once bought, flags and decoration would be pulled from store to celebrate any occasion from a royal wedding to the Wakes which, at least in the 1920s, included a competition to find the best decorated house. The later picture shows members of the Kidd family in front of the fine shop front which, with some careful restoration, survives though the shutters seen in the earlier view are no longer used. The two views also illustrate the addition of cast iron launders and drainpipes to the buildings. The work was undertaken by the Arkwright estate after the 1914-1918 War. The effect of the development of the advertising industry, particularly for cigarette brands, in the intervening thirty or so years is also evident.

Private collections

Bottom right - Wirksworth and Matlock Advertiser, April 18th, 1868.

FIGURE 77. **Entrance to Scarthin, 1911.**

Decorations on the occasion of the coronation of George V and Queen Mary in 1911 included candle-lit coloured glass pots shown here hung around the windows of one of the Scarthin shops and there were illuminated boats on the Greyhound pond after dark. Local newspapers acknowledged Scarthin's renowned celebrations; though 'not a rich community…it united as one man in the cause'. The delayed coronation of Edward VII and Queen Alexandra in 1902 was commemorated with a decorated boat as usual and illuminations in all the windows. 'Loyal Scarthin' was credited with surpassing itself. 'Brilliantly illuminated, the district was a fairyland and crowds gathered from all parts.' Mr Pidcock's illumination of Allen's Hill using car headlights mounted on a boat on the pond is a more recent, 1930s, memory of Scarthin's enterprise.

Private collection

St Mark's Church

When Cromford parish was separated from Wirksworth in 1869, a number of conditions were imposed. The family was again required to enhance its endowment, Frederic Arkwright providing £1,410 to match fund a contribution from the Ecclesiastical Commissioners so increasing the endowment income by £94 per annum. It was also a requirement that the vicar should undertake to make the same provisions and accept the same pastoral responsibilities as the parish of Wirksworth had done. This posed a problem as the new parish of Cromford had no churchyard for public use. The Arkwright family deemed St Mary's itself to be unsuitable because of its location within Willersley Castle park. Instead, Frederic Charles Arkwright as the chief parishioner and then owner of the estate, provided an acre and a half of land in the village. Here, at a cost of about £2000, Mr Parkin, the Arkwright agent, supervised the erection of a chapel which was dedicated to St Mark. The costs were borne largely by the members of the Arkwright family with parishioners making their contributions 'as far as lay in their power'. The new chapel was consecrated in April 1877 but there is some dispute as to whether the ceremony took place on April 25th - St Mark's Day - or on Easter Tuesday, April 3rd. A careful enquiry by the then vicar, Canon G A Hazlehurst in April 1932 concluded that the latter is correct; he reflects 'this seems to me to dispose of the tradition that the Church was dedicated to St Mark because the ceremony took place on April 25th'. He offers no alternative explanation for its dedication.

Though it had been built as a mortuary chapel, it was soon in use for a full range of services

FIGURE 78. **The Favourite, First Empire Day, Cromford, 1902.**

In 1902, the year after her death, Queen Victoria's birthday, May 24th, was chosen as Empire Day, to commemorate the help received from the Empire during the Boer War, 1899-1902.

Private collection

FIGURE 79. **St Mark's Church, Cromford, photograph, about 1900.**

Benjamin Bryan in his *History of Matlock* described St Mark's as 'a small but neat Gothic Church' with the land around it 'laid out as a cemetery', a burial ground having long been desirable 'to save the journey to Wirksworth with the local funerals'. The three-light stained and painted east window in the chancel, made by Messrs Clayton and Bell of London, was dedicated to the memory of Frederic Arkwright (1806 - 1874) and his wife Sabrina and 'erected by the tenantry, agents and workpeople on the Estates in Derbyshire and Cheshire'.

Private collection

though not marriages for which it was not licensed. In the words of the Reverend R M Jones who was curate and then vicar in Cromford from 1838 to 1886 'henceforth the Cromford people commonly attended the Divine Services at St Mark's'.

Popular though it was, St Mark's did not survive. An outbreak of dry rot led to its closure in 1963 and its demolition was authorised in 1970. The fine east window was saved and re-installed at Chinley. The churchyard remained in use for burials until 1992. The lychgate survives and the remnant of the avenue of beeches which lead to it runs off Beech Walk. The *Derby Mercury* recorded that the lychgate was the 'special gift' of James Charles Arkwright of Oak Hill, 'in addition to a previous very liberal money contribution'. Subsequently he added a benefaction of £2,500 which was invested in the names of the trustees of the chapel.

Rock House

The early history of Rock House, when and by whom it was built and when it was first called Rock House, is not known. The earliest known residents were William and Mary Milnes. They had become owners of the manor of Cromford in 1765 and are known to have been resident there in 1768 when Thomas Oldham, a tenant farmer of Aldercar was reported to have been murdered on his way to deliver his £80 half year's rent to William Milnes. When Peter Nightingale purchased the manor from the Milnes in 1776, the house was described as a 'capital messuage or mansion house'. He agreed to lease it to Richard Arkwright at a yearly

FIGURE 80. **Two views of Rock House, snapshot, 1950s and postcard, 1904.**

The picture on the left shows part of the asymmetrical front façade of the house with the service range to the left. The chimney-like structure masking the join between them is thought to be a flue associated with the introduction of a heating system. The door to the left of the principal entrance was originally a window, see the earlier view. The alteration would have been made when the house was converted into flats.

Note that the Mews on the left is in its original form with no window or door openings in this face. Together with the curved curtain walls attached to it on either side, the mews screened the formal entrance to the house from the yards, coach house and piggeries lying behind it. The unusual carved clock face with a single finger in the pedimented gable and two band courses lower down relieve the severity of the front and give it architectural style. The clock mechanism was connected to a clock face on the opposite side of the building facing the yards for the benefit of the servants. The eighteenth century cupola on the roof is a remarkable survival. Its bell was connected to the clock mechanism and would have rung the hours.

Private collection

Rock House: the building

The outward appearance of the main block of the house today dates from the 1860s. The extensive alterations made then, along with the earlier addition of the service wing, have removed or obscured architectural features of the older form of the house which remains a puzzle and awaits explanation.

Attention has been drawn to it in earlier Figures. These are the most informative of the few known eighteenth century images which show a building on the site. They are very small artists' impressions to be treated with some care. John Boydell's print of 1749, Figure 23 suggests there may have been a double pile house on the site. If so, was it altered by spanning the two roof gables with a single wide gable to produce the shape of the house seen at Figures 31 and 32 in the 1780s? This would have been an alteration grossly at odds with Georgian taste. This theory does not explain why the west end of the present Rock House stands on cellars which have been dated to the second half of the eighteenth century.

The view of the house seen from the Greyhound yard, Figure 31 shows an unfashionably wide gable, chimneys at each end and an asymmetrical pattern of windows, a pattern which appears to persist in Rock House today. Was this a new house built by someone after 1749? Again it is difficult to believe that anybody would have built a house in such a style in an age when symmetry was the guiding principle of architectural design. Alternatively, at an unknown date, was an existing house altered by adding the wider bay of building to its east end, under which there are no cellars, to accommodate some larger rooms? The 1924 estate

sale particulars describe the largest rooms, the dining and drawing rooms, occupying two floors at the east end of the house. Such rooms could have offered a setting of suitable scale for the ball which Richard Arkwright gave in September 1778 'at his own House to the neighbouring Ladies and Gentlemen, at which the company was very numerous and brilliant'. But no evidence has been found for an extension being built by that or any date. Whatever its history, the house appears to have deserved Henry Moore's description in *Picturesque Excursions from Derby to Matlock Bath,* 1818 'it is neat but not elegant, and no doubt comfortable within, although the exterior is tasteless'.

The tenants of Rock House in 1860 were relatives of the Arkwright family, the Misses Hurt. They left later that year to occupy the newly built Chase Cliffe at Crich, after which Rock House remained unused for some years. No occupants are recorded in the 1861 census. No tax was being paid on the building in an undated Land Tax record which shows Peter Arkwright's executors as owners so is probably attributable to 1866, the year Peter died, or 1867. In 1867 the *Matlock Bath Telegraph and Advertiser* reported that Francis Taylor fell three storeys 'through the falling of a scaffold at Rock House, where extensive alterations are being made'. These alterations included re-facing or perhaps rebuilding the outer walls, inserting large plate glass windows and redesigning the roof as it is today. Nothing of the structure of an earlier roof survives. The date 1867 appears on the cast iron hopper heads at the house. Francis Taylor survived the fall.

rental of £35. Arkwright was not to plough certain areas of land which would have contributed to the park–like setting of the house without written permission from Nightingale. The reason for this condition is no doubt because at first Nightingale harboured the thought that he himself might like to live there. Arkwright was to have the use of the house for four years but if, after that time, Nightingale should wish to live there, he would build a new house for Arkwright costing not less than £500. In the event , Arkwright remained at Rock House, sometimes referred to as The Rock, until his death in 1792 by which time he had bought the house from Nightingale. Nightingale built himself a new house, Woodend, in 1795.

Richard Arkwright junior moved to Rock House after his father's death in 1792. When later he moved to Willersley Castle, Rock House was retained within the estate becoming home for varying periods of time to descendants and relatives of the family. Richard Arkwright junior's fourth child Peter did not follow the family tradition to go to Cambridge after Eton but instead returned to Cromford to help his father manage the mills. He lived in the house from 1805 until Richard died in 1843. It was scarcely large enough to accommodate his large family of 16 children, 13 of whom survived infancy, and a number of live-in servants. It is considered that at an unknown date, but before 1835 when the house is shown on *Sanderson's Map, Twenty Miles round Mansfield* in an extended form, Peter added the substantial brick and stucco service range.

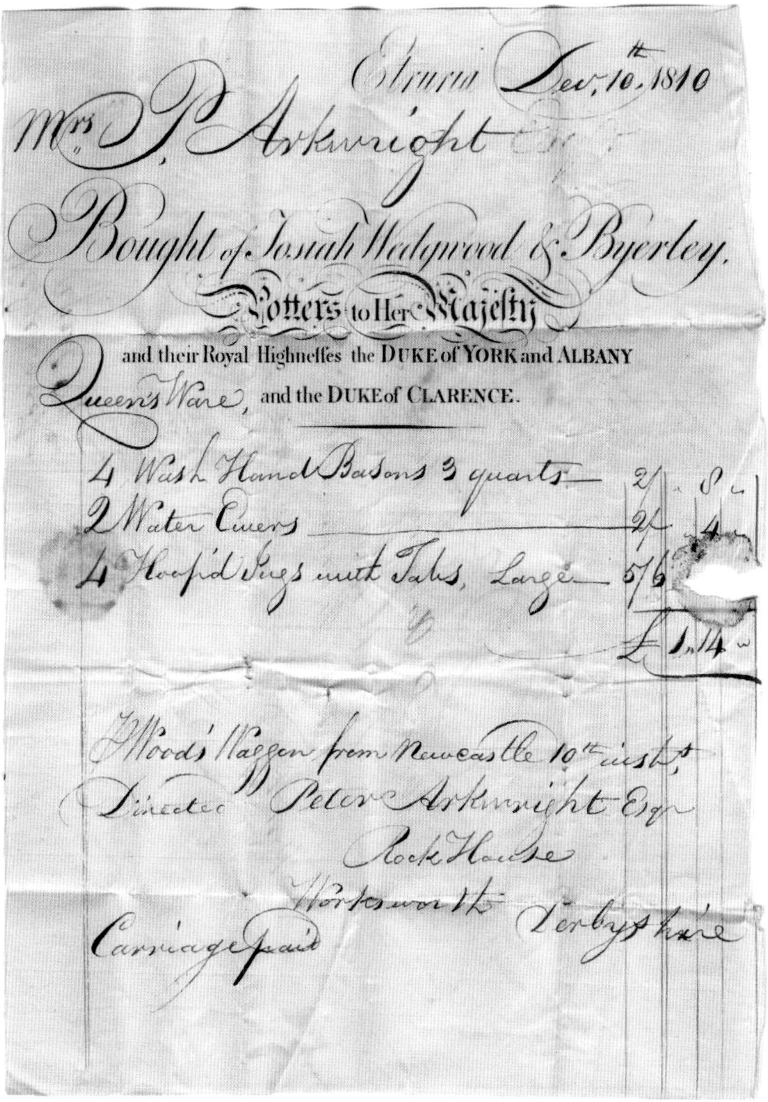
Etruria Dec. 10th 1810
Mrs P. Arkwright
Bought of Josiah Wedgwood & Byerley,
Potters to Her Majesty
and their Royal Highnesses the DUKE of YORK and ALBANY
Queen's Ware, and the DUKE of CLARENCE.
4 Wash Hand Basons 3 quarts — 2/ . 8 —
2 Water Ewers — 2/ . 4 —
4 Hoop'd Jugs with Tabs, Large — 5/6
£ 1 . 14 —
J. Wood's Waggon from Newcastle 10th inst.
Directed Peter Arkwright Esqr
Rock House
Wirksworth Derbyshire
Carriage paid

FIGURE 81. **Invoice to Mrs P. Arkwright from Josiah Wedgwood & Byerley, December 19th, 1810.**

This was one of many purchases by Peter Arkwright and his family in the early years of their occupancy of Rock House. The invoice was accompanied by a note drawing attention to the company's new products. 'I would just observe, that within these few years I have directed my attention to the manufactory of blue and white ware of a very superior description to the common kind hitherto made, and I should be very happy to send you patterns for your selection, if you wished.'

Arkwright Society collection

The next squire, Peter's son Frederic, moved from Spondon to Rock House and, when his mother died in 1872, to Willersley Castle; she had remained at the Castle after her husband's death. Rock House was offered to let the following year and a succession of tenants are recorded in newspapers and directories until 1925 after which it appears to have been empty for some time. In 1885 during Captain Walker's tenancy the house was extended at the back to accommodate a billiard room. In 1929 there were rumours that Rock House was to become a boys' school and the Church Council reported that a headmaster had been appointed and had made several visits but added that 'the For Sale board is still up on Derby Road'. The house was converted into flats in 1933.

The Vicarage and Alison House

These two houses, both listed Grade II, are not recorded in the Cromford Tithe Schedule dated 1840 or on the Cromford Tithe Map dated 1841. Both buildings have been extended but in their original form they were similar in scale and style and have many architectural features in common. The Lodge at the foot of Intake Lane marks the carriage entrance to both properties from Derby Road and there is a later shared entrance from the end of North Street.

The house which became the vicarage was built soon after 1840 by Richard Arkwright at a cost of £1400 as a residence for the Reverend Robert Morgan Jones, the perpetual curate at Cromford Chapel. In 1893 Jones, then living at Spring Cottage, the Dimple, Matlock, recalled that he had been the incumbent in Cromford from 1838 until 1886 and from 1870

also the Rural Dean of Ashover. At the beginning of his career he had lived for about two years at Matlock Bath, (where the first curate of the living, his predecessor the Reverend Richard Ward had also lived), before Richard Arkwright provided a house for him at Cromford. He explained that it was not built as a vicarage but was retained as a private house for which he paid a nominal rent of £1 a year. When

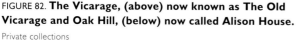

FIGURE 82. **The Vicarage, (above) now known as The Old Vicarage and Oak Hill, (below) now called Alison House.**

Private collections

FIGURE 83. **The Reverend Robert Morgan Jones MA, 1805-1895.**

Reproduced by permission of St Mary's Church, Cromford

Cromford became a separate parish in 1869 the chapel became the parish church and Reverend Jones became the vicar. The Ecclesiastical Commissioners offered to build a vicarage on the basis that Frederic Arkwright would pay half the cost but because there already was a house the Ecclesiastical Commissioners, Frederic Arkwright and the Bishop agreed that the existing house would be used on the same basis as before.

Subsequently in 1898 Frederic Charles Arkwright gifted the Vicarage to the Ecclesiastical Commissioners the gift formalised in a conveyance dated January 1899. When the parishes of Cromford and

Bonsall were combined as a united benefice in 1956, the incumbent at Bonsall continued to live in the parsonage house there and the Assistant Priest in a flat in Cromford vicarage until his death in 1966. The vicarage was sold and converted to offices in 1967. It is now a private residence.

The other house, which retained the name Oak Hill, was built by 1841 for William Melville of William Melville & Co, cotton merchants and spinners. He had earlier moved from Nottingham to Matlock, where he is listed in the Electoral Register of 1835-36. His qualification to be included in the list was his payment of more than £50 for the rent of Masson Mill; he was described as occupier of the mill. In the Register of 1841-42 he was living at Cromford. *Bagshaw's Directory,* 1846 explains that the Cromford and Masson cotton works were now carried on under the name of his company. The terms of the working relationship between Melville and the Arkwright family are not known but the *London Gazette*, August 4th 1846 reported 'The Partnership between William Melville and James Charles Arkwright cotton spinners at Matlock and Cromford dissolved by mutual consent the business to be carried on by J C Arkwright'. Melville died at Oak Hill in 1847.

After Melville's tenancy, Oak Hill was home to members of the Arkwright family including Peter's nephew, the Rev Godfrey Harry Arkwright for a period until 1857; Peter's invalid sister Frances who moved there from Rock House in 1857 and after her death in 1863, Peter's son, James Charles Arkwright. Oak Hill is described as 'being made ready' for him in September 1865 when he was coming to Cromford to help his father in the management of the mills; this was the year before Peter died. The mills were in full work then after a period of four years during the cotton famine when mills at Wirksworth, Cromford and Masson had been on short time, frequently working only three days a week. The *Matlock Advertiser* reported in November 1865 that new hands were being taken on. Masson Mill had been entirely remodelled with 'new and beautiful machinery'. The paper expressed the hope that Cromford should also be remodelled.

James Charles continued to live at Oak Hill until his death in 1896 although for much of that time he retained a house in London. He amassed a large fortune. Bequests in his will of 1895 included £1000 to the trustees of St Mary's Church for cleansing, lighting, warming and beautifying the building and augmenting the stipend of the organist, £1000 in trust to pay the income of the Vicar of Holy Trinity, Matlock Bath for services to Scarthin Mission Church and £1000 to augment the pensions of the inmates of the six almshouses at Cromford in addition to the endowment he had made earlier. James' widow, his second wife, Mary, remained at Oak Hill until 1918.

For the next 40 years Oak Hill was home to George Henry Key, Chairman of the Via Gellia Colour Company. He rented the house in 1918 and purchased it just before the Arkwright estate was offered for sale in 1924. Since 1967 when Toc H (an international Christian movement founded in 1915) became the owner, the property has been known as Alison House, taking its name from Alison MacFie, who established the League of Women Helpers. The League became the Toc H (Women's Section) and is now fully merged with the men's movement. Today (2013) Alison House is a hotel with conference facilities open to the public.

The Meadows

Frederic Charles Arkwright speaking at the Willersley Rent Audit in 1898, reminded his audience that the Meadows were where 'most of those present went for recreation or where their children and grandchildren went for cricket, football, and outdoor exercise'. Speaking today he would have added rugby to that list and no doubt been delighted to find that this flat riverside land still serves the same purpose, providing a popular venue for sporting activities throughout the year. In 1898 he was defending it against their Matlock neighbours' proposal to 'deposit their evil smelling refuse' at a sewerage works there, 290 yards from Rock House; a later threat was a gas works but both plans were abandoned.

F C Arkwright was the President of Cromford Cricket Club and in 1899 he gave half the £100 cost of a new cricket pavilion. By 1893, the Club had built a pavilion, a welcome upgrade in accommodation compared with the existing changing facilities offered by a nearby barn, but in 1898 it was destroyed by fire. F C Arkwright used the occasion of the opening of the replacement pavilion to offer the use of land as far as the railway so doubling the size of the ground for 'a very nominal rent'.

The report of the Church Council for the year 1928 records the great pleasure afforded by the announcement that 'Mr Key intends to give the Meadows to the district for a public recreation ground'. This was George Henry Key who had purchased the Meadows at the Arkwright estate sale. His act of generosity was welcomed by the Vicar in the *Church Magazine* 'in the name of the children, and indeed, of the community as a whole, for it means that

FIGURE 84. **Cricket Pavilion, Cromford Meadows, photograph, September 7th 1900.**

This picture shows the Cromford cricket pavilion erected in 1899. The occasion is a Cromford v W Sugg's Derbyshire XI on September 7th 1900. The *High Peak News* reported that 'the local team had the distinction of being the only one that had faced the County with only eleven men'. The Derbyshire team members were Hulme, Cadman, Ollivierre, Storer, F Sugg, Charlesworth, Yates, W Sugg, Humphries, and Bestwick and for Cromford S Taylor J.Rolley, A Lawton, W Frost, J S Fryer, H Kidd, A E Lawton, J Kidd, R Else, F.Adkin and F.Gillott . The Umpires were ? Roper and J Siddall. The Cromford captain A E Lawton is seated centre, his brother, Arthur, wearing a boater, is standing back left. The visitors scored 424 batting first. Cromford had replied with 48 for 8 when the match was declared a draw 'the light being too bad to allow for a finish'

Private collection

not only will our children be able to enjoy themselves without fear of accident, but that the meadows will never become a building site'.

Alice Taylor, better known as the authoress Alison Uttley, was born in 1884 at Castle Top Farm which overlooks the Meadows from high on the east side of the valley. She wrote of her great pleasure in seeing cricket played there and later of playing herself in a girls' team organised by a cricketing family who came to live in the next valley. She recalled the horse-mower with the horse wearing leather shoes to protect the pitch and visiting teams arriving by horse brake and collecting boxes of beer from the brewery (Matthew Hill's) on their way down the road. The cricketing family she remembered were the Lawtons and when the girls' team played, it included the Lawton daughters. Mr and Mrs Lawton drove down in an open carriage with a big tea basket and all the equipment for the game. Sometimes the telegraph boy came across the fields with a yellow telegram reporting the state of the county game or the Captain's score. This was of special interest to the family when Albert Edward

FIGURE 85. **Cricket teams, Cromford Meadows, photograph, about 1900.**

The date of this occasion when the ladies' team was photographed is not known but was close to that of the men's match described above. May Dawes (see below) was born in 1899.

Not all the people can be named but it may be of interest to list such names as have been attached to the photograph. From the left, indistinct at the left edge of the picture is Mrs Dawes holding baby May. Many local people will have later memories of May Dawes as the piano teacher in Cromford. Standing are: unknown, J Fryer, two Miss Lawtons, unknown, unknown, Miss Mee, Miss Pinder, Miss Parker, Miss Hill, unknown, unknown, J.Siddall, Miss Clarke. Front row: ? Fox, J. Gould, A. Lawton, unknown, S. Taylor?, ? Dawes, J. Rolley, C. Swift, G. Barker.
Private collection

Lawton –'Bertie', the eldest son was playing for Derbyshire County Cricket Club which he did from 1901 until 1910 being captain for much of that time. John Shawcroft in *A History of Derbyshire County Cricket Club 1870-1970*, records that when London County had a cricket match in the area, the famous W. G. Grace sometimes stayed with the Lawtons and played in their family cricket games. John Edward Lawton came from Dukinfield to work with Frederic Charles Arkwright in 1880. Later the family became Matlock Bath residents and before Lawton built Woodbank (now called Cromford Court) in 1901, lived at Glenorchy Villa, the house which stands at the foot of the drive to Cromford Court.

CHAPTER ELEVEN

Scarthin

At the end of the eighteenth century Adam Wolley called the community which stood on the far side of the Greyhound pond in Figure 86 Scarthin Houses. It lay either side of the old road from Cromford to Bonsall on the north side of the Bonsall Brook in Matlock parish. Scarthin retained its association with Matlock parish and in the nineteenth century from 1865 its local government was managed by the Matlock Bath Local Board and from 1895 by Matlock Bath and Scarthin Nick Urban District. In 1924 Scarthin, along with Matlock Bath, Cromford and Tansley was incuded in Matlock Urban District.

In Scarthin, unlike Cromford, the Arkwright's were not the major landowners though Richard Arkwright was awarded land in Scarthin in the Matlock Enclosure Award of 1784 and also purchased some property there. But there were other owners, for example, the inn keeper Isaac North and Anthony Debanke who advertised a newly built house there in 1826, thought to be the property now known as The Old Printing Works. Also, Nathaniel Wheatcroft, who in his will dated 1862, bequeathed property at Chapel Hill (see below) and also a currier's shop, a malthouse and kiln, a building 'now or heretofore used as a Wesleyan Reformer's Chapel' and fourteen cottages all in 'Scarthing Nick'. The late William Stone's property at 'Scarthen Row' and Harp Edge which was offered for sale on September 27th, 1865 included freehold dwelling-houses, joiners' shops with sawpit underneath, store, drying rooms and ground and 'a BEER – HOUSE recently called "Hit and Miss", and now called "The Boat"…brew-house, slaughter-house, pig-stye…occupied by William Allen'. Allen was a boatman on the canal and it seems likely that it was he who changed the name of the beer-house. This advertisement appears to make the distinction between properties at the roadside in Scarthen Row and property which was up the hillside behind them on Harp Edge.

In some respects Cromford and Scarthin were separate entities; in other respects not. In economic terms the two are, and must always have been, inseparable but in the religious and social life of the area Scarthin had a very particular role. This is evident from the significant number of former nonconformist and Anglican places of worship which have survived there though all now are in secular use. Each one of them was brought into existence to bear witness to a particular brand of dissenting worship apart from the Church Mission Chapel which was built as a response to increasingly successful nonconformist evangelism. It was

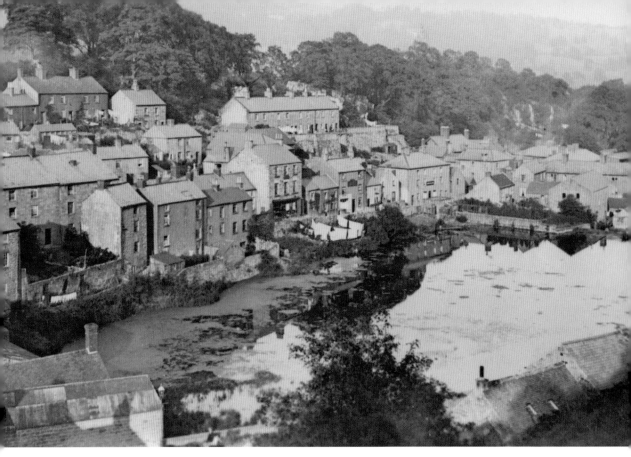

FIGURE 86. **View across the Greyhound Pond to Scarthin, photograph, about 1900.**

Many of the houses shown here on the south facing slope of the ridge known as Harp Edge, have been demolished including the pair of two storey cottages (above the lines of washing) To the right of them the three storey, three bay building prominent in the centre of the picture, today, 2013, houses Scarthin Books. The roof visible immediately above the book shop is of the Wesleyan Reformers' Chapel which was opened in 1862. It was rebuilt and extended forward over the site of the demolished two storey cottages to form the United Methodists' Mount Tabor Chapel in 1907; the design of the building by architects John Wills and Sons of Derby and London is on three levels and reflects the nature of the steeply sloping site. The chapel was purchased in January 1960 for use as a factory packing salt in twists of blue paper for crisp packets and from the late 1960s the building has housed an engineering works.In the cluster of buildings in the right background of the picture note The Boat Inn with its dark roof. The large building standing behind it (shown to the right of it in this picture at the corner where water flows out of the dam) is remembered as the old malthouse.The surviving bottom sections of the outer walls of the building still define the corner.

In March 1908 Matlock Bath and Scarthin Nick Urban District Council bought land from Frederic Charles Arkwright and later in the year began the construction of the promenade in place of the gardens beside the pond. The promenade's surviving roadside railings came second hand from the promenade at Matlock Bath where they had been replaced by unclimbable fencing

The significant feature associated with Arkwright's development of Cromford in this view is the Greyhound pond. It is the lowest of a series of ponds which were created by damming the Bonsall Brook. Some of the ponds along Bonsall Hollow were formed before 1780, see page14, and the Greyhound pond by 1785. Their primary function was to provide water for the mills along Bonsall Hollow and for Arkwright's Cromford mills. William Adam's *Dales Scenery, Fishing Streams and Mines of Derbyshire*, 1861, recorded a secondary purpose - providing a supply of trout and grayling for the Arkwright table. A less salubrious use was highlighted in 1887 when a report to the Sanitary Authority described the Greyhound pond as 'the filthy pond' and Matlock Local Board was admonished for making it foul with Scarthin's sewage.

With acknowledgement to Henry Band

here in Scarthin, rather than in the estate-owned Cromford, that dissenting groups were able to acquire the land on which to plant their chapels and grow their congregations. It was not until 1900 that a nonconformist chapel was built in Cromford on land owned by the Arkwright estate.

Just how far the Church recruited its congregation from Cromford rather than Scarthin is evident in the composition of the Church Council in June 1917. The elected and co-opted members numbered 30. Of these 28 were Cromford residents, some from outlying parts of the parish. The two from Scarthin were Mr and Mrs W. E. Smith. It was Mr Smith who printed the Church magazine. This Council was the first to be elected under rules permitting the election of women as well as men and gave every communicant above the age of 21 the right to vote. The female communicants embraced their new opportunity and no less than 16 of the 30 members were women, among them Mrs Arkwright and the vicar's wife Mrs Hazlehurst. It is likely that this outcome was influenced by the war. Nevertheless it is a remarkable demonstration of female emancipation in a small rural community.

FIGURE 87. **Interior, Mission Chapel, Scarthin, date unknown.**

The chapel was built for about £1800 to a design by J A Wyatt of Manchester. He had earlier designed Holy Trinity Church, Matlock Bath. The chapel appears to be decorated to celebrate Harvest Festival. It closed in 1952; the building now houses Cromford Garage.
Private collection

In addition to the former places of worship the other physical reminder of Scarthin's independent identity is the war memorial on the promenade. This records the deaths in the Great War, 1914-18, of nine Scarthin residents and of three in the World War of 1939-45. Apart from these visible reminders there are the memories of those who grew up in Scarthin in the early years of the twentieth century. They spoke of the fierce loyalty they and their neighbours felt towards Scarthin, of their rivalry with Cromford children and of the occasional scrap or narrow escape on their way to or from school. For the most part it was healthy rivalry adding spice to celebrations and other events. Would Scarthin or North Street produce the best street decorations, the wittiest Wakes stunt or the best carnival float? And which chapel would muster the largest turnout, inter-chapel rivalry being quite as important as the competition between the two settlements?

But Cromford and Scarthin could act together. The Reverend Arthur Hazlehurst writing in the *Church Magazine* recalled the 'real unity of the service' when the anniversary of the unveiling of Cromford's war memorial was celebrated in 1921. 'Church and Chapel goers realised that the sacrifice of the brave men, who gave their lives for us, was a bond of

Chapels in Scarthin

The first chapel in Scarthin, the Wesleyan Methodist chapel was built in 1808 and registered as a Dissenting Meeting House on 18th October that year. Chapel Hill was named after it (see Figure 88). Wesleyans had met somewhere in the village since 1803, probably in a private house; the Register for the Wesleyans in Cromford dates from 1806 and in 1807 Cromford was declared a Wesleyan Home Mission station in the Belper Circuit. The first Home Mission appointments were made in 1806 so Cromford was one of the earliest. William Salt, the first Cromford missionary, was charged to spread Methodism through the Peak. The chapel closed in 1900.

Quarrels within the Wesleyan movement nationally led to groups splitting away from the parent body and in 1829 the Register of Dissenting Meeting Houses for Cromford records the presence of Primitive Methodists. There were also General Baptists. Where their meetings were held is not known but eventually the Primitive Methodists rented a warehouse in Scarthin. By 1853 'with great difficulty' they had raised the money to buy a piece of land there and built a chapel which was opened for worship on February 12th 1854. The chapel underwent considerable alterations in its lifetime and was closed for worship in 1921. It is now a private house distinguished by the commemorative plaque in its red brick roadside façade.

In the 1840s disaffection with aspects of the Wesleyan Connexion's management of affairs led to a serious dispute in which Derbyshire and Cromford congregations were active. The outcome was the formal withdrawal from the Wesleyan Methodist movement of groups calling themselves Wesleyan Reformers. The religious census of 1851 for Cromford records Primitive Methodists and General Baptists continuing to meet but in addition lists 'Wesleyan Reformers and Wesleyan Mithoudist [sic] Reformers'. At about this time two of these groups, the General Baptists and the Wesleyan Reformers were holding meetings in Mart's Clubroom which is thought to have been associated with the Cock Inn but by 1862 Wesleyan Reformers' meetings were being held in a property in Scarthin owned by Nathaniel Wheatcroft and in that year they completed their chapel. This building was extended in 1907 to form Mount Tabor United Methodist Chapel. In 1932, the United Methodists, the Primitive Methodists and the Wesleyan Methodists amalgamated to form the Methodists and met at Mount Tabor. When the chapel closed in 1958 the congregation moved to share the Methodist chapel on Water Lane which the Wesleyan Methodists had opened in September 1900.

The Anglican Church made its contribution to chapel building in Scarthin when Matlock Bath Holy Trinity Church's Mission Chapel was opened in 1869 (see Figure 88). On the occasion of the laying of the foundation stone in August 1868 when garlands were hung across Scarthin Row the *Wirksworth Advertiser* described it as the new church for Scarthin Nick 'in the midst of the poor and exclusively for their use'.

union more potent than the small differences which keep us apart.' The choirs of the several churches combined and were led through the village by the Mount Tabor String Band. Hazlehurst was supported by the Wesleyan Minister, the Reverend B Hughes Smith and Mr Thomas Boden of Mount Tabor Methodist Church. In later years the Friendly Societies joined the annual procession with their officers wearing their regalia and in 1926 the procession was led for the first time by the Middleton Band. The event began at the school and proceeded to the Cromford Memorial and then to Scarthin.

It is our impression that Scarthin's identity was eroded during the inter war years and was further damaged after the Second World War when for a period from the late 1940's many Scarthin houses were declared unfit for habitation and their occupants moved to 'the new houses', the council housing provided on Cromford Hill. Gradually the empty houses were demolished and although some gaps have been filled the former tightly built terraced community has not recovered.

Included in the demolition in the late 1950s or early 1960s was the three storey Temperance Hall which stood alongside the Pitchings and which had a separate entrance door off the Pitchings to each of the upper floors. In 1893, it was described as the Old Temperance Hall and as having been closed for a very long time. It was owned by F C Arkwright who, in that year, had it thoroughly cleaned and renovated, new floors put in and other alterations made. A year or two before 1929, Captain Richard Arkwright 'presented the building to Scarthin'. Older residents remember the two upper storeys as single open spaces, the first floor, where meat and potato pie suppers and Whist Drives were held, had a slightly bowed lime-ash floor and a large fireplace; the second floor was boarded and was used for dances and lantern slide shows. Events were run by Matlock Bath church and organisations such as the Scouts and Brownies met there. The ground floor had uses as a billiard room and later as a garage.

FIGURE 88. **Staffordshire Row, Cromford, about 1900.**

This view, published by G H Brown, Bookseller and Stationer of Cromford shows the three storey houses of Staffordshire Row at the foot of Harp Edge. These appear to be late eighteenth century houses similar to those on Cromford Hill. They stand on land which was awarded to Richard Arkwright in the Matlock Enclosure in 1784 and it is reasonable to consider them as part of his factory village. The footpath over Harp Edge was diverted to accommodate the row.

To the left of Staffordshire Row is Chapel Hill. This road, earlier called Stoney Way Road, was the original route from Cromford to Bonsall over the shoulder of the hill. It took its new name from the Wesleyan Methodist Chapel, the prominent four storey building near the foot of the hill. It is shown here in its final form after it had been extended forward to the edge of the road over a schoolroom built on land belonging to Nathaniel Wheatcroft (see Box overleaf). In 1900 a new chapel was opened on Water Lane and this old chapel building was put up for sale. A bid to purchase it for the manufacture or sale of intoxicating liquors was rejected. In 1904, a John Willn bought it and by 1906 converted it into two houses. The alteration involved the demolition of the front of the two storeys above the former schoolroom. The old chapel is now one house.

John Willn bought all the property on Chapel Hill over a period of 32 years ending in 1905 with his purchase of the two cottages below the chapel and the small building next to them at the foot of the hill which, for a period of 20 to 30 years in the mid nineteenth century, had housed the turnpike toll collector. The Cromford Gate toll-house stood opposite to it on the other side of the road. The collector's house was later used as a bakehouse. Willn demolished it and built Swiss Cottage on the site.

At the bottom right in this view, the building with gothic windows was opened in 1869 as a Mission Chapel of Holy Trinity Church, Matlock Bath. The buildings on the left, opposite Staffordshire Row, are part of the Cromford corn mill complex. The Bonsall Brook which drove the mill now runs in a culvert parallel with and then under the road until it feeds into the head of the Greyhound pond. Below the mill site the path down from Harp Edge crossed the brook and climbed up towards Alabaster Lane through a field called Pennyford, a name which survives in local use. It is reasonable to assume that when the brook ran in its natural course the field extended down to the valley bottom where the footpath crossed the brook via the ford from which the field took its name.

Private collection

Chapel Hill

Chapel Hill as part of Scarthin also belonged to Matlock parish. The Chapel Hill terrace of three storey houses with its stepped lintels may easily be mistaken for Arkwright housing but it is built on land which belonged to John and George Bradley including a small piece of land allotted to them at Matlock Enclosure in 1784. The Matlock's Manor Court records for the period provide detailed information on the later history of the land.

Development on Chapel Hill

The land on which Chapel Hill was developed belonged to John and George Bradley; members of the family added buildings there in piecemeal fashion. In October 1808 Alice Bradley, George's widow and her son George and wife Mary, gave 166 square yards of the land and 'that chapel or meeting house lately erected or built thereon' to the chapel trustees in trust. This was the original Wesleyan Methodist Chapel building, (see Figure 88). Between 1811 and 1832 Nathaniel Wheatcroft bought the other Bradley property on Chapel Hill, four houses and land on which he built further houses. Wheatcroft, an early and successful carrier on the Cromford canal, (see Chapter 12) was a founding trustee of the chapel, a circuit preacher in an area which included Whatstandwell, Ashover, Kirk Ireton and South Wingfield and treasurer of the Sunday School. At first a tenant of the Bradleys, his purchases included a house, garden and a small amount of land for which he paid £300 to George and Mary Bradley in 1811. This must have been a substantial building and was probably the imposing house above the chapel, Via Gellia House, where Wheatcroft lived.

In 1861 he transferred all his property at Chapel Hill, now nine houses, to his son Joseph. He was a tape and smallware manufacturer who developed the Speedwell Mill in Wirksworth and later his family extended the business and took over Haarlem Mill next door to Speedwell. Joseph's legacy from his father included the Little Chapel House which had been attached to the west side of the chapel – perhaps as accommodation for circuit preachers - and the schoolroom built on Nathaniel's land, over which the chapel was extended in about 1840. These were properties which Nathaniel might have been expected to leave to the chapel but he had severed his connection with the Wesleyan movement in 1847. He died

in 1862 and in April the following year Joseph attempted to sell all the Chapel Hill property. The sale proved to be a protracted affair. In 1864 Thomas Outram, the Cromford currier, bought property which included the Little Chapel House and the chapel schoolroom. He sold them later to the Chapel Trustees along with 'the privy across the road'. Little Chapel House was demolished between 1904 and 1911 though the random limestone wall still attached to the chapel building may be a remnant of it. It was not until 1865 that Nathaniel's former residence sold. The house was divided into two dwellings some time between 1911 and 1920.

A monastic legacy?

The other significant sale from Nathaniel's estate was in 1869 when Joseph sold houses and outbuildings to James Hodgkinson of Cromford. By 1873 Hodgkinson had converted the outbuildings to form what is now (2013) Minninglow, the top, south facing house in the terrace. It is of interest that the houses he bought had a right to water 'from a well called Monkstone Well'. This is one of several references to 'monk' in the names of nearby features. Cameron's *Place Names of Derbyshire,* 1959, lists Monkwall in the Duchy of Lancaster records in 1415 and in the Chandos Pole papers in 1620; Monkwell Lane occurs in the Matlock Manor Court Rolls in 1741 and in the Bonsall Tithe Apportionment the field name Monk Hall (Wall?) Close occurs. The names hint at early monastic farming on the common land of Bonsall. In 1297, the *Calendar of Inquisitions post mortem* records Buildwas Abbey (Shropshire) renting pasture for 400 sheep at Bonsall. The abbey held land at nearby Ivonbrook from the twelfth century until the dissolution of the monasteries in the sixteenth.

The Cromford and Scarthin Sewage Scheme

The reference to the 'miasma constantly given off' Cromford's filthy pond, the Greyhound pond, in 1887 was one of a barrage of complaints referring to the inadequacy of the system for dealing with sewage in the district. While using the River Derwent and the Bonsall Brook as sewers had long been recognised as unsatisfactory, years of discussions between the authorities at Matlock, Matlock Bath and Cromford had failed to reach agreement on a joint scheme to deal with the problem. It was not until 1906 that a plan was agreed and 1926 before its implementation was complete with sewage from all three communities being discharged to the sewerage works at High Peak Junction.

By 1888 Cromford was considering its own scheme, F C Arkwright devising a plan for Cromford and Scarthin. The Matlock Bath Board was still discussing joining the project in 1892 but it did not do so, one good reason being that without Matlock's participation in controlling its sewage output, Matlock Bath would still be plagued by a contaminated river. A lifelong resident of Matlock Bath, who as a child in the years just before 1920, had learned to swim in the river there, recalled its condition as obscene.

By 1890 Arkwright had already taken the precaution of reminding Bonsall Local Board that it would be almost useless to carry out his Scarthin and Cromford Sewage Scheme if Bonsall was still allowing sewage to flow into Bonsall Hollow contaminating the water and assisting the silting up of the dams there. He also served notice on the owners of manufactories in the Hollow to 'discontinue damaging the water in the Dams by washings'. Bonsall denied that any sewerage drains were connected to the brook, reporting that the whole of Bonsall was fitted with dry earth closets and the brook course was almost entirely covered. The Board was taking steps to finish covering it in to prevent 'as far as possible any sewerage matter getting in to pollute the Stream'.

The villagers in Scarthin and Cromford had accepted F C Arkwright's recommendation to adopt a system of drainage and sewers were laid to plans drawn by John Parkin and Son of Idridgehay and Derby, Matlock Bath making a financial contribution to the costs of Scarthin's inclusion in the scheme. F C Arkwright took a personal interest in the project going to many parts of the country to view systems for the disposal of sewage and, with his committee, decided 'on account of its efficiency as well as its great economy' to install an Ives patent precipitating tank which would provide for a population of about 1700 and be able to deal with 60,000 gallons of sewage daily. The small sewerage works was built in Cromford Meadows beside the tail race from the Arkwrights' mills site, some 100 yards from the point where the race comes above ground. By the end of 1893 it was in place. The outfall from the works to the tail race and thence to the river was claimed to be 'quite to the sample of the sewerage chemically treated'. How long it satisfied sewerage regulations is not known, nor is it clear how many residents benefitted from the scheme. For example, 'consequent upon an outbreak of typhoid' in 1924, Cromford Parish Council minutes report accepting Mr Slack's offer to empty the cess pools on North Street for five shillings each. Even after the completion of the new scheme in 1926, it would be many years before every house in Cromford and Scarthin was connected to a sewerage system. The nightsoil collectors were still making their weekly visits to properties with outside toilets in the 1960s.

The Wakes

A more joyful undertaking which engaged both Cromford and Scarthin was the celebration of the annual Wakes. Richard Arkwright had begun a tradition of offering his work people a day of celebration at his mill in Nottingham and continued it at Cromford with an event called candlelighting. In September 1776 the day's events began with a 500 strong procession parading round the village led by a band and a boy on a cart working at a weaving loom, (a similar practice was followed in Lancashire textile community celebrations) before returning to the mill for 'buns, ale, nuts and fruit'. The day ended with an evening of music and dancing. In 1776 this occasion also marked the completion of the second mill and included a feast for the more than 200 builders who had erected the mill in the 5-6 months since April. The *Derby Mercury's* report of the event in 1778 drew attention to 'Thousands of Spectators from Matlock Bath and the neighbouring Towns, who testified their satisfaction at so pleasing a Sight'. These festivities appear to have been entirely secular.

At the heart of the traditional Wakes celebration is a religious festival commemorating the patron saint of the local church. There was no church in Cromford when Arkwright's candlelighting tradition began, what remained of the mediaeval bridge chapel by that date had long been in residential use and the chapel which the Arkwrights built was not opened for public worship until 1797. It seems likely that Arkwright's candlelighting ceremony merged into the Wakes celebrations once the new Church, dedicated to St Mary, took a role in the proceedings. Wakes Sunday in Cromford is the nearest Sunday after September 8th, the nativity of the Blessed Virgin Mary. Writing of the Wakes in 1936, Canon Hazlehurst believed the tradition to be as old as Cromford Church itself. The celebrations became a fixture of the village calendar and a major event even to the extent that Richard Arkwright junior, as has been pointed out above, was allowing his workers four days holiday for Cromford Wakes and a half day for Bonsall Wakes. It is not known when this apparently generous allowance began.

Early twentieth century recollections of the Wakes are of the flurry of extra house cleaning which preceded the event and of the excitement when the fair arrived and waited on the Meadows or on Derby Road until after the Sunday evening church service had been held; only then was it allowed to set up in the Market Place. The Vicar expressed delight when, in 1925, the Sunday service was held in the Market Place. In more recent memory it was held there on the already erected fairground Dodgems surrounded by the rides and stalls which would fill the centre of the village for a week.

The practice of a Wakes holiday for the mill workers survived into the twentieth century but the Wakes week holiday which had become a feature of the school year was brought to an end in 1936 by the intervention of the County Council Education Committee when it was decided that school holidays should be uniform throughout the county. The Cromford School Managers protested, objecting to the loss of the Wakes Week holiday, when, with Masson Mill closed, many children were able to visit the seaside with their parents. They wished to retain the three weeks holiday in August plus the traditional Wakes Week in September. The

The Wakes, 1926

For many years the village carnival was an important feature of Wakes week. The Church magazine of 1926 contains the following account of the Wakes in what seems to have been a vintage year. 'The wakes of 1926 have exceeded all previous records, and the Committee are entitled to our warmest thoughts for giving us a very good time. We congratulate the Chairman, Councillor Wright and the Secretaries, Messrs Herbert Gillott and Fred Clay especially upon the success of their efforts. They worked hard and everything was well organised. Of course they had a splendid backing from the village otherwise the result would not have been what it was, but it was the splendid lead which inspired confidence and enthusiasm. The programme was more ambitious than for other years, the Saturday being devoted to the Children's Carnival, which was a new feature and one that can be repeated without hesitation in years to come. The dresses of the boys and girls were a proof that their elders meant turning them out a credit to the occasion. Heralded by the Middleton Band the youngsters had the afternoon to themselves and thoroughly enjoyed it. After parading the streets they gathered in the field behind the school and received their prizes. They were entertained by Mr Snow's Morris Dancers to whom we make our bow and offer our thanks. On the Sunday Mr Harry Hall [the owner of the fair] gave an organ recital at 8 o'clock and a large crowd of 1500 assembled on the Market Place to hear it, the collection for the Hospitals reaching nearly £14. This amount fell short of last year's total by a few shillings, but considering the coal strike and the unsettled weather it was very satisfactory. On the Monday evening came the great attraction – the Carnival proper. The centre of the village was crowded with villagers and residents, so much so that it was difficult for the judges to do their work in comfort. The entries were more numerous than ever and a very picturesque medley followed the ever-willing Middleton Band "up the hill and down again". The little King and Queen must have been proud of their loyal subjects and the Mayor and Mayoress looked superb as they smoked their cigarettes and lolled back in their Carriage-of-state. It was excellent fun and jolly fooling which is very good for everyone at Wakes time. We do not know that any single feature was so mirth-provoking as last year's widow who careered down Cromford Hill with her parasol aloft on a crazy bicycle – we think it will be many years before such a spectacle is seen again - but the general effect was most imposing.' The *High Peak News* reported that the revenue, for the three days including collections and subscriptions amounted to roughly £85 'so that the committee will have a considerable sum available for the Cromford Nursing Association and the Wirksworth and Whitworth Hospitals'.

In his commentary on the Wakes the following year the vicar recorded his regret that the organ recital service in the Market Place on the Sunday evening, though better attended than ever, lacked the reverent touch he had so much appreciated two years earlier 'when every man removed his pipe during the short religious address'

Education Committee was unyielding and there was no Wakes Week holiday in 1936 though the children were given a holiday on Wakes Monday.

The village celebrated Whit Mondays too. The *Wirksworth and Matlock Advertiser,* June 15th, 1867 drew attention to the number of years the day had been observed as a general holiday with people 'making themselves as happy as possible, laying aside all work; appearing in their very best attire; attending church; paying friendly and neighbourly visits, and strolling about the town to see and, in some instances no doubt, to be seen'. The Friendly Societies were at the heart of these activities. There was 'the old club at Mrs Marts, [this was] the "Odd Fellows", [who] for some reason did not show themselves this year, and if we are rightly informed, did not "dine" as they have been in the habit, at the "Cock". The Philanthropic Club at the "Bull's Head" attended Glenorchy Chapel, the one at Mr Kinder's [the Greyhound] attended the Church. Both these clubs, after dinner, perambulated the town, and then returned to their respective inns. There was the usual display of stalls with

FIGURE 89. **Scarthin celebrates VE Day, 1945.**
Private collection

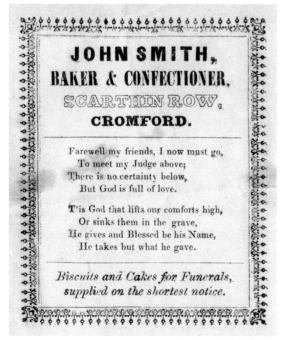

all kinds of good things to tempt the little ones; and towards evening we observed several gentlemen engaged in denouncing the drink and the traffic therein. All passed off quietly'. The significance of these events in the social calendar is evident from their scale and elaborate organisational details. In 1861 this village festival boasted no less than three bands. 'The Provident Society at the Greyhound was led by the village band; the Oddfellows at the Cock, by the Wensley band (both attending Church) and the Philanthropic Society at the Bull's Head, by the Midland Railway Brass Band. All then had "sumptuous" dinners and in the afternoon perambulated the village until evening.'

CHAPTER TWELVE

Transport

A significant road alteration

Attention has been drawn to several improvements to the road system around Cromford including the construction of the road along Bonsall Hollow in 1736 and thirty years later, the turnpiking of the Cromford bridge to Langley Mill road. In 1793 there were further developments with the construction of the Via Gellia road and in 1817-1818 of the Cromford to Belper turnpike along the Derwent valley.

The planned construction of Arkwright's second mill in 1776 was to trigger a significant change in the entrance to Cromford from the north. The new mill was to be built across the line of the public highway which linked Cromford to Matlock Bath via a more or less level though circuitous track, the so-called Roundabout Way. This ran close to the river and round the end of Scarthin Rock to cross the Bonsall Brook over the bridge in what is now the Arkwright Mills' yard. The road could no longer be used for general traffic when the mill was built and when subsequently the mill yard was enclosed.

The alternative way into the village from the north was the road which climbed up to and through the natural nick in Scarthin Rock, the formidable rocky barrier at the

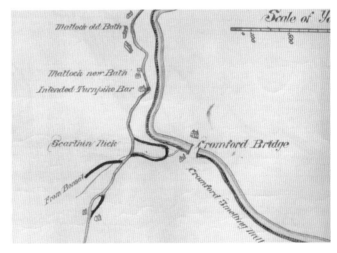

FIGURE 90. **Part of a plan of the roads and cross-roads between Rowsley Bridge & the Cross Post on Wirksworth Moor, 1759.**

This map shows the two routes to the west of the river which linked Cromford and Matlock Bath. One followed the line of the present main road passing the Baths at Matlock Bath and then climbing over Scarthin Rock at Scarthin Nick. This was to be the new turnpike road. The other route, the Roundabout Way, is shown as a solid red loop on the map. This avoided the climb over the rock. It ran beside the river and along the line of what is now known as Church Walk before doubling back around the end of Scarthin Rock to cross the Bonsall Brook and rejoin the main road on the Cromford side of the Nick.

Reproduced by permission of Derbyshire Record Office, reference D1053 Z/P1. Original in black and white.

entrance to Cromford. A Turnpike
Act of 1759 had empowered the
Nottingham to Newhaven Turnpike Trust to turnpike this section
of the road as part of the route from
Wirksworth Moor to meet the Chesterfield to Chapel-en-le-Frith turnpike near Longstone. Part of the
turnpike plan is reproduced here to
illustrate the proposed scheme at
Cromford. No doubt some improvement was made to the road in 1759

The cut through Scarthin Rock

Several writers commented on the effect of Arkwright's
alteration. Bray in 1777 refers to 'a passage cut thro' the
rock which makes a very striking appearance'; Thomas
Newte in 1785 qualifies the cut as 'just wide enough for a
coach to pass' and Warner, *A Tour through the Northern
Counties of England*, 1802, describes 'the narrow pass
into the vale of Matlock, hewn by Sir Richard Arkwright
through the mountain that forms the western barrier of
this enchanting spot'. Pilkington in 1789 reveals that it
had been intended to leave a rock arch over the road which
would have had 'an excellent effect' had it been successful.

but the way remained steep and difficult. Richard Arkwright sought to modify the climb by
cutting the nick down to a lower level thus providing some benefit to road users as the law
required when the closing or diverting of a public highway required travellers to use an
alternative route.

The building of the turnpike road from Cromford to Belper in 1817-1818, now the A6,
was accompanied by the final lowering of the road level at Scarthin Nick (see Figure 93).
Barker, *The Panorama of Matlock*, 1827, commented on the improvement as a 'passage cut
30 feet perpendicularly through the limestone. This bold undertaking is deservedly the
admiration of strangers'. The road remained a relatively narrow carriageway until it was
widened in 1960-61. The rutted riverside route and the way through the Nick are indicated
in the late eighteenth century view looking south over the bend of the river (see Figure
91) and the brow of the cut through the rock in the watercolour of 1789 by John Webber
(see Figure 92).

FIGURE 91. **Part
of the road
from Matlock
to Cromford,
watercolour,
late C18, artist
unknown.**

Reproduced by
permission of Derbyshire
County Council Buxton
Museum and Art Gallery

FIGURE 92. **View near Cromford, Derbyshire, watercolour, 1789, John Webber.**

Reproduced by permission of Derby Museum and Art Gallery

FIGURE 93. **Scarthin Nick, lithograph from a drawing by Eliza Rawlinson of Matlock Bath, published March 28th 1822.**

The dramatic improvement of the road brought about by its final levelling at Scarthin Nick is well illustrated here. Adam in 1838 described it as 'a wide and excellent road' in contrast to his impression in 1812 when it was 'a very narrow lane, very steep and difficult'.

Private collection

The Cromford Canal

Sir Richard Arkwright's last legacy to the industrial scene in Cromford was his agreement to the use of some of his land for the construction of the Cromford Canal.

In 1788 he was involved with a large group of promoters, mainly prominent county business men, bankers and industrialists in the decision to make a canal from Cromford to Langley Mill where it would join the Erewash Canal. Despite his many reservations about aspects of the scheme, he finally threw his weight into securing the Act of Parliament which was needed to authorise the construction. The Act passed into law in July, 1789, three months after Sir Richard had purchased the manor of Cromford from Peter Nightingale. In May of the following year, again with some misgivings, he agreed the terms by which he released such land as was required for the canal. This included part of the grounds of Rock House, his Derbyshire residence, where the canal terminus and wharf were to be built. It seems unlikely that he would have agreed to this choice of location for the wharf had he not already embarked on the construction of Willersley Castle. The agreement also confirmed arrangements to supply water to the canal. The Canal Company paid him £1535-3s-0d. The canal opened in August 1794 and the building of the first warehouse on Cromford wharf began in that year. It is the building now known as 'the gothic warehouse' (see Figure 94).

The construction engineers for the canal were William Jessop and Benjamin Outram. Jessop had encouraged the venture by pointing out that 'at one end of the line was a country populous, rich in its mines, but barren on its surface; wanting for the support of its inhabitants two of the most necessary articles of life – corn and fuel; at the other end it gets into the heart of a country abounding in coal and communication with a canal and river which runs through a fertile vale that would be immediately benefitted by the lime of Derbyshire, the quantity of which is inexhaustible'. This is a reminder of Arkwright's principal interest in the canal, which was not in the advantage it offered for his mill business but in the potential for exporting lime from the area though it was his son who was to benefit from this trade. In his list of canal wharfs with lime kilns Farey includes Cromford and adds 'a great deal of Lime was dug here in the first rock for some years after the Canal was completed, but the principal Quarries nearly in front of Mr Arkwright's House are now shut up: its price here is, I believe, 10d per horse-load of three heapt [sic] bushels'. This would be burnt lime. None of the Cromford kilns has survived. Richard Arkwright junior also advertised limestone from Scarthin Rock for sale at the wharf in 1795.

> **LIMESTONE,**
>
> FROM Scarthin, Rock, belonging to RICHARD ARKWRIGHT, Esq, of a superior Quality, free from any Intermixture of Chirt, to be SOLD at Cromford Wharf at 13d per Ton.
>
> The Tonnage upon Limestone from Cromford to the Erewash and Nottingham Canals, 14½ miles, is 10d. per Ton.
>
> Apply to Mr. KIDD, or J. UNWIN, Wharfinger, both of Cromford.

Derby Mercury, May 21st, 1795

There is no doubt that the construction of the canal compromised the setting of Arkwright's home, Rock House. The canal and wharf would be an interruption in the sweep of land down from the house towards the river which contributed to the park-like landscape setting of the house. But he was able to recognise one personal advantage, the opportunity to have a boat on the canal. It was a benefit he would not reap, for as with Willersley Castle and his chapel, Arkwright was not destined to see the project completed. It was to be succeeding generations, Richard, then Peter, and their large families who were to enjoy the use of the boathouse built into the corner of the canal winding hole at the foot of Rock House garden. In 1837 Peter's sixteen year old son Augustus Peter, who, at an early age had been sent to make a career in the navy, wrote nostalgically to his father from H.M.S Barham in Malta harbour 'How does that old boat of my grandfather's get on do you still go a-pleasuring in her'. Augustus achieved the rank of Commander in the navy and later became M.P. for North Derbyshire.

The agreed supply of water to the canal was 'water from and after same had fallen over the basin between the two mills of the said Sir Richard Arkwright by a trunk underground to the head of the said canal so as not to injure or prejudice the mills of the said Sir Richard Arkwright'. In other words water was piped from the Cromford Mill basin to run under the road and behind the office or 'counting house' which stood at the entrance to the wharf before crossing the wharf to empty into the canal opposite where, soon afterwards, the 'gothic' warehouse was built. This arrangement in part accounts for the unusual shape of the counting house building which has been squeezed in between the line of the pipes, (later culvert) and the wharf gates. The office was later extended outside the wharf. When, in 1795, the Company deemed 'the Pipes' to be inadequate, 'not capable of carrying one half of the water which the Company are entitled to take' Richard Arkwright junior offered an alternative scheme. The Company's précis of the plan was that Mr Arkwright would make 'a navigable communication between the Canal and his limestone rock at Cromford which may also carry the water of Cromford Sough into the Canal'. The rock was 'behind the house of Debanke'. It is not known where Debanke lived but it may have been one of the cottages which stood close to the site later occupied by the mill manager's house. The plan was not implemented; the sharing of the costs of the scheme was not agreed. But the need to increase the water supply to the canal remained and it is thought that the solution was to adopt the plan recommended by Mr Outram, the engineer, to replace the pipes with a culvert. Whether it was Outram's plan or another, a culvert was certainly built; evidence for it on the wharf was found during recent excavations beside the wharf counting house. It is not clear whether any part of this water course which followed the line now marked by the counting house's southern wall emerged from the culvert before it joined the main canal or whether it remained below ground.

It was a plan proposed by Benjamin Pidcock to exploit the adjacent mineral wealth which gave the canal wharf its final form with the creation of what became known as the feeder arm. In 1819 Benjamin Pidcock began negotiations with the Canal Company and Peter Arkwright, then in residence at Rock House, to construct a branch from the canal basin to convey stone from his quarry which was situated behind the mill manager's house on Mill Lane. Pidcock was granted permission in November 1819 'having provided an estimate of the expense of making that part of it which will lead from the Canal near Mr Peter Arkwright's Boathouse to Mr Wheatcroft's Counting House amounting to £250 and undertaking at his own expense to make and compleate [sic] the whole of the proposed Cut and to erect such a fence as Mr Arkwright shall require and in all respects to perform the work to the satisfaction of the Agent of the Company on receiving £130 from the Coy towards such expense'. Sanderson's map published in 1835 and the Cromford Tithe map of 1841 show the watercourse passing under the drive to Rock House from Mill Lane, the Tithe map designating the area behind the mill manager's house as a quarry. The new cut terminated in what is now the garden of the Mill Manager's house, adjacent to the quarry at a wharf. Oral evidence has confirmed the existence of the wharf now buried deep under the garden.

Part of the waterway survives beside Mill Lane and it is possible that the cast iron stanchions there, some of which have recently been recast, are those which Mr Arkwright approved for the new fence. From 1821 the culvert which carried the agreed water supply to the canal from the mill basin to the head of the canal was remodelled to feed more directly under Mill Lane to join Pidcock's cut. This is confirmed by the date 1821 carved in the stone where the culvert joins the cut. The date on the first stone post near this point, now almost obliterated, is also 1821.

Pidcock's arm is narrow and though it widens as it turns at right angles between the entrance to the wharf and the rock, its size and the potential clearance under Rock House drive indicate that conventional canal boats could not have been used. More likely Pidcock used tubs which could be lifted by crane to boats at the canal wharf. Such a system was not unknown on the canal network. No further reference to Pidcock's commercial activity here has been found.

Late in 1823 Nathaniel Wheatcroft made an application to build a warehouse beside the new arm. Mr Arkwright's permission was to be obtained first then details were to be agreed with Mr Martin, the Company's Agent. The annual rent was fixed at one guinea for a term of 14 years and Wheatcroft was to expend not less than £300 on a building two storeys high erected in a substantial and workmanlike manner and to keep it in good repair. This is the building now in use as a restaurant.

Cromford Colour Company bought the wharf from British Waterways some time before 1938 with the intention of re-locating their Cromford, Via Gellia, Bonsall and Matlock Dale works there. This plan was not implemented though the company did occupy the site and made use of some buildings on the wharf. In 1974 Derbyshire County Council purchased Cromford Canal Wharf and the Cromford to Ambergate section of the canal. The wharf is now leased by the Arkwright Society; the buildings, walls and surface have been repaired.

The Cromford to Ambergate canal lies within the Derwent Valley Mills World Heritage Site, the longest length of canal in England to be included in a World Heritage Site. From Cromford to Ambergate it is designated a Site of Special Scientific Interest and from What-standwell to Ambergate a Local Nature Reserve. The towpath has become a much used and attractive pedestrian link to High Peak Junction and the High Peak Trail. Since 2002 the Friends of the Cromford Canal have been working towards the preservation and restoration of the entire canal between Cromford and its junction with the Erewash Canal at Langley Mill. From 2013, following dredging of the canal by Derbyshire County Council, a traditional narrow boat, purchased by the Friends, will operate from Cromford wharf to carry passengers to High Peak Junction, the Leawood Pumphouse and Jessop's spectacular aqueduct across the River Derwent.

FIGURE 94. **Cromford Canal terminus, Cromford Wharf, photograph, 1942.**

In its heyday the wharf was strictly regulated with incoming and outgoing goods stored on separate sides of the canal and space allotted to dealers in coal or timber or stone in proportion to the trade they carried. Boats were loaded or unloaded in order as they arrived. By the time this photograph was taken traffic on the canal was limited to coal from Hartshay near Ripley and the use made of the Nightingale arm by the Lea lead works. The canal was effectively closed to through traffic since the Butterley Tunnel collapsed in about 1900.

The Canal Company appointed John Unwin of Wirksworth as the first clerk at the wharf. He began work in May 1794 and almost immediately was given the job of supervising the erection of the warehouse shown here and the construction of a weighing machine. The warehouse was to be '60 feet long, covered with heavy Welsh slate and with a counting house in the south west corner'. In fact it appears that the counting house was set up in the south east corner (or perhaps it moved); certainly the archaeological evidence places it there and on this basis the counting house window is the upper window shown in the photograph. From this vantage point the incoming wharf could be seen and supervised. The crane lifted goods from the boats into the warehouse to await onward transport. The doors on each floor of the building on the eastern side were used to unload goods onto carts. The Wheatcroft brothers German and Nathaniel leased the warehouse from the Canal Company from 1815. When they divided their business in 1823, German retained the use of this warehouse. In the same year Nathaniel built the other warehouse on the wharf, (just visible on the left of this view) for his use.

The weighing machine appears to have been at work by February 1795 when it was agreed that a penny per ton should be charged on loads being weighed. The Canal Company showed forward thinking with this development as by 1798 it was determined to erect a number of Weighing-Houses on canals where previously the *Derby Mercury* reported 'the quantity of weight allowed to be a Ton, varied at almost every Coal-wharf or place of loading Coals'.

How the wharf was won!

The correspondence between some of the principal promoters of the Cromford Canal, now in the Gell collection in the Derbyshire Record Office, reveals the tortuous debate which heralded the establishment of the northern terminus of the canal. The promoters preferred location was below the rocky outcrop on which Rock House was built and they thought Sir Richard Arkwright agreed with them. But in April 1789 as the Canal Bill was in the final stages of preparation for consideration in the House of Lords they increasingly despaired of him. This was the

FIGURE 95. **The Birdswood at Cromford wharf, August 2013.**

The narrow boat shown here was built by W J Yarwood & Sons in Cheshire and began its working life in 1938. Soon after retirement from carrying goods in 1972, it was converted to a people-carrying trip boat, a use which will continue at Cromford in the hands of the Friends of Cromford Canal.

Friends of Cromford Canal

man they had thought would be their figurehead whose influence among the lords would be decisive. Sir Richard had several grievances. He complained the canal would destroy Rock House garden; the canal horses would 'eat all the meadow up' and spoil the roads in Cromford. It seemed he had turned his back on an earlier agreement and wanted Jessop, the canal engineer, to 'contrive some other spot'. Soon after, an alternative began to emerge though not one which had Jessop's support. Sir Richard would not have 'the Basin' [the wharf] on the Green 'where the Calamy things are' because he wanted to build there. The correspondence does not identify what was to be built but we may assume it was the chapel. Instead he favoured a basin 'on the right of the road'. This proposal placed the route of the canal close to the river with the Basin adjacent to the remains of the Bridge Chapel. Jessop declared the plan 'quite impracticable'

but Sir Richard would not give way and by 30th April was proposing to take water for the canal from the Masson Mill weir via an aqueduct running along the hillside or as Gell describes it 'under the new Mansion', Willersley Castle, and so to the Basin. Mill owners lower down the Derwent were not in favour of taking water from the river. Jessop and Fletcher, the canal surveyors, reluctantly agreed the scheme would be possible though the weir would have to be raised by 16 feet. It is difficult to believe that such a plan was ever seriously considered but it found favour with Gell for a reason which was far from obvious. With remarkable prescience he foresaw the ultimate disadvantage of a water supply to the canal from the Cromford Mills. This was Cromford Sough water available to the Canal Company on the one day a week it was not in use to drive the mills. In Gell's words 'he [Arkwright] stops Cromford Sough every Sunday himself to fill the Dam above the Black Dog [the Greyhound] and the Sough will at a future time be drained by the Birchwood Sough'.

In the event the published plan which accompanied the Canal Bill, contained both proposals, the original described as 'line first proposed', the more northerly route as 'line proposed laterly [sic]'.

It was the middle of July before the Bill was finally passed. Sir Richard had played his part exercising 'a great influence among the Scottish Peers for his deeds in the North'. But the Gells were not likely to forgive him for his earlier intransigence. Capt. Gell writes 'I cannot see we need raise Sir Richard's weir for him as he wants it and us to do it for him'. It is not recorded in the Gell correspondence why the planned northern basin was given up in favour of the original site but there are surely several compelling reasons. The plan to raise the Masson weir and bring water to a canal basin beside the bridge would have been disruptive to the operating of Masson Mill and extremely expensive and, seen from the new Mansion house, unsightly, though not perhaps to Sir Richard who, in May, had threatened to build his own private canal to move limestone from 'opposite the meeting house' [this would be Need's Chapel, later Glenorchy Chapel, close to Masson Mill] to join the Cromford Canal. The northern basin plan led Jessop to comment wryly that the raised water levels would turn the meadows into water meadows. But apart from the expense and the technical problems the other consideration may have been Sir Richard's change of focus. He believed that soon he would be living in the new Mansion house and not Rock House, the garden of which could be sacrificed. In May 1789 Sir Richard agreed to the sale of his land and to the provision of a water supply from the Cromford Sough.

The Wheatcrofts

The construction of the Cromford Canal provided an opportunity which Abraham Wheatcroft and his family from Crich grasped resolutely, using it to develop a range of commercial enterprises, as boat builders, wharfingers, merchants and carriers of goods by canal, road, and later rail to many destinations in England. Abraham's sons and their sons, sons-in-law and relations found roles in the many Wheatcroft businesses. As the rush to build canals spread over the country, the Wheatcroft's offered a service not only from Cromford but also from the many other wharves and depots where Wheatcroft offices had been opened.

Abraham (1747-1812) himself became a boat owner and boat builder and by 1802 is known to have owned nine boats. His son Samuel (1775-1865), a wheelwright, became a boat builder working from a site near Whatstandwell Bridge. Samuel's original trade indicates how the skills that were available locally were adapted to launch this new industry in the district. There cannot have been many existing boat builders in the area at this time. Another son Nathaniel (1777-1862), perhaps began working with his father but had moved to Cromford by 1798 and his reference to his forty years in business when he retired in 1841 suggests he had set himself up independently by 1801; by 1803 he had fourteen boats. The earliest advertisement so far found for his business of May 28th, 1804 is his announcement 'to his friends and the public, that he has lately established a new covered boat, to work regularly every week betwixt Derby and Cromford'. The boat was to leave Cromford on Tuesday afternoon and arrive in Derby on Thursday afternoon; the return journey was to take from Friday afternoon to Monday morning. That the boat was covered implies that it could carry a variety of goods and not only cargoes of a single product such as coal or stone as many of the early boats were designed to do. In 1794 Abraham's eldest son German (1773-1841) was the wharfinger at Bugsworth Basin near New Mills in north west Derbyshire, the first paid employee of the Peak Forest Canal Company. After his dismissal in 1809 he formed a partnership with his brother Nathaniel at Cromford where they leased the Canal Company warehouse in 1815; they had also built a warehouse at Buckland Hollow, near Ambergate, in 1813. Their partnership was dissolved in 1823 and subsequently they formed separate partnerships with their own sons, with widespread long distance carrying becoming the more important business for German and merchant trading for Nathaniel.

CROMFORD.

AT the Cromford Canal Company's Warehouse there is a Twigen BASKET, containing sundry Articles, with the direction defaced. The owner by describing the contents, and paying the charges, may have their own again by applying to HENRY CUTTS, at the Navigation Office, Cromford.

If the same is not owned within 14 days from the date hereof, the contents will be sold to defray the expence that is against them.

25th March, 1805.

Derby Mercury, March 28, 1805

Some idea of the scale of German's enterprise is indicated by the terms of the Deed of Co-Partnership for Messrs German Wheatcroft and Sons, dated May 22nd 1826. German was described as a wharfinger and general carrier at Birmingham, Nottingham, Buckland Hollow and other places and employing capital amounting to £16,000. He offered a seven year partnership to his three eldest sons Alexander, William and David; the youngest son Abraham was too young to be a partner. The prospective partners already worked for their father, managing wharves and warehouses at Nottingham, Birmingham and Buckland Hollow respectively and the terms of the agreement directed them to continue to reside where they were and to send monthly accounts to German at the Counting House at Cromford Wharf. The company would pay £200 a year rent to German for the houses, warehouses and stables belonging to him at Buckland Hollow, Chesterfield and Sheffield. The illustrated advertisements, shown here, give an indication of the countrywide extent of their operations and the variety of transport used in the business.

Nathaniel Wheatcroft formed Nathaniel Wheatcroft and Son with his son, John. The *Derby Mercury* of February 25th, 1835 reported John's death in an accident on Cromford Wharf and it was John's son, also called Nathaniel, to whom Nathaniel senior transferred the business in 1841, retaining only the use of the upper floor of the wharf warehouse at Cromford, which he had built and for which he continued to pay half the rent to the Canal Company, leav-

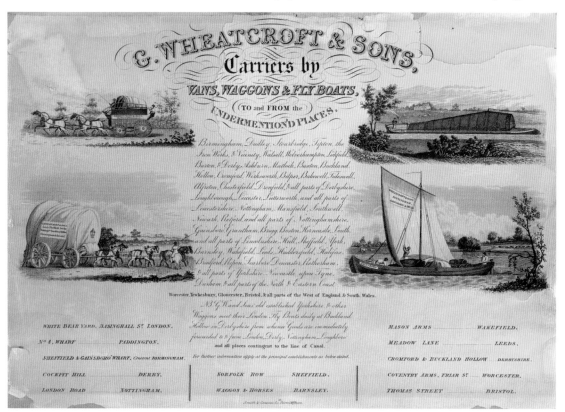

FIGURE 96. G Wheatcroft & Sons, letter heading, bill poster or handout published by Smith & Greaves of Birmingham, 1820s.

The 'undermentioned places' advertised here cover Warwickshire, Derbyshire, Staffordshire, Lincolnshire, Nottinghamshire, Yorkshire, Newcastle upon Tyne, Durham and all parts of the West of England and South Wales. The NB draws attention to: 'G W & Sons' old established Yorkshire and other waggons meet the London Fly Boats daily at Buckland Hollow in Derbyshire where goods are immediately forwarded to and from London, Derby, Nottingham, Loughborough and all places contingent to the line of the Canal. Fly boats were express boats which ran day and night - sometimes to a timetable.

Reproduced by permission of The Waterways Archive, Gloucester

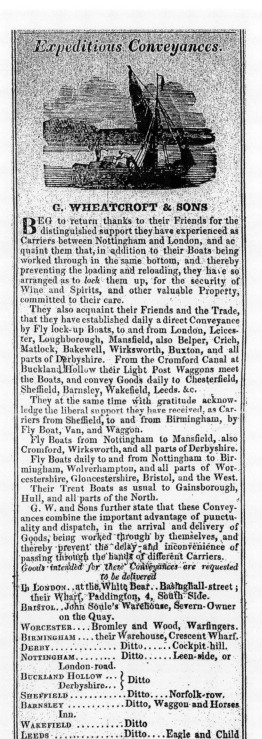

Nottingham Herald, January 18th, 1826

ing the ground floor for his grandson. He had other business interests and his will of 1860, made two years before his death, refers to substantial property in Scarthin and further afield. This included farms, silk mills at Draycott and Derby, a corn mill at Ashover and 'eight houses and a wharf with Dock Cooper's Shop Blacksmith's Shop and Croft' at Bull Bridge, part of which was occupied by his nephew, Samuel's son Abraham. At the time of Abraham's death in 1872 this was described as 'for the build ing of Canal Boats'.

The most important product coming in to Cromford wharf from an early date was coal and any description of Nathaniel's business always included coal merchant. In the *Derby Mercury* of February 6th, 1806, along with Samuel Wragg, who also worked from Cromford Wharf, he gave notice that they were appointed by the Proprietor of 'Swanwick and Summercotes Coals' as the only retailers of his coals at the wharf. Other coal merchants including those 'Coal Higlers or Carriers' who 'made a practice of taking Coals of inferior Quality and sell ing them again for Swanwick Coals' now had to show 'a Ticket from the Cromford Machine' to guarantee their wares. Stone and lime were important outgoing cargoes. Corn, timber, brick, slate, salt, straw and cheese, the speciality of cheese merchant Abraham Wheatcroft, another of John's sons, were some of the other products trad ed through the wharf.

Dealing in chert appears to have become an important strand of the business and this was no doubt associated with Nathaniel's twice weekly boat service to the Potter ies. Chert was used to grind flint to a fine powder for use in the production of white pottery and the best chert was quarried

WANTED IMMEDIATELY,
Upon the Cromford Canal,

A CARPENTER; one that is well skilled in making and hanging Lock Gates. Such an one, being a good Workman, may meet with constant Employment and good Wages by applying to HENRY CUTTS, Cromford Wharf, Derbyshire.—A single Man will have the preference.
Cromford Wharf, 4th June, 1811.

Derby Mercury, June 6, 1811

or mined around Bakewell, a business in which Nathaniel senior had interests. Blocks ranging from three quarters to two and a half tons in weight were transported to the Potteries and though it was a longer trip via Cromford, the canal route avoided the gradients on the more direct overland journeys from Bakewell. Sometimes this required as many as ten horses to pull a single load whereas from Cromford a canal boat could carry several wagon loads at a time. In the transfer of his business Nathaniel senior pledged 'not to carry on the business of coal merchant or dealer in timber tiles slate and chert either at Cromford or anywhere else' so the Nathaniel listed as a chert dealer at Endcliff Quarry, Bakewell in 1852 is likely to have been his grandson.

With the development of the Cromford and High Peak Railway after 1831 the Wheatcrofts' 'boldly utilised' this new form of transport for the development of the various branches of their business and later Nathaniel junior also had depots and wharves on the Matlock to Buxton, and the Wirksworth railway lines. Messrs German Wheatcroft and Sons became the principal freight carrier on the Cromford and High Peak Railway when it opened and in 1833 contracted to carry passengers though this was a short lived arrangement. David Hodgkins in

To TANNERS, BOAT BUILDERS, WHEEL-WRIGHTS, FARMERS, TURNERS, &c. &c.

TO BE SOLD,
In the Wood called CRICH CHASE, near Hotstandwell Bridge, in the County of Derby ;

A Large Quantity of fine OAK BARK, OAK TIMBER (particularly adapted for Wheelwrights, Boat Builders, &c. &c.) Poles, Stakes, Bindings, &c. &c.
The Sale to commence on Wednesday the 7th January, 1824, when attendance will be given in the Wood, and continued every succeeding Wednesday till the whole is sold.
For further Particulars apply to N. WHEATCROFT and SON; Cromford.
Cromford, 5th Jan. 1824.

Derby Mercury, January 4, 1824

his recent history of the Cromford and High Peak Railway states that in 1842 the railway company categorically told the Board of Trade that passengers were not carried on the line.

After 1841 when the Manchester, Buxton, Matlock and Midlands Junction Railway reached Ambergate and before the line was extended to Rowsley in 1849, parties of day trippers sometimes hundreds strong, alighted at Ambergate en route to Matlock Bath and the canal offered them an alternative to walking the next leg of their journey as far as Cromford. *Stephen Mann, Sketches and Reminiscences,* 1854 recalled his trip in 1844 on 'large boats supplied with seats' in which 'we floated past many a boat and warehouse where the eternal name of Wheatcroft appeared conspicuous'.

German Wheatcroft died in 1841 just at the beginning of the era when main line railways began to compete with canals. He had purchased Wingfield Park Farm at Buckland Hollow in 1827 and rebuilt the farm house as his home, renaming it Wingfield Park. After his widow's death their son David lived there until his death in 1864. When it was sold in 1872 it was described as a commodious mansion with 350 acres of land; the ornate entrance lodge, designed by Sir George Gilbert Scott, survives beside the Chesterfield Road at Buckland Hollow.

To BOAT BUILDERS.

WANTED two steady good Workmen, who may have constant employment and wages according to merit, on application to NATHANIEL WHEATCROFT & SON, Cromford, Derbyshire.

Derby Mercury, January 25, 1826

Soon after their father's death, Abraham, Alexander and David began to break up Messrs German Wheatcroft and Sons. Grahame Boyes in the *Journal of the Railway and Canal Historical Society* notes that William had withdrawn earlier to pursue quarrying interests near Wirksworth; he lived in Middleton by Wirksworth. Alexander stayed in Nottinghamshire and became a farmer. Abraham died the year after his father and David and William pursued other business interests. Locally, the most important of these was stone quarrying, in which all four had been involved at different times developing sites close to the Cromford and High Peak Railway. David, still using the name G Wheatcroft and Son, continued to trade in stone and had a stone and marble factory at Sawmills near Ambergate. He leased the Hopton Wood quarry and formed a company the Hopton Wood Stone Company Ltd in 1857 which managed William's quarry near Middleton, his own Hopton quarry and the Sawmills' factory. Both he and William were directors of the company.

Of the other branch of the family, the last to own the firm N Wheatcroft and Son was the founder's great grandson Henry (see also page 26). His partnership with his brother John Adams Wheatcroft was dissolved in 1884, two years after the death of their father Nathaniel. Henry, like his father, lived at Willersley Cottage; he died there in 1912. His obituaries in the *Derbyshire Times* and the *High Peak News,* remind us that the firm became 'one of the largest carriers and general merchants in the Midlands, if not in England' and that it was 'no uncommon sight to see a line of vehicles from the wharf to the Market Place'.

PARTNERSHIPS DISSOLVED.

Alexander Wheatcroft, David Wheatcroft, and Abraham Wheatcroft, of Bull bridge, Derbyshire, stone and marble quarriers.

Alexander Wheatcroft and David Wheatcroft, of Buckland Hollow and Cromford, Derbyshire, and of Birmingham, Sheffield, and Nottingham, wharfingers and general carriers.

James Dixon, William Frederick Dixon, James Willis

From the London Gazette of Friday, February 4th, published in the Sheffield and Rotherham Independent, 12th February, 1842

The canal had effectively closed to through traffic by 1900 because of the collapse of the Butterly Tunnel and a lack of water at the southern end but two firms, Messrs Wheatcroft and Dawes, continued to transport coal from Ripley Colliery and sell it from Cromford wharf. Nathaniel Wheatcroft and Son, continued in the coal trade even after the canal finally closed in 1944 and remained in business until the 1970s. The company signboard survives on Cromford wharf though not in its original and proper place on the counting house. It is a nostalgic reminder of an extraordinary family enterprise.

The Cromford and High Peak Railway

The Cromford and High Peak railway was proposed in 1824 as a solution to the problem of moving heavy or bulky goods over the high ground which separated the Cromford Canal terminus from Manchester. The Act of Parliament needed to put the plan into action was passed in 1826. The railway linked the canal at High Peak Junction, Cromford to the Peak Forest Canal at Whaley Bridge and the entire length was open by 1831 with Messrs German Wheatcroft and Sons as the carriers. In 1837 chains were fixed 'at or near the roads or ways leading from the turnpike to the Wharf of the Cromford & High Peak Railway Company' where. the Cromford to Belper Turnpike Trust collected tolls from users of the wharf.

The railway was constructed in a series of steep inclines linked by level stretches. A stationary steam engine at the top of each incline moved a continuous loop of chain to which the wagons were attached; at first horses and later steam locomotives pulled the trains along the level sections. At different times and on different sections of the line wire rope or hemp rope was used instead of chain. The *Derby Mercury* of February 3rd, 1841 describes the first engine to replace 'animal power', built under the direction of Mr Leonard, the Superintendant of the line, 'now plying with triumphant success' but other accounts of the history of the line report that locomotives were supplied earlier. Whatever its motive power, the line brought hitherto isolated areas of the countryside within reach of the railway and as a consequence a number of quarries and lime works opened near to it and hired its wagons to move their products. Other goods were carried including coal, iron, corn and water. Water, a scarce

**The Cromford and High Peak Railway (C&HPR),
early twentieth century.**

FIGURE 97 (left). The hangers on attaching a chain to the cable
to haul a locomotive tender up the incline.

FIGURE 98 (right). Wheel tapping at the bottom of Sheep
Pasture Incline for the London and North Western Railway.

Ref: Brunel University Transport Collection, Clinker Views nos. C110.2
and C110.5. Prints are available from W.R. Burton, 3 Fairway, Clifton,
York, YO30 5AQ

commodity in the dry uplands, was supplied to mobile tanks for the stationary engines and locomotives and also for domestic use in isolated communities.

The Wirksworth and Matlock Advertiser's report in March 1867 of a fire on the Cromford and High Peak railway is evidence that before the opening of the Midland Railway's main line to the Manchester area, cotton was also carried by this route. The fire, which was supposed to have 'originated from 'a spark from the engine chimney, destroyed almost a full truck of cotton bales, 'the property of Messrs Arkwright and Co'. In the early days raw cotton and thread had been transported by road, carried by pack-horses and later the canal played its part though cotton was never a large part of its business.

Soon after the railway line opened, passengers were carried on the goods trains though they were required to get out and walk up and down the inclines. The service was discontinued before 1842. By 1854 there was a new development; the account of 'a splendid trip' in September of that year reports that the proprietors had recently 'determined to put a passenger train on their line'. The writer, eager to try the service, began the journey at Steeple Houses and four hours and 32 miles later arrived at Whaley Bridge. The train was described as a single carriage 'admirably but plainly fitted up for the comfort of passengers' with seating for about sixteen inside and fourteen outside. It was pulled by a horse along the level stretches and by the stationary engines up the inclines but this time the passengers did not have to dismount. The traveller observed that by this date other railway lines had been built and taken over much of the heavy goods transport for which the Cromford and High Peak Railway (C&HPR) had been designed, commenting that 'it has reduced the traffic to almost a mere local one'.

The other railway line which had been built through Cromford was the Manchester, Buxton, Matlock, and Midlands Junction Railway (MBM&MJR) which was extended from Ambergate through Cromford to Rowsley in 1849. A connection was made between the two railways at High Peak Junction in 1853 but later in 1871 and 1887 respectively, they became the property of competitors; the Midland Railway Company bought the MBM&MJR and the London and North Western Railway Company bought the C&HPR and used part of it to complete a route to Manchester. The Cromford and High Peak Railway continued to decline in importance. The daily passenger service was closed down after an accident in 1877. The Middleton Top to Dowlow section of the line closed completely in 1967 and now is enjoyed by many walkers and riders as the High Peak Trail; the remainder of the line closed in 1973. The early railway workshops survive at High Peak Junction near Cromford and house a small museum which is open to the public.

From Our Iron Roads, 5th edition 1884, F S Williams

The High Peak Railway in Derbyshire was at one time one of the greatest thoroughfares of England. Travellers and merchandise came on to it from the Manchester district down to the Cromford Canal, and thence by the various navigations of the Erewash valley and the Soar to Leicester and the South. But these arrangements have been superseded, and a friend of the writer recently told of one of the last journeys taken by passengers on the High Peak Railway.

'It was in August, 1877' he said, 'and thinking I should like to see the country through which it passed, I went to Stonehouse, generally called 'Stonnis', just by the Black Rocks, where the railway crosses the Wirksworth road, and inquired of a man in the office for the train. 'Do you mean the "fly"?' was the reply. 'Yes'. But the official not knowing whether the 'fly' had passed or not, went out to inquire, and brought back word that it had gone, but that if I followed it up the line, I might catch it at the siding; and if not, I should be sure to overtake it at 'Middleton Run'. I accordingly gave chase, and at length, caught site [sic] of it being drawn up the incline by a rope and a stationary engine. A man at the bottom inquired if I wished to catch the 'fly', and added, 'I will stop it for you at the top', which he did by a signal. A quarter of a mile ahead I joined it. My fellow travellers were then a young woman and a child, and the vehicle in which we sat was like an old omnibus. The guard

stood in the middle and worked the brake through a hole in the floor. A locomotive now drew us up three or four miles to the foot of another incline, up which we were drawn by a rope. When reaching the summit the guard remarked: 'We may have to wait at the top'. 'How long?' I inquired. 'Oh it may be five minutes', he replied, 'or a few hours. It all depends on when the engine comes to take us on. Yesterday,' he added 'it did not come at all'. To while away the time I walked along the line, and my fellow passengers went mushrooming. In about three hours an engine came from Whaley Bridge to fetch us, and after the driver, fireman, and guard had refreshed themselves at a little public-house not far away, and had freely commented on their 'horse', they went back along the line, brought up the 'fly', and having refreshed themselves again, we started. At one part of the journey a flock of sheep were quietly feeding or resting on the line 'Just see them', said the guard as we approached, 'jump the walls'; and they did it like dogs. We reached Park Gates, about a mile from Buxton, at seven o'clock, after a journey of about twenty miles, in six hours. Not long after my journey, a traveller on this line was killed, and the Company decided to close it against passenger traffic. The High Peak may be seen as it joins the Midland Railway on the western side of the line in a wood a little north of Whatstandwell Station. Its summit level is 1,254 feet above the sea.

The Manchester, Buxton, Matlock and Midlands Junction Railway

The station at Cromford was for passenger use only at first and the regular traffic advertised in 1857 was '5 Passenger and 2 Luggage Trains each way daily, and on Sundays, 1 Passenger Train only'. For 19 years from 1852 the line was jointly leased by the Midland Railway Company and the London and North Western Railway Company (L&NWR). In 1869 the Midland Company, fearing that they might lose out to the L&NWR at the end of the lease, prospected an alternative route from Wirksworth to Rowsley. The proposed line would have

FIGURE 99. **Cromford Railway Station, postcard, about 1905.**

On the right hand side in this view of Cromford's elegant railway station is the station master's house in the background and the up line waiting room on the platform on the right of the track, both designed by G H Stokes and built by the railway company in about 1855 and 1860. Stokes had worked in France in the 1850s with his father-in-law, Joseph Paxton, where they designed and built a house at Ferrières near Paris for Baron James de Rothschild; French influence is evident in Stokes' work here at Cromford. The house which originally was a two up, two down building was extended to the rear in 1911. Both buildings are now in private ownership.

By 1874 the then owners of the line, the Midland Railway Company, had procured land adjacent to the station on the opposite side of the track where a new entrance road and the down line building shown here on the left were constructed. In 1885 the Butterley Company was commissioned to supply the ironwork for the footbridge linking the platforms. Previously passengers crossed the track on a wooden walkway but as the lines became busier with both passenger and goods traffic this route was considered to be too dangerous.

Private collection

come through the hill from Wirksworth to a station sited a little higher up and across the road from North Street, then over the Cromford Corn Mill pond on a viaduct before skirting around the valley side at high level to plunge into the hillside again on the Heights of Abraham at Matlock Bath. The scheme was not required; the L&NWR gave up its lease and in 1871 the Midland Railway negotiated sole ownership of the Ambergate to Rowsley line.

In 2009 the station building on the down line which belongs to Network Rail was restored by the Arkwright Society as office accommodation. In the same year the privately owned up line building on the right hand side of the picture was converted for use as a holiday cottage. Trains still stop at Cromford station and the Matlock to Derby service was, in 2011, one of the three fastest growing rural passenger routes in the UK. Ultimately, if the number of visitors travelling to Cromford by train grows large enough, the station will become a Derwent Valley Mills World Heritage Site portal.

The country station master

The construction of such a fine building as the residence shown in Figure 99 for a country station master at Cromford, is likely to have impressed and at the same time confused Cromford society. How was this man to be received? David St John Thomas wrote of the 'classlessness' of such office holders in a 'highly stratified country society' citing Ernest J Simpson's testimony as to the social status of the early station masters who 'were for the most part supplied from the middle class of society, and able to hold their own in a gentlemanly way'. They were also dispensers and recipients of perks and patronage. 'The Jones' who don't associate with the Robinsons meet [at the station]. Mr Jones would not like the station master to touch his cap to Mr Robinson, and pass him without notice, so he sends the station master a hare. The Rev Mr Silvertongue is always wanting to take a party somewhere at single fare for the double journey, or some other concession, so he honours the station master by conversing with him as an equivalent for concessions... the doctor hopes to be sent for in case of a railway accident, so he is polite. 'My Lord' knows he has no right to bully at the railway station, so he brings a brace of pheasants and this adds Mrs Station Master to the train of his servants'.

How the Cromford station masters were regarded by the residents of Willersley Castle is not recorded.

Enlarged detail from G Wheatcroft & Sons advertisement

CHAPTER THIRTEEN

Cromford and the Lea Mills Strike

Cromford station was the scene of one of the most colourful episodes in the strike at Lea Mills in 1911-12. The strike had begun early in December 1911. The factory labour force was drawn from all the settlements around Lea including Cromford so the affair rapidly attracted widespread interest. Meetings supporting the strikers were held in Lea, Crich, Whatstandwell Tansley, Cromford, Matlock and Matlock Bath and the strikers marched to Wirksworth and to Matlock. In January the Lea Mills Prize Band played in Crown Square, Matlock and afterwards paraded the streets of Matlock and Tansley collecting money for the relief fund. From the beginning Councillor Charles Frederick White J.P., (1863-1923) formerly a boot and shoe maker in Bonsall but then living in Chapel Hill, Scarthin and well known locally as a recent Liberal Parliamentary candidate and the Liberal agent for the area, had taken an interest in employment matters at Lea Mills. It was he, or so he claimed, who had first encouraged some of the men of the

DEFINITION of a
BLACKLEG.

At a conspiracy trial the presenting counsel gave the following definition of a Blackleg :—

"A Blackleg is to his Trade what a Traitor is to his Country; although both may be useful in troublesome times, they are detested by all when peace returns; so when help is needed the Blackleg is the last to contribute assistance and the first to grasp the benefit he never laboured to secure. He cares only for himself; he sees not beyond the extent of a day; and for a monetary consideration he would betray his friends, family, and country. In short, he first sells the journeyman, and is himself afterwards sold in turn by his employer, until at last he is despised by both and deserted by all."

"All for each and each for all."

JOIN YOUR TRADES UNION AT ONCE.

FIGURE 100. **Poster or flyer produced in support of the Lea Mills strikers.**
Private collection

firm to form the branch of the union which J B Marsden Smedley, the owner of the firm and one of White's political opponents, refused to recognise. This was ostensibly the principal issue at the heart of the strike. Wherever there was a meeting or parade Charlie White took part and so it was on Monday January 15th 1912 at Cromford station.

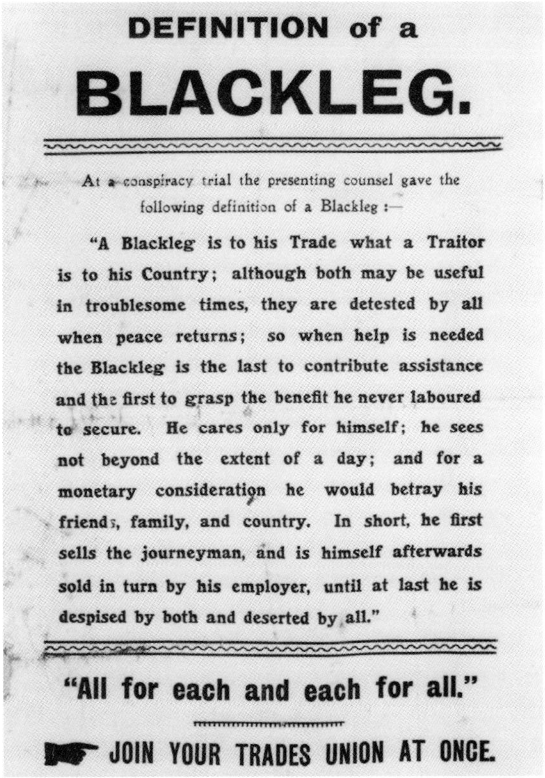

Smedley's had recruited strike breaking labour from outside the area and news reached the strikers that the 10.35 train from Loughborough would be carrying two of these work-

MATLOCK.

A PUBLIC MEETING

WILL BE HELD IN THE

—— ON ——

TOWN

Monday

HALL,

Next,

February

Matlock,

26, 1912,

—— WHEN ——

Mr. Chas. F. White, J.P., C.C.,

WILL GIVE AN ADDRESS

—— ON ——

"The Days We Live In and The Systems By Which We Are Governed, with Special Reference to his Recent Public Experiences."

THERE WILL ALSO BE SELECTIONS OF VOCAL & INSTRUMENTAL MUSIC.

A Hearty Invitation is given to the many people who have shown their practical sympathy with Mr. White in the trying ordeal he has passed through, so that he may publicly thank them for their kindness.

CHAIR TO BE TAKEN AT 7.45 P.M. PROMPT.

FIGURE 101. **Leaflet advertising Charles White's address, 1912.**

Private collection

ers, William Marvin and his daughter Laura, who had been home to Loughborough for the weekend. They were met by a horse drawn brake, sent by the Company to fetch them, and by strikers, numbering according to different accounts 60 or even 150, and by Charlie White.

Two events took place that day which made local headlines. One was the accident which practically destroyed the brake; the other the confrontation between Charlie White and the strike breakers which subsequently brought both parties into court in circumstances which could have terminated White's political aspirations. In fact, rather than causing him damage, his reputation as the local champion of the working man was enhanced. The strike propelled him one step nearer his ultimate goal of a parliamentary seat.

The driver of the brake, John Hawkins junior was in no doubt that as he was turning out of the station, one of the strikers had made a grab at the horse and it was this that had caused him to swerve across the road hitting the wall which stood between the road and the river so overturning the brake and throwing the passengers

FIGURE 102. **Striking workers, local newspaper photographs. December 1911.**
Private collection

onto the road. Mr Amatt, a member of the strike committee, blamed Hawkins who he said had whipped the horse and turned too sharply. In the event when the injuries were found to be no more than cuts and bruises and the conflicting evidence impenetrable, the Police declined to prosecute.

A different view was taken of White's behaviour. According to the evidence presented at the magistrate's court where he faced a charge of intimidation, White had been at the station to catch a train to Derby where he had County Council business and had not known that the Marvins were on their way until he met strikers in the road. Marvin claimed that White had greeted him 'in a very threatening manner' [wanting] 'to know what b........ train he was going back to Loughborough by', and reminding him that there was one coming in [going that way]. Asked what he had to do with it White said 'because you are not going to Lea Mills, if you do we shall chuck you in the .... river'. Miss Marvin intervened prompting White to say 'if you were a .... man I'd hit you in the .... mouth'. Luther Buttery of Rowsley, the relief signalman and acting station master at Cromford judged White's manner 'as not at all peaceable' and said 'he clenched his fists and ground his teeth' but he was not able to support Marvin's claims. His colleague, Joseph Pickering, a porter at the station confirmed that White had told the Marvins to return to Loughborough but added that Miss Marvin had told White 'You are the scum of the earth.' But despite the evidence of 21 witnesses many of them strikers (or perhaps because of their evidence, they were hardly unbiased bystanders), nearly all of whom contradicted Marvin's claim, the magistrates were unimpressed. Despite the hundreds who had gathered outside the court in Matlock to cheer their man and to boo the magistrates, White, their fellow magistrate, was committed for trial at the Assizes.

At the Assizes at Derby, a jury found White guilty but urged leniency, his actions not being premeditated. He escaped prison but was fined £20 which with prosecution costs awarded against him amounted to a penalty of over £200. His supporters, undaunted by the verdict, cheered him up St Mary's Gate and along Iron Gate. Within weeks the White Defence Fund had dealt with the debt.

Cromford's destiny as the administrative hub of the thirteen week long strike at Lea Mills was sealed as early as September 29th 1911 when four or five men met together to form the Lea Mills branch of the Hosiery Workers' Union. The meeting took place in Charlie White's house and as he lived in Cromford or more precisely Chapel Hill, Scarthin, the committee came to regard Cromford as their headquarters. Meetings were held in the Greyhound club-room and it was here that the first distribution of strike pay was made. A Courier reporter was on hand. 'One looked in vain for signs of grumbling or dissatisfaction. On every hand, one saw, instead that the operatives viewed the situation with great enthusiasm and unbounded confidence tempered by a deal of grim humour'. Many of the workers had trudged for miles through pouring rain and after they had received their money were 'hospitably entertained to cups of steaming hot tea in Mount Tabor Schoolroom'. When Christmas came the weekly rates were increased from 7/6d to 9/- for females and from 15/- to 18/- for males with an extra 1/- for married men for every child instead of the previous 1/- only. Where will the money come from the paper asked and answered its own question with a report of the band touring the county with 'gratifying' results. J B Marsden Smedley tried to persuade the bandsmen to return their instruments but they refused on the grounds they had received insufficient notice.

In Cromford as in other parts of the Lea Mills labour catchment the strike divided families and tempers were roused. Those who continued to work, 'the blacklegs', were 'tin-panned' – followed along the road to the mill by strikers carrying old tins and pans and banging them with sticks. Smedley's was forced to send a charabanc to collect its workers. It is clear that there was widespread support for the strikers but this was not always apparent from the local press which, while it gave them a fair hearing, included lengthy correspondence from those who supported Marsden Smedley, opposed Charlie White or doubted that good would come from unionisation. They feared a change to the old order of master and servant. The composition of the strike was in itself shocking to some observers in that the women and girls outnumbered the men and the boys by a wide margin. The company monitored the workforce week by week and its record for week one revealed that whereas 100 men and boys had joined the strike, the figure for women and girls was 316. A slightly different survey indicated that of 824 employees 466 were on strike and 358 remained loyal. Some parts of the works were decimated. What is described as Factory 3 was left with a labour force of 29 in place of the usual 138. The behaviour of the women was considered objectionable by at least one observer. These were the days before women had won the right to vote and action by them was regarded with suspicion. Did they understand the issues? Did they need to join the strike? What had they achieved asked one correspondent when the strike was about a month old? 'They have paraded the district in great pomp and made a great-to-do, openly insulted persons on the highway, and made themselves a nuisance generally, magnifying petty grievances into cases of tyranny, and belittling the privileges hitherto enjoyed at Lea Mills to the most minute and even microscopic dimensions.

26th Dec 1911

TO THE WORKERS OF LEA MILLS.

VICTORY IN SIGHT!

Fellow-workers :—

All sorts of promises and inducements will be held out to you to-day to return to work.

Turn a deaf ear to everyone but your Union leaders, who rely on you to stand firm.

Enjoy your holidays, and if from any cause funds run short, apply to your Union Secretary, and help will be forthcoming.

Continue to show the courage you have shown up to now, and in a very short time victory will crown your efforts.

Yours faithfully,

(Signed) H. BASSFORD, General Secretary;
    „ H. MILLWARD, Chairman;
    „ F. HALL, Secretary;
    „ W. AMATT, Relief Fund Secretary.

P. S.—
An Open-air Meeting will be held in the Market Place, Crich, at Mid-day, Wednesday, Dec. 27th.

Howling hordes of well-clad persons have hooted and booed helpless women and children; young ladies whose modesty would not have allowed them to be seen in the company of any inferior persons in daylight, roamed the streets at 10pm, without any apparent distinction, and made night hideous by joining the Rum Tum Bands, beating time upon tin pans with their fingers on which shone and sparkled rings of gold set with precious stones.'

The end came in early March 1912 when the strike pay had run out and the strikers agreed to accept the terms the company offered. Recriminations included blame for the union for poor tactics and weak leadership; and for the Derby Trades Council, accusations of interfering in a dispute which was none of its business. The company agreed to some increase in wages but did not recognise the union. Those deemed not to be ringleaders were taken back to work. But J B Marsden Smedley could not forgive the Lea Mills bandsmen for supporting the strikers and the band was broken up. Charlie White's reputation was enhanced.

From time to time in the public pronouncements he made during the Lea Mills strike Charlie White alluded to the legal disputes he had begun and which would soon be coming to court. The litigation, begun in 1911 but relating to incidents a year earlier, reached the High Court in March 1913. White accused the High Peak News of slander and Ernest Barnes of Matlock

Bath, a reporter working for that paper and Joseph Henry Rose, a former Cromford resident and a long standing political opponent, of libel. Barnes alleged that White had sat as a magistrate in a case concerning Mrs..... of whom Barnes had said '[White] slept in a field in the Via Gellia with her for a week when he was on the booze'. He also claimed 'White [had] run into a house naked and [had] been chased out by a woman with a poker'. Rose's claim had been in a political debate with White in Cromford schoolroom. 'If anyone does pub crawling it is Mr White' Rose said [he] 'spends freely and I know of his being frogmarched from the top and lying beside it' an event said to have taken place at Clatterway, Bonsall. The High Peak News, which until November 1910 had been a liberal paper supporting White but which had changed sides, published some of Barnes's material and so the editor found himself embroiled in the case.

The allegations questioned White's integrity, moral standards and sobriety and as the case unfolded the term pub-crawling revealed a sinister meaning. In making this charge Rose was accusing White of influencing voters by buying them drinks and, if true, of breaking the law.

White might have won the case but he found himself confronted by one of the greatest advocates of the day, Marshall Hall KC. In his concluding remarks Hall described White as 'one of the class of men who do more harm to the political life of this country than good [he was] a public danger'. The jury agreed. Losing the case cost White over £1000 and led to his bankruptcy and so to an enforced absence from public life. This changed in February 1918 when £200, said to have come from friends, secured his discharge so allowing him to stand as the Liberal candidate for West Derbyshire in the General Election later that year. He took the seat from the sitting member, the Earl of Kerry, brother in law of the Duke of Devonshire, by a handsome margin. In his maiden speech in the House of Commons he recalled starting his working life 'at 10 years of age for one shilling per week for a year, increased by another shilling, and so on, to sixteen years of age' so he claimed 'to know something of what the cottager's life is'. He retained his Parliamentary seat much less convincingly in the 1922 election. He died at his home, which by then was in Matlock, in 1923.

The Cromford vicar, the Reverend Hazlehurst, did not witness Charlie White's pre-war political activities, not having come to the village until 1915 but by 1923 he had seen enough to be able to deliver a characteristically even handed assessment of a man who for so many years had aroused in his followers the strongest loyalties and loathing among his adversaries. He wrote in the Church Magazine 'He was a good speaker, though he would be the last one to claim the title of orator. His gift lay in his power to persuade, and his appeal was more often to the heart than to the reason. For that very reason he was a dangerous foe politically, for it is only the inexperienced who fancy that elections are won by the force of logic. And behind his persuasive tongue Mr White was an untiring worker. When he helped a cause it was with all his enthusiasm and with an indefatigable brain. Had he not worked so hard he might have been with us still.'

CHAPTER FOURTEEN

The last Squire: the end of an era

Frederic Charles Arkwright

FIGURE 103. **Frederic Charles Arkwright, 1853 -1923.**

Arkwright Society collection

Frederic Charles Arkwright was the last resident Arkwright squire and the youngest to accede to the family's estates in Cromford, Mellor and Marple, the two latter acquired from the Oldknows, the outcome of the substantial funding Richard Arkwright junior had made available to them and which they were unable to repay. When he succeeded his father Frederic in December, 1874, he was just 21 and unmarried. His marriage to Rebecca Olton Alleyne on his thirtieth birthday, November 7th, 1883, at Hazlewood was the occasion of huge celebrations. They began in Cromford two days before the event when 'magnificently bound and richly illuminated addresses' were presented to the groom from 'the historic cotton factories at Cromford, Masson and Mellor'. John Edward Lawton, who, earlier in the year, had entered into a business partnership with Arkwright, described them as 'an inadequate but sincere expression of the good will and gratitude of five hundred people'. Mr Young and Mr Webster represented the 200 employees at Cromford and Masson and Mr Furniss the 300 work people at Mellor. They spoke of their indebtedness that 'at a considerable sacrifice you have for a long period found us work, thus continuing the generosity of your ancestors who kept the work people employed during the cotton famine caused by the American Civil War, when for years almost all the Lancashire operatives were dependent on outside help for their daily bread'. They expressed thanks for the recent improvements and 'valuable and judicious' capital outlay at the mills 'which have already materially improved our position and prospects' and hoped the result would be continuous prosperity to all concerned. In the evening other gifts were presented including a 'handsome silver tea tray' from the agents, tenants and workmen on the estates.

On the wedding day the Cromford estate and mill workers had a paid holiday, the school was closed, the church bells rang and cannon were fired. There was unlimited refreshment of which 'the workmen availed themselves largely'; the mill hands had an excellent tea followed by dancing at the Greyhound Hotel. In the evening the Drum and Fife Band paraded and on Allen Hill, witnessed by great crowds of spectators, there was 'the grandest display of fireworks ever seen in this district'. In May the following year in commemoration of their marriage, Mr and Mrs Arkwright 'gave a grand party at Willersley for all their tenants on their Marple, Mellor, Bonsall, Cromford, and other estates. For the convenience of those at Marple, special train arrangements with free tickets there and back were issued'. A thousand invited guests sat down to dinner in a specially erected marquee.

Frederic Charles Arkwright left an indelible mark on Cromford village. In his 49 year tenure he was to oversee the building of St Mark's Church and the Institute; he initiated and masterminded the alterations to St Mary's Church and the enlargement of the school; he gave the Vicarage to the Ecclesiastical Commissioners, guided the village through the First World War and defended the Meadows from industrial development.

As his workforce testified at his wedding, he also sought to secure employment for his tenants, facing up to the difficulty of making Masson Mill pay its way, something his father had considered in 1872 but failed to do. In 1880 he recruited John Edward Lawton, a cotton spinner, from Dukinfield and three years later the two men formed a partnership taking the name Arkwright and Company in which Lawton was

FIGURE 104. **Donkey Cart at Willersley Castle, July 1890.**

Frederic Charles Arkwright's snapshot taken at the terrace door of Willersley Castle, shows the young Frederic Arkwright, born October 1885 and his elder brother Richard, born September 1884.

Arkwright Society collection

the managing partner. Lawton's brief was to revive the fortunes of Masson Mill. He found it with archaic machinery, an unreliable power supply and uncompetitive products. He reported that it had been worked for many years past at a heavy loss explaining Arkwright's reason for having continued to run it in these words 'The sole influence which has operated in his mind has been a deep-rooted, inborn consideration for the people employed here; and an anxiety to promote the welfare of the district'.

Not all Lawton's efforts to modernise the business were successful. In 1884 he organised a sale of the 'ancient machinery' at Cromford Mill which attracted little interest. Two years

BY MR. ALLEN MELLOR.

CROMFORD MILLS, CROMFORD, DERBY-
SHIRE.

SALE of ANCIENT, ANTIQUE SPINNING,
DOUBLING and CARDING MACHINERY,
&c. &c., similar to that made by Sir Richard
Arkwright, in the year 1769, very suitable
for Museums, Exhibitions, and such like
purposes.

MR. ALLEN MELLOR respectfully an-
nounces the receipt of instructions from
Messrs. Arkwright and Company to prepare,
catalogue, and SELL by AUCTION, at
the above Mills, on WEDNESDAY,
August 27th, 1884, the following ancient
and interesting MACHINERY :—11 sets
of finisher carding engines, 6 sets of breaker carding engines, 34 finisher carding engines, 17
breaker carding engines, 20 carding engine frames
(in parts), 35 wood cylinders, 8 lengths of drawing frames, lap machine, two roller frames, 31
wood reels, three twisting Mills, doubling
machine, spooling table (for six heads), spool-
measuring machine (with table), two bundle
presses, old printing press (with type), wood and
iron shafting, pulleys and drums, quantity of
metal, old spindles and rollers, weigh beam and
scales, and a considerable quantity of stores,
sundries, &c. &c. These machines will be found
remarkably interesting to municipal corporations
and others, not only from their old associations,
but by way of comparison with the present
improved construction of cotton spinning
machinery.

Sale at Eleven (for Twelve) o'clock prompt.

Catalogues are in course of preparation, and
may be had seven days prior to date of sale upon
application to the AUCTIONEER, 21, Queen-street,
Oldham.

Derby and Chesterfield Reporter, 15th August, 1884

later in 1886 he resurrected an earlier company name Sir Richard Arkwright and Company. But he did much more than attempt to clear out the attic and rebrand the business. He set about solving the problems he had found.

In 1888, to supplement the water power, Lawton installed a steam engine which was christened Rebecca by Frederic Charles' wife Rebecca. Two years later he installed new machinery and brought in skilled operatives from Manchester who trained the local workforce to use it. Without neglecting the company's extensive overseas markets, the mill's main branded product – sewing thread – was concentrated on the new market for sewing machine thread serving the cheap and reliable sewing machines which had become available for home use. These developments secured the future of the mill and employment for local people. Many of these were Arkwright's tenants, and secure employment in turn promoted the well being of the Cromford community. The evidence has not survived that would determine whether the rent income from the houses occupied by mill workers in Cromford was a significant factor in Frederic's and then his son's acceptance of losses from the mill over so many years nor indeed the extent to which Lawton made the firm profitable.

The Arkwright family's association with Masson Mill came to an end with the formation of the English Sewing Cotton Company in 1897. Frederic Charles conveyed Masson Mill and the adjacent paper mill to the company for £33,504. Lawton had played a key role in the formation of the new conglomerate and held the position of Vice Chairman; his influence with the Board ensured that investment at Masson and in Belper and Milford would continue. Under the heading 'The Great Cotton Combine', the *High Peak News* of December 11th, 1897 described how the rush for shares in the company had resulted in an estimated £20 million being subscribed, of which £540,000 was believed to have come from the Matlock district. 'Mr J E Lawton, the Chairman of Matlock Bath Urban District Council' the paper reported 'has now earned the title of the "Cotton King". It is admitted in the cotton world that none but Mr Lawton could have succeeded in bringing the gigantic scheme of amalgamation to so successful an issue. The general public will never know the amount of work it entailed upon him and his coadjutors; for weeks they were travelling in railway trains night and day between Glasgow, Manchester and London. The project has taken thirteen months hard work on the part of Mr Lawton to bring it to its present position. His business acumen has produced what even the most sanguine held to be an impossibility twelve months ago..... Matlock Bath and Cromford will both benefit enormously.' F C Arkwright acting as one of 3 trustees for the debenture holders was said 'to inspire the utmost respect and confidence and speak volumes for the solidity and future prospects of the company.'

This account gives little indication of Frederic Charles's personal qualities or of his daily engagement with those around him whatever their social standing. Glimpses of him at work in the village emerge from the *Cromford Church Magazines*. For a time in 1922 he took a service for the men of the village on Sunday afternoons at St Mark's. This ran through the winter and was aimed at those who were not regular attenders at the other church services. He served as a churchwarden and subsequently on the Parochial Church Council and whenever there was a good cause to promote, for example money for the schools, he would take

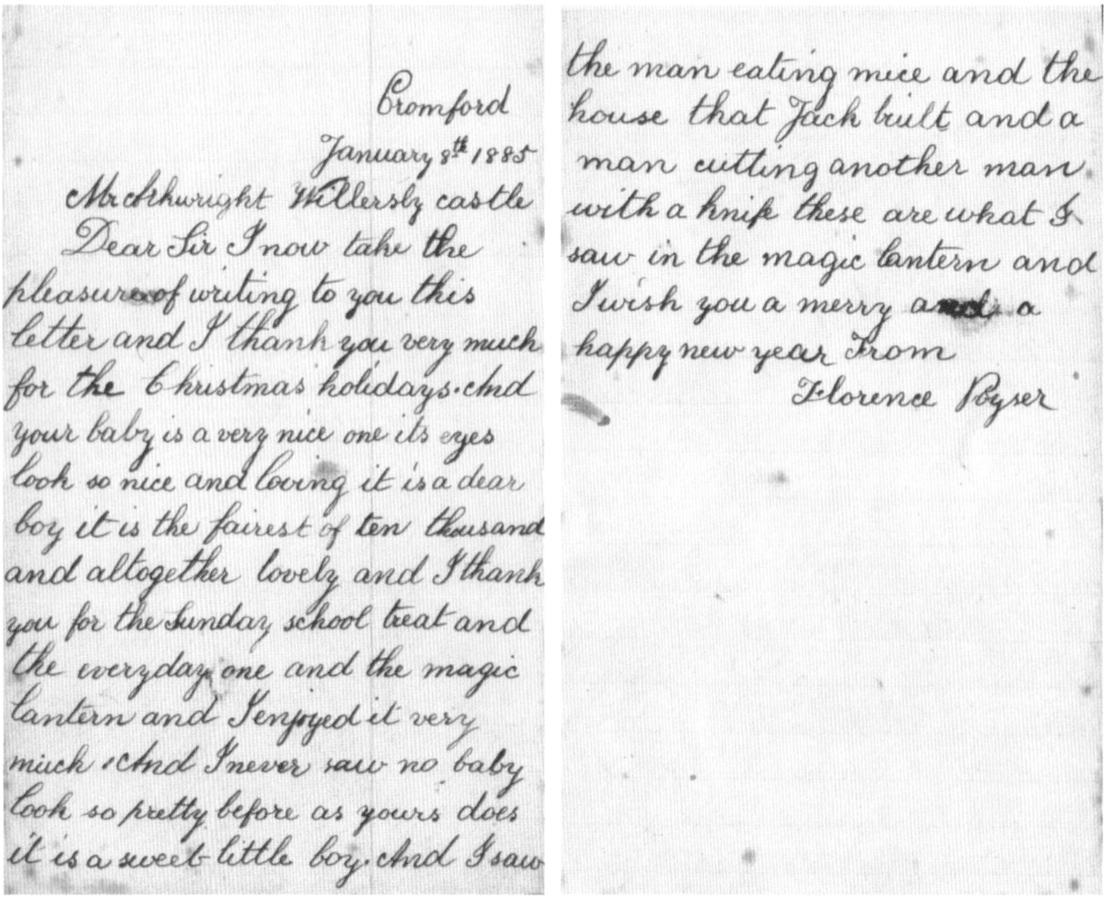

Cromford
January 8th 1885
Mr Arkwright Willersly castle
Dear Sir I now take the
pleasure of writing to you this
letter and I thank you very much
for the Christmas holidays. And
your baby is a very nice one its eyes
look so nice and loving it is a dear
boy it is the fairest of ten thousand
and altogether lovely and I thank
you for the Sunday school treat and
the everyday one and the magic
lantern and I enjoyed it very
much. And I never saw no baby
look so pretty before as yours does
it is a sweet little boy. And I saw
the man eating mice and the
house that Jack built and a
man cutting another man
with a knife these are what I
saw in the magic lantern and
I wish you a merry and a
happy new year from
Florence Pyser

FIGURE 105. **A schoolchild's letter.**

Arkwright Society collection

the lead. The Vicar, the Reverend Arthur Hazlehurst who had worked closely with the squire since his arrival in Cromford in February 1915, saw him as 'a father of his people'. As he wrote in July 1923, reflecting on the squire's death, 'one of the earliest memories I have of him occurred when he first brought my wife and myself up to the Vicarage, little Daphne Humphreys catching sight of him ran and threw her arms round his neck…when anyone was in trouble, there was always a friendly visit from the squire and anything he could do to help lift the burden he did at once'.

There are also reminders of the roles of Frederic Charles as the squire and of his wife Rebecca in surviving letters from schoolchildren written in response to their visit to the school to show the children their first baby, Richard Alleyne in 1884. Clearly there had been guidelines about what the letters were to say, not only about the baby but also about the treats enjoyed at other times of the year, races and cricket in the Willersley paddock and the magic lantern show at Christmas. Young Frank Adkin's closing advice to the family in his letter 'that all of you will enjoy the priviliges [sic] you have got around you and make use of them' appears to be his personal independent addition. The arrival of the baby had been greeted with festivities in the village which was decorated with flags, fairy lamps, garlands and a variety of banners proclaiming Welcome, Long life to the Heir and Here's Health to the House of Arkwright. A year later the members of the Mothers Meeting drew attention to the role of Mrs Arkwright in the community when they wrote to express their sympathy with her after the birth of her second son, Frederic, when it seems both mother and baby were unwell. The letter spoke of her kindness and of 'the interest you took in the Meetings when you so willingly took all the work yourself'.

The Arkwright family's role in World War I

During World War I, Frederic Charles Arkwright and his wife, Rebecca, played an active role contributing to and promoting the war effort in Cromford. They retained the use of two rooms at Willersley Castle while, for the period from October 1914 to March 1919, the rest of the house was used as a Red Cross auxiliary hospital. The undertaking was funded by the Arkwright family and Mrs Arkwright acted as Matron for which service she was awarded the Order of the Royal Red Cross in the Second Class in October 1917. The strain of the work looking after up to twenty patients at a time lead to a serious breakdown from which she was slow to recover. Her widowed daughter Kathleen, whose husband, Captain Guy Bonham-Carter, was killed in France in 1915, helped with nursing the wounded soldiers who were patients there. Later in 1915 the family suffered a further loss when Frederic Charles' and Rebecca's second son Frederic who served in the Royal Flying Corps was killed in a flying accident in Scotland.

The contribution which Frederic Charles Arkwright made to the war effort has been extensively recorded by Charles Berresford in his book *The Bath at War*, 2007. As a Deputy Lord Lieutenant of the County and on other occasions as a prominent Conservative, Arkwright chaired meetings throughout the district, sometimes imploring his listeners to encourage their young men to enlist, frequently raising money for causes such as the Belgian refugees living in the Matlocks or for comforts for the troops. In Derby in 1917 he launched the Tank

Bank to which he himself contributed £1000. The war for him was 'a crusade to prevent the domination of this barbarous foe'. His war work brought him company he must have found unfamiliar. Frequently he shared a platform with Charlie White who, following his prominence in radical politics and his role in the Lea Mills strike of 1911, was regarded by most local conservatives as a dangerous rabble rouser. White claimed that he, White, 'got more recruits than any man for the Army in the country'.

Taking the lead in public meetings would have been a sufficient contribution for most people in Arkwright's position but not for him. Somehow he was able to accommodate his campaigning within working weeks that included two long days in a Derby munitions factory from which we are told he returned on an evening train with hands sore and blistered. He also founded and joined the Cromford Home Guard and as 'Private Arkwright' he was required to drill with his unit three times each week at Cromford Mill or in the Meadows. 'Private White' was also a member.

In his personal life and as squire he set as good an example as in his other capacities. He gave up beer, wines and spirits and, he claimed, new clothes, for the duration of the war. He may not have been entirely serious about the clothes. He was a man with a sense of humour. The people of Cromford, his tenants, were kept informed of the wartime initiatives he wished them to support. So it was that his agent for the Willersley estate, William Barker, wrote to the domestic tenants 'if any tenant finds it impossible to set his garden, it must be arranged for someone who is willing to set it, and have it free of charge for the season...Any tenant unable to provide seed or manure should make application to the Estate Office'. His farm tenants were released from restrictions on ploughing grassland so that they might grow more feed crops for their cattle. Permission was also given to plough the Meadows to grow corn.

These were the actions of a patriotic landowner keeping step with the war effort. But the Cromford squire was one of a more select group who part-funded those enlisted from his own pocket. For the Cromford tenants this took the form of a concession to any family with a husband or son in the forces to live rent free until the war was over. The arrangement ran until January 1919; a local newspaper estimated it had cost Arkwright £3000.

Sale of the estate

Cromford's metamorphosis from estate village with a resident squire who relished his paternalistic role to an open community having to create its own leadership was brutally sudden. The old squire died in July 1923 and just a month later his heir, Captain Richard Arkwright, announced he would be selling the outlying farms and seeking a tenant for the Castle. But if that was the position at the end of August, by November it had become clear nothing short of the sale of the entire estate would meet the death duties Captain Richard faced. Early in 1924 the estate tenants were given the opportunity to purchase their properties.

The vicar, the Reverend Arthur Hazlehurst, writing in the *Church Magazine* in December 1923 looked ahead and reminded them that 'it will be a strange year for many of you, for

FIGURE 106. **Illustrations from the estate sale catalogue, 1924.**

Lot 256 The Greyhound Hotel. Lot 54 The Cromford Colour Mills.

you will be property owners for the first time, and when the tap starts dripping or the door hinges give way there will be no Estate workmen to send for, and you will experience the pleasure of being your own landlords and paying for repairs out of your own pockets. On the other hand, when once the purchase is complete there will be no rent to pay, though where borrowed money has been used its place will be taken by the interest, and the advantage will not be felt until the debt has been redeemed.' In January 1924, he added 'The cottages have been sold to the tenants at such nominal prices as have enabled the great majority to become their own landlords, whereas at a public auction they would have realised at least half as much again.' The three storey North Street houses sold for £50 each. In 1924 that part of the village which remained unsold was offered for sale.

By 1925, the family had decided not to return to Willersley and the Castle and its estate were offered for lease. No tenant was found and on June 2nd 1927, the remaining Arkwright property including Willersley Castle and its grounds and the Cromford Mills site, then in use as the Cromford Colour Works and the Troy Laundry, were put up for sale. The sale catalogue was misleading in that the buildings occupied by the Cromford Colour Company had been purchased by its parent company, the Via Gellia Colour Company in 1923 and did not form part of this sale.

Sir Albert Ball, a former Mayor of Nottingham bought property to the value of £19,750 including Willersley Castle and its grounds which he immediately advertised for sale for £8,500. Within days agreement was reached for their purchase by representatives of the Wesleyan Methodist Connexion in Derbyshire whose spokesman, the Reverend C H Taylor, President of the Derby and District Wesley Guild Council, expressed delight in ending their four year search for suitable premises for their planned guest house. The castle was opened as a Wesley Guild Holiday Home in May 1928. It is now known as Willersley Castle Hotel.

A five day sale of the Castle's contents began on June 7th 1927. The catalogue included Adam mantelpieces, Sheraton, Chippendale, Adam and Hepplewhite furniture, paintings, books, silver and china. Some items did not sell and were bought in by the family. The *High Peak News* report considered that the latter was true of the Adam fireplaces and the eventual owners of the house later confirmed that arrangements had been made to retain the fireplaces and other precious antiques. Oral evidence from a person associated with the purchase challenges this assertion alleging that one or more of the fireplaces was removed and replaced by a replica.

The family continued to put other items up for sale over the next ten years.

In World War II, from 1940-46, Willersley Castle became a maternity hospital. Staff and patients from the bombed Salvation Army Mother's Hospital in Clapton, London, were evacuated there and later in the period some mothers from the local area were accommodated and were able to claim that their babies had been born in a Castle.

Years later, reflecting on the Arkwright family's migration to Willersey, a village near Broadway in the Cotswolds, there were Cromford residents who had known the family who believed the departure was as much to do with loss of appetite for the old life as resident squire as it was financial. It may be significant that F C Arkwright had embarked on the sale of a small number of outlying properties immediately after the war. Before the war when he had offered to sell some property to tenants, the interpretation by the Press was that it was because of a shortage of money. This was repudiated by him. In a letter to his relative 'Jack' (Richard Arkwright junior's grandson John Arkwright) at Hampton Court in April 1911 he explained that in the light of much national publicity about 'the advisability of increasing the number of occupying owners of land' he had offered some 16 tenants, 'all smallholders as all my tenants are' the opportunity to buy their holdings on easy terms. He was testing to see if there was a 'land hunger' and offering to 'satisfy any such feeling' if there was. He considered he could sell and reinvest 'at the same or better interest without the bother connected with land and its increasing taxation'. In the event, only 3 tenants, together occupying about 50 acres, 'expressed a wish to purchase'. F.C. concluded 'it is satisfying to have proved that nearly all the tenants are wise enough to realise they are far better off as they are than they would be as owners'.

Cromford without the Arkwrights

It is clear that there were those who felt deeply the loss of a resident squire for practical and social reasons. The schools, the church, the Institute and many good causes no longer enjoyed the financial comfort the family had provided. At the same time the hierarchical order of society had been destroyed. Where now was leadership to be found? Who now would open the garden party and launch social and fundraising events? It was not as if Cromford possessed a prosperous middle class groomed to shoulder the burden. But while the vicar was surely not alone in identifying and regretting irreversible change, just as surely there were those who relished Cromford's deliverance from what they saw as social subservience. So it was for the young girl who had been denied a place on the canal boat to Ripley for the Sunday School outing because she had refused to curtsey to Mrs Arkwright when they met in the street. She was glad to see the back of the Arkwright family. She knew Cromford could manage without them.

In the event Cromford endured a period of austerity which, given the economic climate nationally, would have been bleak enough had there been a benign resident squire but inevitably was more severe without such leadership. So despondent had the vicar, the Reverend Arthur Hazlehurst, become by November 1927 that he used the pages of the monthly Church Magazine to reflect on the opportunities provided by emigration to the colonies and offered to put any boy aged between 15 and 19 in touch with a Church scheme for migration. 'What he asked has Cromford to offer young men? Practically nothing except work in the mills' was his answer 'and that is not over-attractive in view of the fact that in times of trade depression the dole takes the place of wages for weeks at a time'. A number of Cromford's young people did emigrate and two years later Hazlehurst was able to compile a roll of 22 Cromfordians living abroad in Canada, the United States and Australia. When the results of the 1931 census became available in 1934 the decline in the population of the village was seen to be severe, too great to be attributed to the loss of the Willersley Estate or some temporary employment problems. Since 1911 the population had fallen by 177, just over 17%, and now stood at 839.

The combination of hard times and the loss of the Arkwright family's generosity placed a strain on the community's self help networks. In July 1929 it became clear that the schools must be painted but this would cost £30 and none of this money was available. Without the Arkwrights at their shoulder the School Managers turned to the community. They argued nearly everyone in Cromford and Scarthin had some connection with the schools which '[had] earned the goodwill of all'. They proposed every house should contribute a shilling. They estimated with 400 housed this would bring in £20 and perhaps more, some houses having more than one wage earner. In fact the house to house collection raised only £14 and the shortfall had to be found through a rummage sale. The bill was not paid until February 1930.

Since the middle of the war in 1916 the prudent Cromford housewife had been able to call on the Cromford Clothing Club to help her with the family clothes budget. This issued cards to its members on which to record payments made to the fund in instalments of threepence or more between October and the following September. Over many years Mrs Mee of the Bell Inn administered the scheme. In 1928 she received contributions on alternate Monday evenings at the British Legion and in later years at the Institute and by 1935 at the Schools. Between 1916 and 1925 nearly £1000 had been paid in but the annual contributions fluctuated; in 1934-35 it was only £83. The benefit for the members took the form of a small bonus and a discount of 2/6d in the pound for goods bought in all the participating shops. A list published in November 1930 included two Matlock shops, Marsdens and the Manchester Stores and six Cromford shops; Messrs Chapman, J R Gould, Fletcher, Wright, Mrs Bond and Miss Kidd though it was claimed any other shop could be added to the list if the shopkeeper was willing. Within this period, in January 1933, the first meeting of the Women's Institute was held in the village.

Late in the same year it 'ought to have been done years ago' was one response to the improvement in village life when Derby Road, Mill Lane and Cromford Hill got a new water supply. Other comment makes clear how welcome that change must have been - there was now 'no necessity to leave the pail under the tap for half an hour before the miserable trickle has filled it'.

In 1927 the absence of a doctor in Cromford or Bonsall was recognised and a service was established in the two communities to handle some of the medical needs. This was the Cromford and District Nursing Association. By becoming a member at the cost of twopence a week all the members of a family could call upon the services of a nurse. During the year 1934-35 Nurse MacKeman, in return for a salary of £146, made 1,588 visits dealing with midwifery, medical and surgical cases. Income from the members' subscriptions was supplemented by a grant from the County Council and a donation from the Cromford Carnival and with some difficulty the association contrived to break even.

In April 1930 an Evening Branch of the Yorkshire Penny Bank opened in the Schools. It was limited to an hour each Friday evening and was intended for adults, there already being a school bank. It accepted deposits from a penny upwards and offered a rate of interest 'slightly better than the Post Office'. Cheque books and home safes were provided. Each Thursday evening between 6 and 6.30pm the Schools were also home to the Derbyshire County Library.

By means of another local initiative tennis arrived in the village. Help came from George Henry Key, the owner of the Colour Works who gradually emerged in the decade after the departure of the Arkwrights as Cromford's leading resident. Two tennis courts and a pavilion were created through a process which began in 1921 when Key loaned the tennis club £60 to level ground in the Meadows on which to build the two courts with the promise he would refund £20 if the debt was repaid within five years. The courts were in use in June 1922 and early in 1925, with the courts complete and the loan repaid, Key's £20 was put towards the pavilion described by those who remember it as a small wooden shed.

In 1935 the village celebrated the King's Silver Jubilee. George Henry Key chaired the committee which planned the event. It began with a procession from the Market Place to the Meadows where the beech tree he had donated was planted. Children's sports followed and Mrs Key presented the children with Jubilee beakers and sixpences. In the evening a bonfire on Allen's Hill and a firework display completed the festivities.

The *Church Magazines* create the impression of a community comfortable in its insularity. In May 1930 the vicar proposed taking a party to Ashbourne for a missionary service in the church and tea at the Green Man. He pointed out Ashbourne is not far from Cromford 'but there are many in our village who have never visited it'. He would not have said the same about Derby to which the village was linked by rail and where the Infirmary provided medical services for those with financial means or charitable access and whose needs were not met by the hospitals at Wirksworth and Matlock. The importance of the Derbyshire Royal Infirmary was acknowledged in the donations of the annual Church Harvest Festival collection, modest though it might be. In 1931 it was so tiny, £7-11-1, the smallest the vicar had witnessed since coming to the village, that he implored his flock to do better; and to good effect the collection increasing to £9-5-0 a year later. Cromford also responded to the DRI's regular appeal for eggs, sending nearly 1000 in 1927. Donations were left at the school and the vicar took them to Derby.

Derby or more precisely the Alvaston Recreation Ground was also a favoured venue for the annual children's outing. As Hazlehurst recorded in August 1932 'when you have a lake with a real motor-boat, a sunny afternoon, and a Woolworth's Store within easy reach, what more is wanted to make you happy, except a good tea? And that was also provided'.

In May 1929 the vicar attempted to encourage his parishioners to look beyond their familiar horizon. 'HAVE YOU A SPARE ROOM?' he asked. 'If so why not give a holiday to two or three children from London?' He appealed to their good nature and their need for an extra income, each child being worth 10/- a week. 'Try to picture their life in London, their homes consisting of one or two rooms in a crowded house in a crowded, noisy street, with no playground but the dusty paper-strewn pavement'. The rules were carefully drawn up and included the following. Not more than two children may occupy one bed, and a child may not share a bed with an

FIGURE 107. **Reverend George Arthur Hazlehurst.**
Reproduced by permission of St Mary's Church, Cromford

adult. Boys and girls must not occupy the same room but special leave to do so may be given by the County Correspondent. It is essential that every child should have at least one hot bath or complete wash once a week and a weekly wash of underclothing and additionally for the girls, a frock and pinafore. It is not known whether the scheme was taken up.

Our account of life in Cromford in the inter-war years relies heavily on the pages of the Church Magazines and on the Reverend Hazlehurst's comments on the lives of his parishioners. A more extensive study would include the commercial life of the village, the shops, the pubs and the significance of such developments as the opening of the Wirksworth and District Co-operative Society's new shop on 'the Co-op garden' on Water Lane in 1928. The Co-op was previously located in the red brick shop at the bottom of the Tap Road, the slope down from the end of Scarthin to the tap in the wall opposite the shop. Such research is for another day.

But a dramatic change in the village in the twentieth century which it is not possible to over-look is the effect of quarrying with its attendant dust and lorry traffic. Cromford lies across the boundary where millstone grit and limestone meet and the area has had many quarries providing gritstone, principally for building but also for millstones until foreign stones were available more cheaply, and limestone for many uses. Some small quarries were developed often for temporary use and often close to where the stone was needed for a particular purpose, for local buildings, for dry stone walls, and for the raw material for lime burners as land improvement became important. There is evidence for these abandoned sites in many small hollows and exposed rock faces in the district. There was reworking of lead mine spoil heaps as commercial uses were found for the minerals earlier discarded by the lead industry such as calcite, fluorite and barite. A little further afield there were quarries like Hopton exporting stone to embellish stately homes, a trade greatly enhanced when the Cromford canal was built. The canal also transported local stone to the ironworks in the Black Country.

The twentieth century's extractive industry has worked on a grander scale as the major quarries still at work close to Cromford show. At the edge of the village, at Ball Eye in Bonsall Hollow, a small disused working was opened up again after the area was sold in the Arkwright estate sale in 1924. Slinter Top Quarry began on land belonging to Braeside Farm in the 1930s and the awesome hole which is Dene Quarry claims a precise birth date to which the commemorative plaque on its lip bears startling witness. It reads 'to the memory of Don Harris who on the 6th May 1942 walked onto this hillside with a wheelbarrow and hand shovel and started Dene Quarry'. He was working for Herbert Hardy and the quarry was originally called Steeple House Quarry but changed to Dene in March 1943. In recent years in Tarmac's ownership, the quarry's annual production has been about a million and a half tons.

Over the years much of the Dene has disappeared and with it lengths of the routes which criss-crossed the hillside, much of Yeats Lane and of Bakers Lane, which ran across from west to east, and Longload Lane, (for which Cameron's *The Place-names of Derbyshire* gives a reference date 1309) which ran up the hillside to the guide post (now missing) on Halli-car Lane and the turn left to Middleton or right to the rim of the valley and so to Bonsall. Middleton miners were still using this route to Bonsall on their way to work at Millclose Mine in the early twentieth century. Dean Hollow where the rifle butts were in use in 1878 has gone. Evidence of the pattern of farming at the surface and of the widespread lead mining activity below has been dug away. In 1947 the Barmaster transferred the title to 43 mines on Hardy's land to his company, The Dene Quarries (Derbyshire) Ltd, as the Dean Hollow Consolidated Title.

Today, 2013, the quarry is closed.

CHAPTER FIFTEEN

Recognition for Cromford

The rescue of North Street from demolition after World War II did not immediately raise local awareness of Cromford's historic importance. That took time and the principal trigger was the Arkwright Festival held in the summer of 1971 to commemorate the bicentenary of Arkwright's first Cromford mill. The Festival was a success financially and socially and there is a direct link between its legacy in Cromford and the inscription thirty years later of the Derwent Valley Mills World Heritage Site.

FIGURE 108. **Young volunteers removing debris from the Bear Pit, May 1977.** Private collection

The long term impact of the Festival owed much to the way in which it was organised. The plans were conceived in Cromford; it was delivered largely by local people and it was this group, the Arkwright Festival Committee, which was then able to invest the money raised by the Festival in bricks and mortar and on the development of the Arkwright Society. Planning the event began in 1969 when the central and a number of subsidiary committees were established each with particular targets and responsibilities. It was an ambitious programme which included three exhibitions, musical and theatrical productions, lectures, walks, site boards, history trails and the daily opening of many of the Derwent Valley's industrial heritage sites, a number of which had not been opened to the public before. To achieve all this, an army of volunteers was enrolled and it is estimated that over 100 people took part manning sites, supervising exhibitions, writing trails and leading tours. Specialist help was enlisted from the University of Nottingham, Department of Adult Education which provided an office and secretariat and from Derbyshire County Council County Record Office and Matlock College of Education which devised the principal exhibition and the schools' and education programmes respectively. Two local companies were central to its success, the Cromford

Colour Company which made available the former laundry building to house the largest of the exhibitions and permitted visitors more or less unfettered access to the Colour Works site and English Sewing who housed the exhibition of textile machinery and allowed tours of Masson and Belper North Mills. The third exhibition which focused on the Arkwrights in Cromford was set up in Cromford school.

So for four weeks between mid July and mid August, later extended because of the programme's popularity, Cromford was inundated with visitors. The organisers had expected an audience of some hundreds selected from among the aficionados of industrial archaeology. In fact there were thousands and they were drawn from all walks of life. The experience was as moving for some local people as it was for the visitors. In North Street where site boards had been erected to inform visitors of Cromford's history as they followed the Festival trails a sense of local ownership emerged. Householders debated whether one house was a better or less good example of its type than another. The residents of longest standing claimed their rightful position as neighbourhood soothsayers and within a day or two, quite spontaneously, many of the North Street houses were open to visitors entirely free of charge.

Local pride and a sense of self worth – perhaps these were the most significant legacies of the Festival though this was by no means the entire inheritance. The Festival Committee found itself with money and with property to protect. It became clear that a permanent legal entity would be required and a registered charity, the Arkwright Society, was formed. The local car dealers Lehane Mackenzie and Shand (Matlock Motors) presented the Cromford corn mill and maltings site to the Society which also acquired the lock-up. The Festival had spawned the first practical initiatives to protect and repair Cromford's historic sites. Teams from Bilborough School in Nottingham excavated many tonnes of waste material to reveal the archaeology of the Bear Pit and the Ernest Bailey School, Matlock cleared a part of the northern water course of the first mill uncovering a wartime mortar bomb in the process. At the corn mill the rubble which had filled part of the mill pond to create hard standing for cars awaiting delivery was removed so returning the pond more or less to its original configuration. This work was undertaken by local volunteers.

The decade that followed the Festival firmly established Cromford's heritage credentials. In 1971 the Cromford Conservation Area was designated and a number of buildings were listed; the Greyhound pond was cleaned out and taken over by the local council; and in 1975, European Architectural Heritage Year, the Arkwright Society restored the water wheel at the head of the Greyhound pond, and the sluice which controlled the flow of water to and from the Bear Pit.

But while the new found enthusiasm for Cromford's historic buildings, engendered by the Festival, had played its part in clearance, repair and research and would continue to do so, the residents of North Street were not alone in coming to regard the visitors as guests who had outstayed their welcome. What had been fun for five or six weeks in the summer of 1971 had become a nuisance. Within two or three years of the Festival the Arkwright Society's teams of volunteers were showing round more than a thousand people per year. It was said Cromford 'had become a goldfish bowl'. More recently, though overall visitor numbers are likely to be greater than forty years ago, there is more to see at Masson and Cromford Mills so there are less organised groups in the village and it is to be hoped the pressure on householders is less intense.

There have also been some rewards for householders as a result of heritage recognition. Over the last 25 years conservation area grants under several different titles funded jointly by English Heritage, Derbyshire County Council and Derbyshire Dales District Council have helped property owners meet the cost of repairs to their buildings. The availability of grants has also encouraged owners to reinstate lost architectural detail, such as historic window and door patterns.

FIGURE 109. **Photograph, 1974.**

Lady Dartmouth, later Countess Spencer, Chairman of the European Architectural Heritage Year Council for the United Kingdom visiting Cromford in December 1974 to inspect the water wheel at the head of the Greyhound pond. The Council had agreed to grant aid the Arkwright Society's plan to restore the wheel.

Private collection

It was during the 1980s, soon after the Arkwright Society purchased the Cromford Mills' site, that the Society's President, Andrew, the 11th Duke of Devonshire, suggested that the significance of the Derwent Valley was such that there should be international recognition of its importance. So began the long campaign for inscription by UNESCO, the United Nations Educational Cultural and Scientific Organisation, as a World Heritage Site which was not to be achieved until December 2001. In the early years the difficulty lay with the determination of successive British Governments to avoid adding new World Heritage Sites in the UK. This changed in 1997 when the incoming Labour Government resolved to resume work with UNESCO, put forward potential UK World Heritage Sites accepting recommendations that the UK should give priority to its industrial heritage. Proposals were invited for a new UK tentative list. This was the opportunity the consortium of organisations supporting a Derwent Valley bid needed. The Secretary of State at the Department of National Heritage called for letters of support and though figures were never published it is clear that Derwent Valley residents responded positively overwhelmingly welcoming inscription. Inclusion on the tentative list in 1999 was no more than a first step. There followed months of intensive work with English Heritage to establish the boundaries of the proposed site and to prepare the intellectual case for presentation to UNESCO and to the International Council on Monuments and Sites, ICOMOS.

When finally in December 2001, World Heritage Site status was achieved for the Derwent Valley Mills the citation from UNESCO read:

'The cultural landscape of the Derwent Valley is of outstanding significance because it was here that the modern factory system was established to accommodate the new technology for spinning cotton developed by Richard Arkwright. The insertion of industrial establishments into a rural landscape necessitated the construction of housing for the workers in the mills, and the resulting settlements created the exceptional industrial landscape that has retained its qualities over two centuries.'

Many agencies, many workers and many volunteers have been and continue to be involved in restoration and conservation work, interpretation and education at Cromford fulfilling the obligation which World Heritage Site designation imposes worldwide - 'to identify, protect, conserve, present and pass on to future generations, cultural and natural heritage considered to be of outstanding value for everyone'.

FIGURE 110. **The Royal Mail's First Day Cover celebrating the 250th anniversary of Sir Richard Arkwright's birth, 1982.**

Private collection

The Arkwrights of Willersley Castle: a family tree

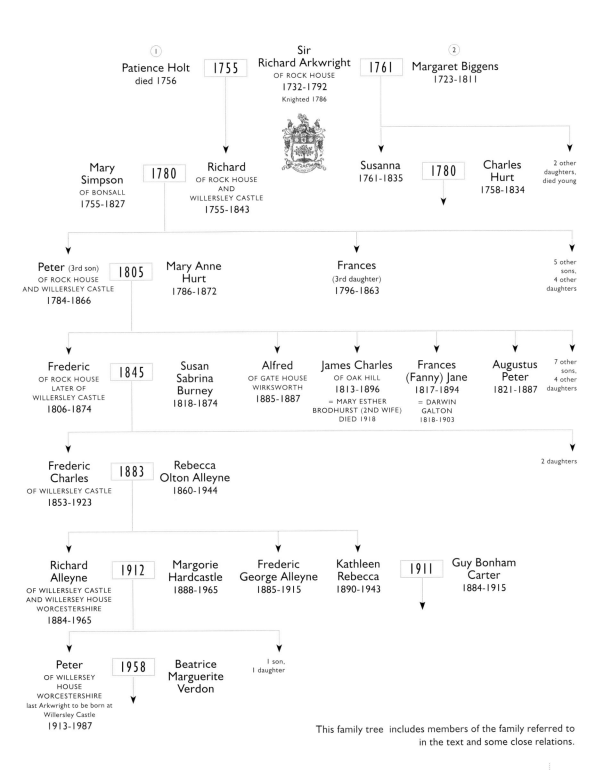

① Patience Holt died 1756	1755	Sir Richard Arkwright OF ROCK HOUSE 1732-1792 Knighted 1786

Sir Richard Arkwright — 1761 — Margaret Biggens 1723-1811 ②

Mary Simpson OF BONSALL 1755-1827 — 1780 — Richard OF ROCK HOUSE AND WILLERSLEY CASTLE 1755-1843

Susanna 1761-1835 — 1780 — Charles Hurt 1758-1834

2 other daughters, died young

Peter (3rd son) OF ROCK HOUSE AND WILLERSLEY CASTLE 1784-1866 — 1805 — Mary Anne Hurt 1786-1872

Frances (3rd daughter) 1796-1863

5 other sons, 4 other daughters

Frederic OF ROCK HOUSE LATER OF WILLERSLEY CASTLE 1806-1874 — 1845 — Susan Sabrina Burney 1818-1874

Alfred OF GATE HOUSE WIRKSWORTH 1885-1887

James Charles OF OAK HILL 1813-1896 = MARY ESTHER BRODHURST (2ND WIFE) DIED 1918

Frances (Fanny) Jane 1817-1894 = DARWIN GALTON 1818-1903

Augustus Peter 1821-1887

7 other sons, 4 other daughters

Frederic Charles OF WILLERSLEY CASTLE 1853-1923 — 1883 — Rebecca Olton Alleyne 1860-1944

2 daughters

Richard Alleyne OF WILLERSLEY CASTLE AND WILLERSEY HOUSE WORCESTERSHIRE 1884-1965 — 1912 — Margorie Hardcastle 1888-1965

Frederic George Alleyne 1885-1915

Kathleen Rebecca 1890-1943 — 1911 — Guy Bonham Carter 1884-1915

Peter OF WILLERSEY HOUSE WORCESTERSHIRE last Arkwright to be born at Willersley Castle 1913-1987 — 1958 — Beatrice Marguerite Verdon

1 son, 1 daughter

This family tree includes members of the family referred to in the text and some close relations.

Glossary

Baryte, barite (barites) – barium sulphate, a heavy mineral locally called caulk or cawk. Was bleached and substituted for white lead in paint to produce Dutch white lead paint. Now has uses in oil and gas drilling as heavy mud, in chemical industries, in medicine and in glossy paper production.

Black jack, blende – zinc sulphide, an ore of zinc, now known as sphalerite.

Calamine, calamy – zinc carbonate, an ore of zinc. The term is commonly used for the metal extracted from the ore though this is now named smithsonite. Has uses in cosmetics, medicine and paint; formerly used with copper to make brass.

Calcining – reducing rock minerals, for example calamine, by roasting to a powder or friable substance.

Calcite – calcium carbonate or calc spar, principal constituent of limestone and marble. Many uses in the construction industry - in decorative renders, for terrazzo flooring and in aggregates and fillers. Used for agricultural lime and in pharmaceuticals.

Conservation Area – an area of special architectural or historic interest the character or appearance of which it is desirable to preserve or enhance and which once designated by the local planning authority enjoys a degree of legal protection. The concept was introduced to the planning system in the 1967 Civic Amenities Act.

Culvert – a built, underground drainage tunnel.

Enclosure – the process of dividing common land into individual allotments or enclosures by agreement or as directed under the terms of Acts of Parliament called Enclosure Acts.

Fluorite – calcium fluoride, locally fluorspar. Used in smelting as 'flowing stone' to help slag to run off freely. Now used in many processes including plastics production and fluorination of water.

Fustian – a fairly coarse cloth originally made with a linen warp and cotton weft. Later any of several stout twilled cotton fabrics such as corduroy or moleskin.

Galena – lead sulphide, chief ore of lead.

Gangue minerals – non-metallic minerals, in Derbyshire found in association with lead ore eg baryte, fluorite and calcite.

Goit, (goyt) – an open man-made watercourse frequently associated with the delivery of water to a water wheel.

Horse gin – device whereby horsepower is used to turn machinery.

Lantern – a small structure on top of a dome for light, ventilation or ornament.

Launder – a wooden trough. This term is encountered most frequently now referring to the shallow gutter set below the edge of a roof to catch rainwater and pass it to a downspout. But it was also used to describe much larger man made troughs associated with water mills.

Lead – heavy base metal, Pb, soft and malleable.

Lime ash – literally the lime and ash - the waste products from the lower parts of a lime kiln – which when poured wet over a framework of wood and straw produced a long lasting floor as hard as concrete.

Lime kiln – a furnace in which limestone is burnt in layers with coal to produce quick lime. With the addition of water, slaked lime is produced.

Listed buildings – the 1947 Town and Country Planning Act required the production of a list of buildings of special architectural or historic interest. This list now controlled by English Heritage divides buildings into 3 grades; grade I; grade II* and grade II each of which enjoys a certain degree of protection under the law.

Litharge – PbO, yellow oxide of lead, prepared by calcining lead in a furnace. Used as a pigment.

Malting – where grain is turned into malt for use in brewing and the name for the process.

Messuage – a legal term for a dwelling house which could include its associated outbuildings and yards and or garden. The capital messuage of an estate was usually the dwelling where the owner of the estate lived.

Overshot – the description for a water wheel driven by water delivered near the top of the wheel or 'beyond' the top of the wheel.

Ovolo – a quarter rounded or convex moulding

Pentrough – a trough constructed to control the flow of water across the water wheel of a water mill.

Pier glass – a pier glass is a mirror placed on the wall between two windows. It is likely to be tall and may be either a hanging mirror or mirrored glass fixed flush to the pier (ie the wall) between the windows.

Pilaster – an architectural feature resembling a square or rectangular column or pillar projecting from the surface of a wall.

Red lead – Pb3O4, a red oxide of lead known as minium; formed by roasting litharge in a furnace. Largely used as a pigment, in anti-corrosive paint for example.

Register of Parks and Gardens – historic designed landscapes entered in a register which is compiled by English Heritage to draw attention to their importance.

Roving – the act of converting, (or the product of converting) cotton, wool, etc into a thin rope with a slight twist which can then be fed into a spinning frame to produce a spun yarn.

Shearing – the clipping or cutting off of the fleece of an animal, a sheep for example.

Slag – molten and cooled refuse produced during the smelting of lead ore.

Slag hearth – a furnace for re-smelting slag.

Slag mill – a water powered building which housed a slag hearth. The water wheel provided power for the bellows.

Smelting mill – a general term for a smelting works.

Sough – an underground channel which drained water from a lead mine.

SSSI, Site of Special Scientific Interest – SSSI's were originally established in 1949 but the current legal framework is provided by the 1981 Wildlife and Countryside Act as amended in 1985 and 2000. An SSSI may be designated on any land considered to be of special interest for its biological or geological importance. Once designated SSSI's are legally protected from damaging development and from neglect..

Stereocard (stereograph, stereo-scopic photograph, stereoview) – Two photographs of the same subject taken from slightly different positions so that when mounted side by side on a card and viewed through a stereo-scope the subject appears three dimensional. The two photographs were taken with a special twin-lens stereoscopic camera, or by moving a single camera between exposures.

Turnpike – a road managed under the terms of an Act of Parliament called a Turnpike Act on which barriers, toll-gates, were erected where a payment, a toll, was collected from users of the road.

Undershot – description of a water wheel driven by water passing under it to drive wooden paddles attached to the rim of the wheel.

White lead – a compound of lead carbonate and hydrated oxide of lead. Historically used as a component of paint, including artists'oil paints and in pottery glazes and made using lead and vinegar in small pots which were covered with dung or spent tanner's bark.

World Heritage Site – under the terms of the Convention concerning the Protection of the World Cultural and Natural Heritage adopted by UNESCO in 1972 a World Heritage list was established for properties forming part of the cultural and natural heritage which are judged to have Outstanding Universal Value.

Sources

Manuscript sources:

Arkwright family Mss,

Arkwright Society Mss

Cambridge University Library, Ms 3955 f43

Devonshire Mss, Chatsworth House

Evans of Darley Abbey Papers, (Taylor Simpson Mosley deposit, DRO unsorted)

Oxford University Bodleian Library, Gough Maps 41A fols 53-81 William Thomas's drawings

Public Records Office, Board of Trade Papers, Cromford Canal Company Minutes

Derbyshire Record Office, Matlock:
    Bagshawe Collection, (formerly in Sheffield)
    Cromford Parish Council Minutes
    Gardner's Building Accounts for Willersley Castle
    Gell/Evans Papers
    Journal of an Excursion into Derbyshire, DRO 395 Z/Z1
    Land Tax Returns for Cromford and Bonsall,
    Manor Court Rolls for Matlock and Bonsall,
    Nightingale Papers
    Poor Rate Records for Cromford and Bonsall,
    Taylor Simpson Mosley Deposit D769, Box 2, Miners' depositions
    Tithe Redemption Schedules and Maps for Cromford, Bonsall, Matlock, Middleton,
    Wilson Furnishing Accounts for Willersley Castle

Sheffield Archives
    Tibbitts Collection

Derbyshire Local Studies Library, Matlock:
    (now incorporated in the Derbyshire Record Office)
    Census Enumerators Returns (microfilm)
    Wolley Mss, (microfilm)

Simmons Collection (Derbyshire), Science Museum Library, London

Published electronically:

Bradley, John, Before the Snapshot & the Postcard: Victorian Photography & Photographers in Matlock and Matlock Bath

Charlton, C. and Strange, P., Sir Richard Arkwright's Cromford Mills Conservation Statement. The Arkwright Society, 2007

Printed primary sources:

Acts of Parliament:
    Enclosure Acts for Matlock, Bonsall and Middleton
    Tithe Acts for Bonsall, Cromford and Middleton
    Turnpike Acts

English Law Reports, Exchequer of Pleas E.T. 1839, Meeson and Welsby Exchequer, 5 (1852), (referred to here as the Meerbrook Sough enquiry)

Parliamentary Papers, Minutes of Evidence before Select Committee on State of Children Employed in Manufactories, 1816-17

Second Report: Employment of Children in Factories, 1833-34

Maps:

Ordnance Survey Maps published 1880, 1899, 1922, 1993

Sanderson's Map, Twenty Miles round Mansfield, 1835, George Sanderson

Newspapers:

The Belper News, The Courier, (Chesterfield), Cromford Church Magazines 1917-18; 1921-1936, Derby Mercury, The Derby and Chesterfield Reporter, Derbyshire Times, High Peak News, Leicester and Nottingham Journal, London Gazette, Manchester Guardian, Manchester Mercury, Nottinghamshire Guardian, Nottingham Herald, Wirksworth Advertiser

Secondary Printed Sources:

Directories: Bagshaw 1840, 1846,: Bennett 1899, 1906-7, Brewer 1823-4, Bulmer 1895, Freebody 1852, Glover 1829, Harrison, Harrod & Co 1860, 1870, Kelly 1881, 1887, 1891, 1899, 1900, 1904, 1908, 1912, 1916, 1922, 1925, 1928, 1932, 1936, 1941, Melville 1854, Pigot & Co 1821-2, 1828, 1831, 1835, 1842, Post Office 1848, 1876, Slater 1862, White 1852 (Sheffield), 1857

Adam, W., Gem of the Peak, 1838, 1840, 1843, 1845, 1851, 1857
    Dales Scenery, Fishing Streams and Mines of Derbyshire, 1861

Aikin, J., A Description of the Country from 30 to 40 Miles round Manchester, 1795

Aitken, W.C., Birmingham and the Midland Hardware District, 1859

Anon, Four Topographical Letters written in July 1755, printed 1757;
    Journal of an excursion into Derbyshire, 1782. DRO D395 Z/1

Audubon, J.J., The 1826 Journal of John James Audubon, transcribed by Alice Ford, 1967

Arkwright Festival Committee, Arkwright and the Mills at Cromford, 1971 and revised editions

Barker, H., The Panorama of Matlock, 1827, 1828;
    The New Panorama, 1834, 1868

Barton, David A., Discovering Chapels and Meeting Houses, 1990

Barton, David A., "By Schisms Rent Asunder": The Wesleyan Reform Movement in Derbyshire, Proceedings of the Wesley Historical Society, Vol. 52, 1999

Beckett, J.V. and Heath, J. E. eds Derbyshire Record Society, Derbyshire Tithe Files 1836-50, 1995

Berresford, C., The Bath at War, 2007

Boyes, Grahame, Journal of the Railway and Canal Historical Society, Vol. 36 Part 6, German Wheatcroft and the Wheatcroft Family of Canal Carriers, Nov. 2009

Bray, W., Sketch of a Tour into Derbyshire, 1778, 1783

Britton, J. and Brayley, E. W., The Beauties of England and Wales, 1802

Brown, Thomas, A General View of the Agriculture of Derby, 1794

Brumhead, D., The Estates of Thomas Eyre of Rowtor in the Royal Forest of the Peak and the Massereene Connection, New Mills Local History Society Newsletter No. 9 Autumn 1992

Bryan, B., History of Matlock, 1903

Burnett, John, A Social History of Housing, 1815-1985, 1986

Butcher, Rev Edmund, Excursion from Sidmouth to Chester, published 1805

Byng, J., The Torrington Diaries, 1781-94, 4 Vols. 1934 edition

Camden, W., Britannia Depicta 1695, 1806

Cameron, K., The Place-names of Derbyshire, eds English Place-names Society, 1959

Chapman, S., Textile History, James Longsdon (1745-1821), Farmer and Fustian Manufacturer

Colvin, H.M., Dictionary of British Architects 1600-1840, 4th edition 2008

Cooke, G. A., Topographical and Statistical description of the County of Derby, 1811

Cox, J.C., Churches of Derbyshire, Vol. II, 1886

Craven, M., and Stanley, M., The Derbyshire Country House, Vol.1, 1982

Croston, J., On Foot through the Peak, 1862, 1868

Curl, James Stevens, Encyclopaedia of Architectural Terms, 1993

Davies, Rev D. P., A New and Historical View of Derbyshire..., Vol. 2, 1811

Day, J., Bristol Brass: The History of the Industry, 1973

Defoe, D., Tour through the Whole Island of Great Britain, 1724, 1727, Revised 1742, 1748, 1753

Derwent Valley Mills World Heritage Site Nomination Document, 2000

Farey, J.A., General View of the Agriculture and Minerals of Derbyshire, 3 vols, 1811, 1813, 1817

Farington, J., The Diary of Joseph Farington, Vol. 5, 1801-1803

Fiennes, C., The Illustrated Journey of Celia Fiennes, c.1682 – 1712, 1947

Fitton, R.S. and Wadsworth A.P., The Strutts and the Arkwrights, 1958, reprint 1973

Fitton, R.S., The Arkwrights, Spinners of Fortune, 1989

Flindall, R., What the Papers Said. Derbyshire in Nottingham Newspapers 1714-1776, 2000
    Calendar of the Barmasters' Derbyshire Lead Mining Records, arranged and described by Roger Flindall, PDMHS, 1998

Glover, S., The History and Gazetteer of the County of Derby, 1829
    The Peak Guide, 1830

Grant, E., Memoirs of a Highland Lady, 1797-1827, 1911

Grant, J. A., London Journal of a Three Weeks' Tour in 1797 through Derbyshire into the Lakes. Printed in The Britsh Tourist's Companion, 1800

Hackett, R.R., Wirksworth and Five Miles Around, 1863

Hall, I., A neoclassical episode at Chatsworth, Burlington Magazine, Vol. 122, No,927, June 1980

Hodgkins, D., The Cromford and High Peak Railway, Journal of the Canal and Railway Historical Society, Vol. 35, 2007

Hopwood, D. and Dick, M., The Brass Industry and Brass Workers in Birmingham

Jewitt, A., The Matlock Companion, 1832, 1835, 1837, 1838

Jewitt, L., The Matlock Companion, 1862

Kiernon, D., The Derbyshire Lead Industry in the Sixteenth Century, Derbyshire

Record Society, Vol. XIV, 1989

La Rochefoucauld Brothers, Tour of England in 1785

Lipscomb, G. A Description of Matlock Bath, 1802

Lysons, D. and S., Magna Britannica, 1817

Malcom, J. P., A Journey from Chesterfield to Matlock, Gentleman's Magazine Vol. 63, 1793

Mann, S.J., Sketches and Reminiscences, 1856

Martin, Thomas, Circle of the Mechanics Arts, 2nd edition, 1818

Mavor, W., The British Tourist Vol. 5, 1800,

Moore, H., Picturesque Excursions from Derby to Matlock Bath..., 1818;
    The Pilot, a new Matlock, Buxton and Castleton Guide, 1818;
    The Stranger's Guide through the Peak 1833, 1837

Mynors, C., Listed Buildings, Conservation Areas and Monuments, 2006

Moritz, C. P., From letters published 1795 describing a Visit to Derbyshire in 1782

Nicolson, Benedict, Joseph Wright of Derby, 1968

Pigott, S., Hollins: A Study of Industry, 1949

Pilkington, J., A View of the Present State of Derbyshire, 1789

Plumptre, J., James Plumptre's Britain; The Journal of a Tourist in the 1790's, 1992

Rees, Abraham, Rees's Manufacturing Industry, 1819-20 edited by Neil Cossons 1972

Rhodes, E., Derbyshire Tourist Guide, 1837

Rieuwerts, J. Lead Mining in Derbyshire, Vol. 3, 2010, Vol. 4, 2012
    Early Gunpowder Work in Longe or Cromford Sough, Peak District Mines Historical Society Bulletin, Vol. 3, No 6, 1998

Shawcroft, J., A History of Derbyshire County Cricket Club, 1870-1970, 1972

Stukeley, W., Itinerarium Curiosum, 1724

Thomas, David St John, The Country Railway, 1976

Ure, A., Dictionary of Arts, Manufactures and Mines, 1840

Victoria County History, Derbyshire, 2 Vols. 1905, 1907

Ward, Rev R., The Matlock, Buxton and Castleton Guide, editions 1814, 1818, 1824, 1826, 1827

Warner, Rev R., A Tour through the Northern Counties of England..., 1802

Watson, R., Chemical Essays, Vol. IV, 1786

Wells, E. A., Hollins and Viyella, 1968

Woolley, W., History of Derbyshire, Derbyshire Record Society, Vol. VI, (1981)

Young, A., A Farmer's Tour through England, 1770

Index

Slinter Wood 15,16,22
Smalley, John 40,44
Smedley, John (Matlock Bath) 32
Smelting Mill Green 38
Smith, John 140
Smith, Mr and Mrs W E 133
Smith, Rev B Hughes 134
smithy 35
Soresby, William 1,41,107
Speedwell Mill, Wirksworth 136
Sperrey, William 26
spinning wager 34
Sproul, James N and Co 66
Staffordshire Row 135
Stagalls, James 82-83
Staley, Francis 79
Stamp, Leonard 32,103
Statham, George 116; -Maria 116
Steeple Grange 76
Stevens Bros, Messrs 26
Stevens, Henry Isaac 101
Stokes, G H 157
Stone, William 131
Stonehouse, workman 44
Stoney Way Road 13,135
St Mary's Church, 38,86,99-106,
122,128,166
see also under Chapels
Street, William 46,62
Stretton, William 41
Strutt, Jedediah 31,40,41,57,76,
77; Strutts 37,75,82,111
Sutton's Wharf, Derby 20
Swann Minerals 20
Swiss Cottage 135
Sykes, Robert 79

T

Talbot, Henry 35
Tap Road, Scarthin 175
Taylor, Alice 129; - Francis 124
Taylor, Rev C H 171; -William 93
Taylor Colour Company 27
Temperance Hall 135
tennis lawn/courts 84,174
Thomas, William, 85-92,95,99
Thomisson, William 6,8
Thornley, David 40
Tiremare Lane 13
Toc H 128
toll charges 37
toll gate/house 13,38,135
Torrington, Lord 87,88,92,100,
118,119
Trout Farm 74
Troy Laundry 64,65-68
tubs on the canal 146
tufa 32

Tufa Cottage 3,24,32
turbine 18
Turner, John 30,86
Turner Brass House 30
Turnor, Mrs 13
Turners of Swanwick 2
turnpikes/Acts:
Cromford to Belper 37,141,142
Cromford to Five Lane Ends 13
Cromford to Langley Mill 2,141
Nottingham to Newhaven 13,
Wirksworth Moor to Longstone
2,142
Tyack, Thomas 65
typhoid 137

U

United British Basalt Company 20
United Steel Companies Ltd 20
Unwin, John 96,147
Uttley, Alison 129

V

Venetian Fete, Matlock Bath 113
Venture Rail 106
Via Gellia 3,11,13,23,26,82,83,141,
163
Via Gellia Brook 3,23
Via Gellia Colour Co 23,26,53,65,
68,128
Via Gellia House 136
Via Gellia Shooting 32
Via Gellia Spinning Co 12
Vicarage, the 126,166
Victoria Row/Terrace 38,118
Viyella 14

W

Walker, Captain 125
Walker, T H 32
Wallace, Mr, Lincoln's Inn 44
Wallpainting Workshop of
Faversham 105
Ward, Rev Richard 93,100,103,
110,126
Water Lane 28,32,118,134,135,175
water rights 11,14,17,39
Watson, Mr 51,53
weavers' workshop 45,48,53
Webb, John 95
Webber John artist 38,143
Webster, Mr 165
Wedgewood, Josiah & Byerley 125
weighing machine 96,147
Weston, William 46,62
Wheatcroft, James Walter 31
Wheatcroft family (Crich)
Abraham (1747-1812) 149
Abraham, Samuel's son 151

Abraham, John's son 151
Abraham, German's son 149,153
Alexander 149,153
David 149,152,153
German 147,149,150,151,152,154
Henry 25,26,153
John 150
John Adams 153
Joseph 136
Messrs & Sons 64
Nathaniel (1777-1862) 131,134,
135,136,146,147,149,150,151,
152,153
Nathaniel, John's son 150,152
Samuel 149
William 149,155
Wheeldon, George 20,
Whiston Copper Works, Staffs 24
White, C F 159-164,170
white lead 20
White, Samuel of Ashford 34
White Tor, Via Gellia 10
Wilkinson, William 111
Willcock, Colin Clive 26
Willcock, Henry of Bonsall 29
Wildgoose (Bonsall) Ltd 14
Willersley Castle 38,58,68,84-96,
124,144,148
Willersley Lodges 93,97,98
Willersley Park 95-97,112
Willersley Cottage 153
Willersly Farm Estate 1,84-5,95
Willn, John 65,135
Wills, John & Son of Derby 132
Wilsons of London 92,93,100
Wilson, Edward 89; -Walter 89
Wilson's of Sheffield 32
Wingfield Park Farm 152
Wirksworth 1,2,5,11,13,34,36,40
Wirksworth and District Co-op
175
Woodend 54,96,124
Wolley, Adam 13,57,86,87,131
Wragg, Samuel 151
Wright, Councillor 139; -John 31
Wright, Joseph 50,53,61,94
Wyatt, J A, architect 133

Y

Yarwood, Ernest 116
Yates, John 49
Yorkshire Penny Bank 174
Young, James 35; -Sibyl 22;
Young, William 76
Young, Mr 165

Z

Zinc 24,29; -oxide 29; -carbonate
31; -sulphide 31